Stephen Sondheim's
Sweeney Todd

Stephen Sondheim's *Sweeney Todd*

Behind the Bloody Musical Masterpiece

Rick Pender

BLOOMSBURY ACADEMIC
NEW YORK • LONDON • OXFORD • NEW DELHI • SYDNEY

BLOOMSBURY ACADEMIC

Bloomsbury Publishing Inc, 1359 Broadway, 12th Floor, New York, NY 10018, USA
Bloomsbury Publishing Plc, 50 Bedford Square, London, WC1B 3DP, UK
Bloomsbury Publishing Ireland, 29 Earlsfort Terrace, Dublin 2, D02 AY28, Ireland

BLOOMSBURY, BLOOMSBURY ACADEMIC and the Diana logo are trademarks of Bloomsbury Publishing Plc

First published in the United States of America 2025

Copyright © Bloomsbury Publishing, 2025

Cover design: Sally Rinehart
Cover image © iStock.com/tiero, iStock.com/iantfoto, iStock.com/vistoff

All rights reserved. No part of this publication may be: i) reproduced or transmitted in any form, electronic or mechanical, including photocopying, recording or by means of any information storage or retrieval system without prior permission in writing from the publishers; or ii) used or reproduced in any way for the training, development or operation of artificial intelligence (AI) technologies, including generative AI technologies. The rights holders expressly reserve this publication from the text and data mining exception as per Article 4(3) of the Digital Single Market Directive (EU) 2019/790.

Bloomsbury Publishing Inc does not have any control over, or responsibility for, any third-party websites referred to or in this book. All internet addresses given in this book were correct at the time of going to press. The author and publisher regret any inconvenience caused if addresses have changed or sites have ceased to exist, but can accept no responsibility for any such changes.

Library of Congress Cataloging-in-Publication Data
Names: Pender, Rick, 1949- author.
Title: Stephen Sondheim's Sweeney Todd : behind the bloody musical masterpiece / Rick Pender.
Description: New York, NY : Bloomsbury Academic, 2025. | Includes index. | Summary: "A deep dive into this unique, murder-filled masterpiece-its slimy roots, original production, characters from killers to lovers to bakers, soaring score, gripping storytelling, and lasting power"—Provided by publisher.
Identifiers: LCCN 2025011484 (print) | LCCN 2025011485 (ebook) | ISBN 9781538196441 (hardback) | ISBN 9798765148976 (pdf) | ISBN 9781538196458 (epub)
Subjects: LCSH: Sondheim, Stephen.—Criticism and interpretation. | Sondheim, Stephen. Sweeney Todd. | Sweeney Todd (Motion picture : 2007) | Musicals—20th century—History and criticism. | Musicals—21st century—History and criticism. | Musical films—21st century—History and criticism. | Musicals—Production and direction—History.
Classification: LCC ML410.S6872 P46 2025 (print) | LCC ML410.S6872 (ebook) | DDC 782.1/4—dc23/eng/20250321
LC record available at https://lccn.loc.gov/2025011484
LC ebook record available at https://lccn.loc.gov/2025011485

ISBN: HB: 978-1-5381-9644-1
ePub: 978-1-5381-9645-8
ePDF: 979-8-7651-4897-6

Typeset by Deanta Global Publishing Services, Chennai, India
Printed and bound in the United States of America

For product safety related questions contact productsafety@bloomsbury.com.

To find out more about our authors and books visit www.bloomsbury.com
and sign up for our newsletters.

Contents

1 Attend the Tale of *Sweeney Todd* 1
2 Sweeney's Bloody Roots 13
3 First Blood on Broadway 37
4 Blood on the Big Screen 79
5 Sweeney Swings Back … Again and Again 107
6 Sweeney Settles the Musical Score 149
7 Take Sweeney Home to Listen 169
8 "Isn't that Sweeney there beside you?" 185

Appendix 1: Sweeney Todd Productions Worldwide 195
Appendix 2: Song-by-Song Commentary 205
Notes 226
Index 247
About the Author 252

1

Attend the Tale of Sweeney Todd

"Attend the tale of Sweeney Todd!" Do those words make you shiver with fear, tremble with anticipation, sit up and listen, possibly even dread what's coming next? That's the first line sung in Stephen Sondheim's masterpiece musical about the "Demon Barber of Fleet Street" (Figure 1.1). What follows is a horror story dripping with blood, told with dark humor, macabre events, scandalous behavior, heartrending tragedy, and magnificent, soaring melodies.

In the late 1970s, as news began to spread about the next Broadway musical from composer and lyricist Sondheim and director Harold Prince, many theater fans were shaking their heads. Say what? A musical about a legendary serial killer and bogeyman named Sweeney Todd, a bloody vengeful barber, as its central character? An incorrigible baker, Mrs. Lovett, who lusts after the barber and moves on from filling meat pies with the remains of stray cats to ground-up human flesh from

Figure 1.1 *Stephen Sondheim (1930–2021). Photofest.*

the victims of Sweeney's murderous swath through Victorian London? A corrupt jurist, Judge Turpin, and his sleazy accomplice, Beadle Bamford, who conspired to send Sweeney to a penal colony to clear the judge's lustful path to the barber's wife, then take Sweeney's beautiful daughter as his ward and eventually marry her? These were not the kind of heartwarming or redeemable musical theater characters that audiences were used to finding on Broadway stages through most of the twentieth century.

Sondheim's previous shows did not point to a horror story as his likely next subject. His first work on a Broadway stage—initially as a lyricist working with eminent composer Leonard Bernstein—was *West Side Story* (1957). With a script by veteran playwright Arthur Laurents, it was an updated story based on Shakespeare's *Romeo and Juliet* about gang warfare and star-crossed lovers in New York City.

Sondheim's second engagement, again as a lyric writer, was *Gypsy* (1959), was another show with a book by Laurents. It was the story of ecdysiast Gypsy Rose Lee (that's a fancy word for a striptease "artist") and especially Rose, her domineering, manipulative stage mother. For that production, Sondheim worked with another brilliant Broadway composer, the prolific Jule Styne, to assemble a score showcasing the vocal talents of theater legend Ethel Merman. *Gypsy* is often considered one of the best shows from Broadway's so-called "Golden Age." Merman's clarion voice was a perfect fit for the larger-than-life Rose, and Merman dug deep to take on this serious, demanding role. Sondheim's talent for writing lyrics again shone forth. But he was ambitious and impatient to expand his work to composing.

His first show combining his skills as a composer and lyricist was a slapstick farce, *A Funny Thing Happened on the Way to the Forum* (1962, with comic writers Burt Shevelove and Larry Gelbart). It was followed by an absurdist, nine-performance musical flop, *Anyone Can Whistle* (1964, yet one more with a book by playwright Laurents) that starred a young Angela Lansbury as a corrupt town mayor. Neither *Forum* nor *Whistle* pointed toward the success Sondheim would find in the 1970s when he worked in tandem with his friend Harold (Hal) Prince, one of Broadway's greatest directors who also produced many of Sondheim's musicals throughout the decade.

Sondheim's First Venture in Underscoring

Sondheim created a work in 1966 that certainly foreshadowed his potential for writing a score for a creepy tale. He and playwright James Goldman crafted a fifty-two-minute filmed musical, *Evening Primrose*, for an ABC television series, "Stage 67." It was based on a mysterious 1961 short story by John Collier, a frequent contributor of fiction to *The New Yorker* from the 1930s to the 1950s. Several of his imaginative stories were adapted for popular television series such as *Alfred Hitchcock Presents* (1956) and *The Twilight Zone* (1960). "I've always liked John Collier stories," Goldman said, "and *Evening Primrose* had a macabre quality that appealed to Steve."[1] Sondheim said they settled on this "bizarre and romantic piece" as a notch above the material the ABC series had been presenting. The result was a tale—featuring Sondheim's effective underscoring—that landed "somewhere between a hallucination and a nightmare," according to biographer Meryle Secrest.[2]

Evening Primrose starred actor Anthony Perkins, a friend of Sondheim, as Charles Snell, an unhappy, idealistic poet who seeks refuge from the cold, cruel world by hiding out in a department store where a society of kindred tender spirits comes out at night. He falls in love with Ella, a young woman left behind in the store as a child by her distracted mother. She has become a prisoner of the nocturnal community. The pair try to escape but are caught by "Dark Men" who enforce the society's secret presence and transform them into store-window mannequins whom we see in the show's final moments.

Evening Primrose was produced six years after Perkins's star-making performance as Norman Bates in Alfred Hitchcock's *Psycho* (1960), a sophisticated psychological thriller that included a bloody murder and composer Bernard Herrmann's screeching score of violins, violas, and cellos. Herrmann's music intensified the iconic scene of the violent murder of Marion (Janet Leigh) in a shower. Sondheim and Perkins both loved films, so he surely knew how bloody scenes could pack a frightening emotional wallop.

Evening Primrose had just four songs, but Sondheim also composed a dozen instrumental melodies used for evocative accompaniment and underscoring for the compact TV musical. It was his first time to compose more than songs.

In fact, he created a moody, often frightening score for the entire story. Of course, *Evening Primrose* was much more genteel than *Sweeney Todd*, but it certainly demonstrated that Sondheim could compose music to enhance a tale's pulse-inducing terror. *Evening Primrose* was a harbinger of more sophisticated work to come a decade later.

Moving into a Whole New Territory

In the 1970s, Sondheim and director Hal Prince embarked on a series of musicals that firmly cemented his reputation and career as a noteworthy Broadway composer and lyricist. *Company* (1970, with a book by actor and playwright George Furth) focused on a single man whose married friends were pushing him toward romantic commitment. *Follies* (1971, working again with playwright James Goldman) explored the unhappy lives of two couples who first met during extravagant Broadway shows in the 1930s and 1940s. That show featured a score full of musical pastiche, with numbers that mimicked delightful popular tunes from that era. *A Little Night Music* (1974, with a script by novelist and playwright Hugh Wheeler, who adapted Ingmar Bergman's 1955 film, *Smiles of a Summer Night*) charmed audiences with a lush, waltz-time score and a series of mismatched romantic triangles.

A lot of people didn't know quite what to make of *Pacific Overtures* (1976, Sondheim's collaboration with young playwright and historian John Weidman), which told the story of traditional nineteenth-century Japan being forced to join the modern world by American political and military dominance. These shows all stemmed from ideas brought to Sondheim by his various creative partners. But his personal predilection for emotive melodrama was about to surface.

In a *New York Times* interview in 1979 about *Sweeney Todd*, Sondheim stated forthrightly that he endeavored to do something new and different with the score for each of his productions. "I try to use muscles I haven't used before. That's the fun of writing, I think. It's no fun going over territory you're familiar with. And in the process of exploration, one always learned."[3] Six years earlier he had stumbled on a story that would evolve into his greatest show—profoundly unlike anything he'd written before.

Seeking Grand Guignol

Sondheim was in London in the spring of 1973 to see the first British production of his 1959 Broadway hit, *Gypsy*. Actress Angela Lansbury, who was coaxed by Sondheim into a leading role in the short-lived production of *Anyone Can Whistle* in 1964, was stepping into Ethel Merman's original role as Rose, *Gypsy*'s fearsome stage mother, singing brassy lyrics by Sondheim.

A lifelong and self-described Anglophile, Sondheim relished his visit to London and casually decided to take in a performance of a British melodrama he'd heard about. It was by Christopher Bond, a young Liverpool actor and playwright. In 1968, Bond had adapted an old melodrama script about a murderous barber named Sweeney Todd into a play that was first produced by a theater in the English Midlands. It met with enough success that it traveled to a series of regional stages. Five years later, it was produced at London's Theatre Royal, Stratford East.

Sondheim thought Bond's play might be a chance to experience "Grand Guignol," a sensational theatrical form developed by a tiny Paris theater late in the nineteenth century that specialized in graphic horror shows. Shows were inspired by horrific revenge plays from the sixteenth and seventeenth centuries, such as Shakespeare's *Titus Andronicus* (1588), a bloody story about an ambitious Roman general who baked the heads of two of his enemy's sons into pies, and John Webster's *The Duchess of Malfi* (1613), a tragedy with a final act of terrible carnage. The Parisian shows seldom rose to the level of great drama. Rather, their most predictable elements were almost exclusively blood and gore. But the category appealed to some audiences, just as today's splatter films have followers, and Sondheim was intrigued by such material.

In fact, he had attended an evening at Le Théâtre du Grand-Guignol in Paris in the 1960s to see what it was like. "There were three extremely bloody one-act plays," he told interviewer Daniel Gerould in 1979.

> Each had a plot at least as simple as *Oedipus*, only far less interesting, and each had one climactic, bloody, gory effect, exactly like *Oedipus*. . . . The three plays were extremely boring because, bloody as the effects were, if you were squeamish, you hardened yourself, and if you weren't squeamish, it

was just red tomato sauce and a lot of people in terrible make-up overacting. Melodrama, for me, has to be a great deal purer than that, and it has to be at least as interesting as other drama.[4]

Such productions might be compared to twentieth-century horror films such as *Halloween* and *Friday the 13th*. These movies offer shocking violence, blood and gore, and are popular with thrill-seeking audiences but seldom provide much in the way of serious acting or aesthetic value. Sondheim, a lifelong film buff, was up for a spine-tingling evening when he headed to see a performance of Bond's *Sweeney Todd, The Demon Barber of Fleet Street*. That wasn't exactly what he experienced at Stratford East in Newham.

Sondheim told biographer Meryle Secrest that Bond's *Sweeney* "turned out to be not Grand Guignol but this charming melodrama, and melodrama and farce are my two favorite forms of theatre because . . . they are obverse sides of the same coin."[5] In an introduction to the libretto of *Sweeney Todd*, Bond explained that he drew upon "Penny Dreadful" tales from the 1840s that were subsequently adapted into popular late Victorian London theatrical melodramas. These productions "possessed at least some of the essential ingredients that go to make good theater: energy and commitment crackling between the stage and the audience; involvement; passion and fun."[6]

Convincing Hal Prince

Unlike their previous collaborations, Sondheim had to work hard to persuade Hal Prince to direct this one. He was moving away from producing and increasingly focused on directing. He had already achieved success staging *She Loves Me* (1963), *Baker Street* (1964), *It's a Bird . . . It's a Plane . . . It's Superman* (1966), and *Zorba* (1968). *Sweeney Todd* was the first Sondheim show with the director not serving also as a producer. He did not share Sondheim's enthusiasm for melodrama and farce, as evidenced by his original productions of Jerry Bock and Sheldon Harnick's *Fiddler on the Roof* (1964) and John Kander and Fred Ebb's *Cabaret* (1966), as well as several of his earlier Sondheim shows, especially *Company* (1970) and *Follies* (1971).

Sondheim eventually won Prince over when the director found a way to make the story meaningful from his own point of view. "It was only when I realized that the show was about revenge," Prince told Sondheim chronicler Craig Zadan,

> that I knew how to do it. And then came the factory and the class struggle—the terrible struggle to move out of the class in which you're born, and suddenly it became about the Industrial Age and the incursions of machinery on the spirit . . . that was very important. It made it possible for me to conceive it.[7]

Prince's insight drove his decision to build a massively physical Broadway production, vastly larger and quite different from what Sondheim had imagined. As will be discussed in subsequent chapters, one of the most surprising features of Sondheim's *Sweeney Todd* is how it has been successfully revived in productions ranging from immense to intimate. But for its first outing, Prince pulled out all the stops.

Seeking Help with the Script

Although Sondheim had already proved himself a genius with many facets of musical theater creation, book writing was not in his arsenal. His previous shows each had book writers who provided spoken words for each show: Arthur Laurents for *West Side Story*, *Gypsy*, and *Anyone Can Whistle*, Larry Gelbart and Burt Shevelove for *A Funny Thing Happened on the Way to the Forum*, George Furth for *Company*, James Goldman for *Follies*, Hugh Wheeler for *A Little Night Music*, and John Weidman for *Pacific Overtures*.

Sondheim wrote brilliant lyrics, but he had never drafted a libretto. He imagined he could simply carve out space in Bond's script to make room for songs.

> I started it, trying to write everything myself because it was really all going to be sung . . . it was going to be virtually an opera. I did the first twenty minutes, and I realized I was only on page five of Bond's script. So at that rate, the show would possibly have been nine hours long. And I realized I didn't know how to cut it, so Hal suggested I call Hugh [Wheeler] because

he had written mysteries, and he was British, and he would understand the tradition of the play.[8]

Wheeler had collaborated with Sondheim and Prince as the book writer for *A Little Night Music*. Their endeavor had been productive and pleasant, and Wheeler's involvement solved the puzzle of getting a workable script for *Sweeney Todd*.

Melodrama and Farce

Sondheim took pains in a 1979 interview to clearly distinguish his notion of melodrama from "villains twirling mustaches and lashing young virgins to railroad tracks." That kind of melodrama is almost always humorous. Sometimes it's a condemnation of overheated reactions: "Oh, don't be so melodramatic." Sondheim preferred to think of melodrama as "high theater . . . the kind of theater that takes place in an auditorium with a proscenium arch . . . theater that is larger than life—in emotion, in subject, and in complication of plot." He suggested that Sophocles' tragedy *Oedipus Rex* could be considered a melodrama: "It is a mystery with a stunning surprise solution (surprising for the hero, that is), and that has a violent and bloody dramatic conclusion: Oedipus blinds himself."[9]

Sondheim also expressed his love of farce, that is, satirical comedy, which he saw as the flip side of melodrama. "We find the same qualities in both," he explained.

> Complications of plot, larger-than-life characters, grand gestures, and non-naturalistic acting are common to both melodrama and farce. The only difference is that in melodrama what we could call tragic events occur, events with truly unpleasant consequences. In farce, annoying events happen with comic and generally happy consequences. . . . The point is that melodrama and farce are essentially the same form, and they represent for me the heart of the theatrical experience. . . . The theater is the one place where you can create larger than life, and melodrama and farce represent the two forms best suited to that kind of circusy quality that I love in the theater.[10]

Both melodrama and farce are obvious components of *Sweeney Todd*, particularly represented by the characters of Sweeney and Mrs. Lovett. The barber is generally dead serious, often maniacal (as in the song "Epiphany"), while the baker is silly and frivolous in "A Little Priest," in which she momentarily draws Sweeney into her farcical perspective.

Sondheim was certain that melodrama would fuel the power of *Sweeney Todd*'s story. The musical is populated with larger-than-life characters, some of whom—such as the mountebank barber Pirelli—are comically exaggerated. But Sondheim's intention was to present the story seriously so it would "be taken seriously by an audience today, the way the original *Sweeney Todd* was taken seriously in the nineteenth century."[11] Sondheim and Wheeler shaped *Sweeney Todd* as "theater that is larger than life, in emotion, in subject, and in complication of plot."[12] Sondheim enhanced the story with musical amplification to tell Sweeney's story with heightened emotion and a complicated plot.

Sondheim wanted his version of *Sweeney Todd* to be serious about profoundly frightening people in attendance,

> but not by suddenly opening doors in the dark, which can always terrify audiences and produce little shrieks of surprise, but that is not the kind of scare I am referring to. The true terror of melodrama comes from its revelations about the frightening power of what is inside human beings. And if you write about kings and queens and are a great poet, you end up with a first-class tragedy; if you write about ordinary people and are an ordinary writer, you end up with a melodrama.[13]

Of course, Sondheim and Wheeler were far from ordinary, and the terrible, terrifying melodrama they crafted for *Sweeney Todd* pushed the story painfully close to tragedy.

A Horror Movie?

"What I wanted to write," he told theater chronicler Craig Zadan,

> was a horror movie. The whole point of the thing is that it's a background score for a horror film, which is what I intended to do and what it is. . . . I

figured the only way to tell a horror story is to keep musical texture going, because in most horror films what really scares you, apart from the lighting and makeup, is the music. You know you don't have to see a single shark's tooth in *Jaws*: the minute the lights go down and that score starts, and you hear all those double basses, you get frightened right away.[14]

With the architecture of Wheeler's carefully constructed libretto, Sondheim had the perfect infrastructure for his musical horror tale.

Throughout his long life, Sondheim was a fan of films, often material well outside the commercial mainstream, cinema that was more esoteric, avant-garde, and artistic. He included several from the horror category in a set of his favorite films published in 2010, around the time of his eightieth birthday. *Dead of Night* (1945), a black-and-white British anthology of supernatural horror tales, was one he listed. But perhaps the most important example was *Hangover Square*, another film from 1945 that he saw when he was fifteen. With his friend Jamie Hammerstein (son of Sondheim's musical theater mentor, Oscar Hammerstein II), he attended a showing in a Times Square movie theater of the eerie melodrama set in the London gaslight era (Figure 1.2). He was so captivated by composer Bernard Herrmann's score that, after sitting through a 7:00 p.m. showing, he slipped back in at 9:00 p.m. to see it a second time so he could memorize a sheet of music from Bone's piano concerto and subsequently play it himself.

Figure 1.2 *John Brahm's Hangover Square, a 1945 noir classic with a score by Bernard Herrmann, was an inspiration for Sondheim's "horror musical." 20th Century Fox/Photofest.*

Hangover Square is about Henry Bone, a schizophrenic composer, driven to commit murders whenever he hears a particularly dissonant musical chord. Director John Brahm's noir classic features a score by Herrmann, who earned his first Oscar in 1941 for Orson Welles's *Citizen Kane*. He subsequently composed memorable scores for Alfred Hitchcock's *Vertigo* (1958) and *North by Northwest* (1959) and—especially pertinent to *Sweeney Todd*—the score for *Psycho* (1960). The notes that triggered Henry Bone's murderous deeds in *Hangover Square* were musical forebearers of *Sweeney Todd*'s deafening factory whistle. The melodies and musical themes from Herrmann's menacing movie scores were essential cinematic elements that captivated Sondheim during his teenage years. They were also a significant inspiration for his score for *Sweeney Todd*.

As noted, Sondheim had to convince Hal Prince to direct *Sweeney Todd*. They differed both on the scale of the production and on what story the show was actually telling. "For me, what the show is really about," Sondheim said,

> is obsession. I was using the story as a metaphor for any kind of obsession. Todd is a tragic hero in the classic sense that Oedipus is. He dies in the end because of a certain kind of fatal knowledge: he realizes what he has been doing. I find it terribly satisfying—much more so than any kind of accidental death, which often occurs in flimsy forms of melodrama.[15]

That certainly speaks to *Sweeney Todd*'s tragic final scene when the barber realizes that he has murdered his long-lost wife.

Prince recognized that he and Sondheim differed on the show's message. "I think it's also about impotence, and that's quite a different matter," Prince explained. "The reason that the ensemble is used the way it is, the unifying emotion for the entire company, is shared impotence. Obviously, Sweeney's is the most dramatic, to justify all those murders. Impotence creates rage, and rage is what is expressed most by Sweeney's behavior."[16] While Sondheim's and Prince's perspectives diverged, they staged a show that still resonates—and induces fear and horror—more than a half-century later.

Sweeney Todd, The Demon Barber of Fleet Street: A Musical Thriller is perhaps one of the greatest works of onstage horror, comedy, and tragedy—a strange, fascinating, and, yes, bloody stew. In 2021, blogger Graham Skipper put it succinctly: "For us horror fans, there is no more seismic moment in horror theatre than *Sweeney Todd*. It is bold, daring, dangerous theatre, both fun and frightening, entertaining and introspective. There is truly nothing else like it, nor will there ever be."[17]

Before digging into Sondheim and Wheeler's creation from Christopher Bond's stage script, it's important to explore the roots of this frightening legend as well as its existence as a creepy nineteenth-century publishing phenomenon and subsequently a horrifying stage show. All these elements converged to cement the terrifying tale of *Sweeney Todd* in the psyches of superstitious Brits and to lay a firm, if bloody, foundation for Sondheim's masterpiece.

2

Sweeney's Bloody Roots

A frequently asked question about the story of Sweeney Todd is whether there was a real person of that name who perpetrated horrifying crimes and inspired these frightening tales. The simple answer is no. But plenty of bloody threads from horror stories wove their way together across several centuries before they became a sensational print version in the 1840s, the catalyst for another century of terrifying storytelling.

Very possibly the earliest published account of a murderous barber dates from the thirteenth century, 1206, in Paris. He was said to have killed his customers and transported them from his cellar to a nearby pastry shop where they were ground up for meat pies. A house named "Marmousets" (a French word meaning a "grotesque figurine") on Paris's Île de la Cité was on a street that still bears that identification today. The name was surely a hint that dark deeds happened there. As the story goes, once authorities discovered the home of the barber and his partner the pastry maker, he was arrested and executed. The house where these ghastly crimes occurred was demolished, replaced by a small memorial shaped like a pyramid. (The shop of the pastry maker was said to have been on the corner of the Rue des Deux Hermites.) The barber shop's lot was said to remain vacant for many years out of fear and respect. Finally, in 1536, King Francis I was said to have granted permission for a house to be built on the site.

During an era when literacy was a rare skill, oral storytelling perpetuated similar stories, tales that were repeatedly embellished and expanded. Such narratives especially focused on monsters, ogres, trolls, and other evil beings.

In 1598 a French tailor from Châlons was sentenced to be burned alive by the Parliament of Paris after he was charged with "lycanthropy," a belief that he could transform himself into a wolf or some other nonhuman animal. He had reportedly drawn children into his shop or attacked them in a nearby forest, torn them with his teeth, then dressed their remains and eaten them. An incriminating barrel of bones was reportedly found in his shop.

Centuries later a similar story from Polomia in southern Poland described an impoverished beggar who killed and ate fourteen children. His behavior was said to have been triggered when a jail caught fire and burned down, roasting one of the prisoners. The starving beggar happened by and could not resist the temptation of making a meal of the charred body. He developed an irresistible craving for human flesh, including a nine-year-old orphan girl. He too was discovered and punished. Stories like these were easily heard, repeated, and used as cautionary warnings to wayward children.

Much in the same way that ghost stories get retold, exaggerated, enlarged upon, and believed, the tale of the Rue de Marmousets evolved from the thirteenth century and continued to flourish—and frighten people—for centuries, as recorded in Jacques du Breuil's *La Théâtre des Antiquités de Paris* in 1612:

> Since time out of mind, it has been rumoured abroad that there was once in the city of Paris, on the Rue des Marmousets, a murderous pastry-cook who killed a certain man in his house; he was helped in doing so by a neighbour of his—a barber—who slit the man's throat while shaving him. From the flesh of this man they made meat pies that were found to be better than all others, insofar as human flesh is more tender, because of its diet, than that of other animals. And the murderer having been discovered, the parliamentary court ordered that in addition to the punishment of the pastry-cook, his house be razed to the ground and that a pyramid or pillar be built on the site in its place, in shameful memory of this disgraceful fact—a part of which aforesaid stands to this day in the rue des Marmousets.[1]

Peter Mårtensson Lindeström, a seventeenth-century Swedish artist, cartographer, and engineer, left a manuscript at the time of his death in 1691 that reported on his travels in 1654 to North America. His manuscript (unpublished until 1925) contained a story he claimed to have heard from merchants and residents of Calais, France, when he passed through that port. It closely resembled the tales of other crimes perpetrated by a vicious barber and a pastry maker, suggesting that the root story of Sweeney Todd and Mrs. Lovett is an archetypal and legendary one.

The seedy Parisian neighborhood of the Rue de Marmousets was a place of narrow alleys and rotting tenements, the sort of locale where wicked things were likely to happen. It was a setting for numerous fearsome stories written during the following centuries. The street name in the story shifted to an adjacent—but equally dismal—street, the locale for "A terrific story of the Rue de la Harpe, Paris," in a very similar narrative published in 1824 in *The Tell-Tale*, a weekly London magazine that provided a constant stream of sensational narratives. So popular was the story that, in the days before copyright laws provided some legal restraint, it appeared in another London publication, the *New Wonderful and Entertaining Magazine*, in 1825 bearing the title "The Murderous Barber."

Sweeney Swings His Razors in London

Quite naturally some of these stories crossed from continental Europe to England. London, where the population doubled in the late eighteenth century from 750,000 in 1780 to 1.4 million by 1815, was the perfect breeding ground for such salacious tales. Rampant poverty and unemployment, particularly in the blocks surrounding Fleet Street, meant violence, disorder, and brutal punishment were commonplace. The profusion of taverns and alcohol encouraged increased lawlessness, and the environs, replete with byways, alleys, and tunnels, provided hiding places and escape routes for criminals.

People lived in extreme, overcrowded tenements with shabby, sparse furniture and little clothing aside from what they wore day in and day out. Violence was rife, and the exploits of felons, their crimes, and their executions were constantly and breathlessly reported in the press and the literature of the era. These fed into even more sensational stories, particularly focused on individuals, even adolescent children, often sentenced for largely inconsequential crimes to time in prisons such as the massive grim fortress of Newgate. More than 200 crimes were punishable by hanging, including simple acts of petty theft such as picking pockets or stealing small items from a shop. Wealthier Londoners paid to enter the filthy, disease-ridden Newgate to stare at criminals in their cells. (One such visitor, author Charles Dickens, was inspired to write about child pickpockets in his novel *Oliver Twist* in the 1830s.)

Newgate had at least one prisoner who reportedly had been a barber. From the dank halls and cells he was said to have served affluent inmates in need of grooming and medical assistance. Barbers in this era often were both hairdressers and primitive, untrained surgeons, addressing minor bodily complaints and injuries—ranging from harshly extracting a decayed tooth or amputating a gangrenous arm or a leg. (From medieval times the red-striped pole that still serves as a symbol of a barber shop was inspired by flowing blood or bloody bandages that resulted from bloodletting.)

Newgate became a regular source of ghastly information, *The Newgate Calendar; or, Malefactor's Bloody Register*, first published in the early 1700s by the prison's keeper as a bulletin of executions. By the mid-eighteenth century it was appropriated by other publishers of sensational materials; it lasted for more than a century. Over its long existence *The Newgate Calendar* likely published more than a thousand cases. It reached countless eighteenth-century British homes, outnumbered only by copies of the Bible and John Bunyan's Christian allegory, *Pilgrim's Progress* (1678).

A forerunner of nineteenth-century crime fiction and today's scandalous tabloids, one of *The Newgate Calendar*'s most prominent publishers was J. Cooke, a crafty entrepreneur, who featured "Genuine and Circumstantial Narratives of the Lives and Transactions, Various Exploits and Dying Speeches of the Most Notorious Criminals of Both Sexes." Employing tiny type in double columns on cheap paper, these publications typically featured lurid drawings of a crime on the front page, intended to draw readers into the gruesome stories of robbery, forgery, and murder on the following pages.

Such publications perpetuated myths about urban cannibalism. Perhaps the most sensational product was an 1844 novel *Sawney Bean: The Man-Eater of Midlothian*. The legendary sixteenth-century figure, Alexander "Sawney" Bean, was supposedly the scion of a forty-five-member clan in Scotland that murdered and cannibalized more than 1,000 people over a quarter-century. The tale allies Bean with Black Agnes Douglas, a vicious woman often accused of being a witch. According to tall tales of their early crimes, they took shelter in a deep coastal cave in Scotland, where—married or not—they spawned six daughters, eight sons, fourteen granddaughters, and eighteen grandsons, all said to be the products of incest.

The infamous clan supposedly ambushed people at night and brought bodies back to the cave where they were butchered, roasted, eaten, and sometimes pickled. Eventually public outcry supposedly caused the king of Scotland to send a posse to hunt them down. By some accounts Bean and his family were captured and gruesomely executed; by others they were trapped in the cave by detonated gunpowder, which suffocated them. There is no hard evidence of Sawney Bean's existence, but stories of his grim crimes were recycled over the years. A prominent example is S. R. Crockett's *The Grey Man*, a popular novel, published in 1896. Sawney Bean's name might have been at least an inspiration for the nefarious Sweeney Todd.

In late December 1784 an article appeared in *the Annual Register*, a respected London publication edited by statesman and philosopher Edmund Burke. He wrote and published this reputable reference work annually, reliably reporting the year's major events, developments, and trends. The article was titled, "A Barbarous Barber."

> A most remarkable murder was perpetrated in the following manner by a journeyman barber that lived near Hyde Park Corner, who had been jealous of his wife, but could in no way bring this home to her. A young gentleman, by chance coming into the barber's shop to be shaved and dressed, and being in liquor, mentioned having seen a fine girl in Hamilton Street, from whom he had had certain favours the night before, and at the same time describing her person. The barber, concluding this to be his wife, and in the height of his frenzy, cut the young gentleman's throat from ear to ear and absconded.[2]

Despite the perpetrator being unidentified, this incident, first reported in the *London Chronicle* (December 2, 1784), was subsequently incorporated into many accounts purporting to be about the "real" Sweeney Todd. Scholar

Robert L. Mack commented, "The persistent search for the 'genuine' historical incidents that inspired the narrative of Sweeney Todd suggests that at least on some level there is part of our collective psyche that actually wants or even needs his story to be true; to have it reduced to a mere fiction among other fictions would somehow detract from its aura."[3]

A claim in a popular pamphlet published by James Catnach in 1818 offers another example. His cheaply produced chapbooks and broadsheets at first offered British nursery rhymes and fairy tales. But early in the nineteenth century he expanded his focus to the equivalent of today's "fake news"—using rumor and innuendo to boost his circulation. On June 1, 1818, he issued a libelous handbill titled "A Number of Human Bodies Found in the Shop of a Port Butcher" that said Thomas Pizzey, a butcher on London's Drury Lane, had been selling pork sausages actually stuffed with human flesh. Catnach's scandalous account provoked hysteria:

> We have just been informed of a most dreadful and horrible discovery revolting to every feeling of humanity and calculated to inspire sentiments of horror and disgust in the minds of every individual. . . . Great flocks of people were assembled from all parts of the town at Marlborough Street in expectation of the offender having a hearing.[4]

The butcher sued Catnach for his malicious libel, and the printer was sentenced to a six-month stay in a house of correction. Such unfounded stories circulated easily and frequently. One that made its way into more serious literature appeared in Charles Dickens's *Martin Chuzzlewit* (1843). The character Tom Pinch wonders whether his friend is

> afraid I have strayed into one of those streets where the countrymen are murdered; and that I have been made meat-pies of, or some horrible thing. . . . Tom's evil genius did not lead him into the dens of any of those preparers of cannibalistic pastry, who are represented in many standard country legends as doing a lively retail business in the Metropolis.[5]

London's gullible, lower-class population was rife with fears and anxieties, but also had a voracious appetite for shocking true crime stories. Cheaply published eight-page broadsides, generally referred to as "Penny Dreadfuls" or "Penny Bloods"—because they were sold for just a penny—were stuffed with overheated accounts of horrifying crimes. Once read, such tales were certainly repeated by word of mouth and exaggerated even further. They built upon one another creating an undertow of belief and an opportunity for an ever-increasing stream of sensational publications, the nineteenth-century predecessors of today's supermarket tabloids.

Edward Lloyd's Salisbury Square and Penny Dreadful Tales

This historic stew of obscure horror tales, known murderers, folklore and the very human fear of cannibalism formed the foundation of a sensational publishing series by Edward Lloyd (1815–90), probably the most influential publisher of such items starting in the 1830s. These were cheaply produced serial literature about the exploits of detectives, criminals, and supernatural beings. By the 1850s there were as many as 100 publishers of such horror fiction, typically released in weekly editions of eight to sixteen pages and sold for a penny. The principal content was usually bloodthirsty tales of vampires, pirates, highwaymen, and murderers.

Lloyd was the third son of an impoverished family; his father declared bankruptcy several times. Lloyd left school at the age of fourteen and quickly found his way to a lifelong career in printing. Growing up during the Industrial Revolution, he was fascinated with inventions and machinery. He recognized that people living in poverty could improve their lives by learning to read, so he initially printed inexpensive educational items such as cards and songs. In 1832 he launched the *Weekly Penny Comic Magazine*. By 1835, at the age of twenty, he established his own print shop with presses.

The growth of literacy caused a growing demand for written works, especially for entertaining and affordable reading material. Women were important customers, so Lloyd's publications, at first, needed to be decent and morally sound. As he sought steadier revenue, he began to print serialized romantic fiction. He launched several periodicals: *People's Periodical and Family Library*, *Lloyd's Entertaining Journal*, and *Lloyd's Penny Weekly Miscellany of Romance and General Interest*.

The content of his publications was far from intellectual and seldom original. He often appropriated other people's good ideas. Adopting familiar plots wholesale in an era when copyright laws were largely nonexistent, Lloyd's retellings were eagerly consumed by readers. Plagiarism was the order of the day for such publishers. He had considerable success with slightly adapted knockoffs of novels by Charles Dickens with minimally changed titles: *The Penny Pickwick*, *Oliver Twiss*, and *Nickelas Nickleberry*. His *Pickwick* issue was a bestseller: roughly 50,000 copies were snapped up at a penny each—rather than Dickens's own novels, which cost considerably more. (The Parliamentary Copyright Act of 1842, championed by Dickens, significantly reduced the rampant plagiarism by Lloyd and others.)

If a romance cranked out by one of his stable of Salisbury Square freelance writers failed to sell, Lloyd simply had the writer conclude it quickly and move on another far-fetched tale. Starting in the 1830s and continuing until the early 1850s, he published roughly 200 romances, extravagant tales of love and adventure. He had pool of engravers who created sensational, graphic woodcuts (Figure 2.1) to illustrate tales written by his corps of authors, men often paid by the line or by the page. In particular, he frequently employed James Malcolm Rymer (1814–84) and Thomas Peckett Prest (1810–59).

Figure 2.1 *"Penny Dreadful" publications in the 1840s and 1850s featured sensational graphic woodcuts, such as this one depicting Sweeney Todd slashing a throat. A historic woodcut illustration.*

The String of Pearls

The String of Pearls: A Domestic Romance first appeared in *The People's Periodical and Family Library*, Lloyd's most memorable serialization, published in eighteen weekly installments from November 21, 1846, to March 20, 1847. (It was subsequently retitled *The String of Pearls: A Sailor's Gift*, and in a later "collected" version subtitled *The Barber* of *Fleet Street: A Domestic Romance.*) *The String of Pearls* was the first time the characters of Sweeney Todd, the barber, and Mrs. Lovett, the meat-pie baker, were named in print. Here is a quick synopsis of the plot of *The String of Pearls*.

> ## SYNOPSIS
> ## *The String of Pearls*
>
> London, 1785. Lieutenant Thornhill, a sailor, has disappeared after entering Sweeney Todd's barber shop on Fleet Street. Thornhill had with him a string of pearls, a gift he was to deliver to Johanna Oakley from her missing lover, Mark Ingestrie, possibly lost at sea. Colonel Jeffrey searches for his friend Thornhill with the aid of Hector, the sailor's faithful dog, and concludes that Sweeney is responsible for the sailor's disappearance. Johanna, seeking to find out what has happened to her lover Mark, joins the search. Colonel Jeffrey is suspicious that the greedy Sweeney is responsible for other disappearances, so Johanna dresses in boy's clothing and goes to work in the barbershop to observe his actions more closely. She fills an apprenticeship recently held by young Tobias Ragg. After he accuses Sweeney of being a murderer, he is incarcerated in a madhouse. It's revealed that Sweeney dismembers his victims' bodies and, through underground tunnels, delivers the remains to Mrs. Lovett for her meat pies. The chimney fumes from the baking of flesh send a revolting smell throughout the neighborhood, especially in St. Dunstan's Church. Bones and remains of Sweeney's victims are discovered in the church's crypt. Johanna's lover Mark Ingestrie has been held captive in Mrs. Lovett's cellar and forced to bake the meat pies stuffed with butchered human flesh. He escapes using the lift that delivers pies from the cellar to the shop. To the assembled customers, he announces, "Ladies and gentlemen—I fear that what I am going to say will spoil your appetites; but the truth is beautiful at all times, and I have to state that Mrs. Lovett's pies are made of *human flesh!*" Sweeney poisons Mrs. Lovett, but he is quickly apprehended and executed. Johanna and Mark are married.

Lloyd's writers remained anonymous. Thomas Peckett Prest, who likely wrote at least half of Lloyd's 200 penny novels, was long considered to be the principal author of *The String of Pearls*. But scholarship early in the twentieth century more accurately and conclusively identified James Malcolm Rymer, another prolific writer in Lloyd's employ.[6]

Rymer was born in 1814 to a working-class family in Clerkenwell, a seedy London neighborhood outside the jurisdiction of the city and home to three notorious prisons. Rymer's writing was for people like himself. He began his literary career with his own publication in 1842, *The Queen's Magazine: A Monthly Miscellany*. It failed after just five months. He then went to work for Edward Lloyd and contributed several tales and soon became a mainstay of Lloyd's writers. Rymer's first bestseller was *Ada the Betrayed; or, Murder at the Old Smithy*, which remained in print from 1843 to 1858. In 1844 he likely authored *Joddrel, the Barber; or Mystery Unraveled*, published in the second volume of *Lloyd's Penny Atlas*. The title character, Lewis Joddrel, was a French-Irish barber whose customers mysteriously disappeared from his Bishopsgate barbershop. (This work likely inspired the invention of Sweeney Todd, another murderous barber who appeared in the first versions of *The String of Pearls* in 1846.) Rymer's greatest publishing success prior to *The String of Pearls* was *Varney, the Vampyre; or, The Feast of Blood* in 1846.

It is likely that Rymer was not the sole author drafting stories for *The String of Pearls*. Modern editor Dick Collins conducted a close reading of Lloyd's chapters in his 2008 introduction to the Wordsworth edition.[7] For instance, he surmised that Rymer was absent at least twice during a period in early 1847 when he was forced to deal with a bankruptcy filing. During that time, Lloyd apparently interpolated extended stories by other writers, likely the prolific Prest and perhaps Edward Peron Hingston, another occasional Salisbury Square contributor.

The seed of the Sweeney Todd legend was surely planted by the aforementioned short 1825 piece in *The Tell-Tale*, "A Terrific Story of the Rue-de-la-Harpe, Paris." It contained all the elements: the murderous barber, the unlucky customer, a faithful dog, an angry mob, and an accommodating pastry cook next door. Of course, Rymer's rendition of *The String of Pearls* contained vastly more material than this brief item. Lloyd's *The People's Periodical* where *The String of Pearls* was serialized was largely written for women, as indicated by several exemplary titles: *Rose Somerville*; *Helen, or the Forced Marriage*; *The Pride of Our Village*; and *The Ordeal by Touch*, all now attributed to Rymer.

Additionally, Collins identified an actual neighbor of Rymer who was a "pearl-stringer." He writes,

To find Samuel Todd . . . living a few doors away from James Malcolm Rymer is too much to be a coincidence. He must be the original of Sweeney Todd, at least in his link to pearls. As to his physical characteristics, it is well within belief that he would have been a low-slung, long, low-jointed sort of a fellow; stringing pearls by hand is a remarkably arduous task, requiring great concentration, and hours of staring at a tiny, fixed point down a magnifying glass. Leaning over his work all day, for years on end, Todd the pearl-stringer could well have been "sweeny."[8]

If Rymer's actual neighbor were known as "Sweeney" Todd, then it's not too far of a leap to suggest that was why he used that name for his fearsome character. Collins quickly adds, "It goes without saying that, however many characteristics the pearl-stringer shared with the barber, murder and cannibalism were not among them."[9] Collins simply offered this as a possible explanation for the character's name, not suggesting that Rymer's neighbor was a "Demon Barber."

It's apparent that Rymer crafted his text for *The String of Pearls* with young female readers in mind. But other story elements were clearly added to expand the narrative from the brief piece that appeared in *The Tell-Tale* in 1825. For example, the pearls of the title were an added feature. The central character of Johanna Oakley took considerably more initiative than typical Gothic heroines. Her aggressive search for her missing lover is another element that Rymer likely conceived to attract eager young female readers.

Sweeney Comes to the Stage

Just as best-selling novels in the twentieth and twenty-first centuries have become popular movies, *The String of Pearls* didn't take long to morph into another form of entertainment. On February 22, 1847, a month before Lloyd's serialized tale was finished, playwright George Dibdin Pitt (1795–1855) produced a stage adaptation, *The String of Pearls; or, The Fiend of Fleet Street*, at the Royal Britannia Saloon and Theatre in Hoxton. His play became a long-running and influential hit that inspired many later versions and variations of Sweeney's tale. Pitt dramatically embellished the role of Sweeney and coined the Demon Barber's menacing catchphrase, "I'll polish him off," that originated with his theatrical version. A later editor of Pitt's script pointed out that the playwright "made the great discovery that there was no need to whitewash the criminal; on the contrary, he were better black-washed. The important thing is to make him a supreme criminal, a demon."[10]

George Pitt (1799–1855) was the son of a musician and an actress. His uncles, composer Charles Dibdin and dramatist Thomas John Dibdin, encouraged and supported his pursuit of a theatrical career, so he took their surname as his middle name. Starting in 1830 George Dibdin Pitt became an actor, a stage manager, and a prolific playwright, having a hand in creating more than 250 scripts. The majority of his works were melodramas with sensational plots, powerful emotions, and stereotypical characters who spoke in bombastic or sentimental terms. His popular plays included *Rookwood* (1840), the first onstage tale of eighteenth-century highwayman Dick Turpin, and *Susan Hopley; or, The Vicissitudes of a Servant Girl* (1841), which was performed 343 times over an eight-year period.

In 1843 Pitt became the actor-manager of the Royal Brittania Saloon and Brittania Tavern, a Hoxton venue that could seat 1,000 patrons. There he presented numerous sensational melodramas such as *Pauline the Pirate* (1845) and *Margaret Maddison, The Female Felon* (1846). Many of his works told stories so abhorrent that the Lord Chamberlain's Office refused to license them, which could well have enhanced their notoriety in the same way that today's X-rated movies have a powerful fascination for contemporary audiences, even when condemned by conservative, moralistic, and religious leaders.[11]

Pitt's 1847 production of *The String of Pearls; or, The Fiend of Fleet Street* adapted the serial tale as it was being published weekly in Lloyd's *The People's Periodical and Family Library*. His stage rendition, written specifically for his audiences at the Brittania, made Sweeney Todd the amoral, unremorseful central character, a kind of villainous antihero. Pitt was the first to conceive of the mechanical barber chair that ejected Sweeney's victims down to his shop's basement cellar where he would "polish them off" if the fall failed to break their necks. (Around 1880 an edition of his adaptation mistakenly asserted that Pitt's play was first performed in 1842. That led to him sometimes being misidentified as the author of the tale, rather than the team that wrote Lloyd's 1846–7 *People's Periodical* serialization.)

Sweeney's Horror Expands

Thanks to instant success of Lloyd's 1846–7 serial publication of *The String of Pearls* and the expanded popularity and broad availability of Sweeney Todd's tale in print and onstage, Lloyd called upon his Salisbury Square freelancers to generate more material in late 1847 and 1848. They expanded the original 18 installments of 39 chapters to 92 stand-alone eight-page numbers sold for a penny each, encompassing 173 chapters. This enlargement was built out with numerous additional subplots that greatly extended the period of sales—89 weeks in all—and the length of the tales. But it also considerably reduced the narrative tension of the story. In 1850, Lloyd gathered all of this expanded matter into a bound, single-volume edition of 732 pages. This version of *The String of Pearls* had a new subtitle: *The Barber of Fleet Street: A Domestic Romance*.

The Demon Barber's story spread far and wide, especially to the rough-and-tumble United States. In 1852 American author Justin Jones (1814–89), who wrote under pseudonyms including Harry Hazel and Captain Merry, published a plagiarized version of Lloyd's expanded text, a thirty-six-chapter novel, *Sweeney Todd: or the Ruffian Barber. A Tale of Terror of the Seas and the Mysteries of the City*. Jones was an American printer and "dime novelist." The printer of the weekly *Hartford Pearl and Literary Gazette* as well as *Harry Hazel's Yankee Blade*, he also published children's books, short stories, and numerous novels of sea tales.

Throughout the 1860s numerous stage adaptations of *The String of Pearls* continued to be performed throughout England. In March 1861, Alfred Rayner's "popular drama" of *The String of Pearls* was onstage at London's Victoria Theatre. In April of that year at London's Marleybone Theatre in the West End, there was a production of *The String of Pearls; or, Sweeny Tod, The Barber of Fleet Street . . . Occurred in London, based on fact*. In June an anonymous dramatic version of the tale was performed at a saloon in London's East End. Mrs. Henry Young's adaptation, *The String of Pearls; or, The Life and*

Death of Sweeny Todd, was presented in July 1862 at the Effingham Saloon on Whitechapel Road. The same month there was a "revival of the great Drama," *The String of Pearls* at the City of London Theatre.

Around 1865 a dramatic adaptation by British actor and playwright Frederick Hazleton (1825–90) was performed at The Old Bower Saloon on Stangate Street in Lambeth. Almost all the plays produced at the seedy Bower in the 1860s were based on Penny Dreadfuls and appealed to blue-collar workers. The saloon seldom paid its actors and was often closed. (It disappeared altogether in 1879.) Hazleton was likely the Bower's house dramatist. A decade after his adaptation was produced, its script appeared as one of "Lacy's Acting Edition of Plays," a series that provided texts of classic and popular dramas for amateur theatricals. Across the final decades of the nineteenth century there were many onstage productions of the story, most based on texts by Pitt or Hazleton. These were performed both in London and in the provinces. Additionally, puppet versions of Sweeney Todd's story using marionettes and scripts adapted from Pitt's melodrama were staged in London and throughout England.

In the late 1870s the Fleet Street publisher Charles Fox and Co. brought out *Sweeney Todd, The Demon Barber of Fleet Street*, a 48-part, 576-page novelization likely by Charlton Lea, a later Penny Dreadful writer who also wrote *Spring-Heeled Jack: The Terror of London*. Lea's *Sweeney Todd* was very loosely drawn from Lloyd's original 1847 edition. In 1885, *The Boy's Standard*, a popular sensational periodical full of violent action and tales of cliff-hanging suspense, published *The String of Pearls; or Passages from the Life of Sweeny Todd, the Demon Barber*. This magazine and others like it were seriously criticized as worse than Penny Dreadfuls.

In 1892 publisher A. Ritchie of Red Lion Court, London, issued a shortened, thirteen-chapter version of the story, *Sweeney Todd the Barber of Fleet Street: A Thrilling Story of the Old City of London. Founded on Facts*. It was based on Lloyd's original text from 1846–7. On December 31, 1898, *The London Journal* began to reprint another slightly abridged version of the 1846–7 series.

In the twentieth century an appetite for tales of Sweeney's crime and murder continued unabated. In 1910 the Daisy Bank Press started to publish short versions of such tales with illustrations. Between 1910 and 1922, fifty tales were separately issued, each of thirty-two pages. One was a short version of Lloyd's text. The constant search to identify a real person behind the legend continued in 1915 with a short biography of Sweeney Todd written by Felix McGlennon, a British songwriter and publisher. His work was popular in music halls in the late nineteenth and early twentieth centuries, certainly venues where the existence of the Demon Barber was often debated—and believed.

The Legend Spreads

The nineteenth-century tales took on new forms in the twentieth century as they found their way into modern media and audiences beyond the UK. In 1925 a melodramatic Australian radio production of *Sweeney Todd, the Barbarous Barber* was broadcast in Melbourne. A script by J. P. Quaine subsequently published in Australia in 1932 might have been used for that radio production. It was billed as being "an entirely original version for the radio" and set "in the Reign of George the Second." (Around 1947 a radio version of Pitt's script was broadcast by the Canadian Broadcasting Corporation.)

In 1926 a short fifteen-minute silent film version starred actor G. A. Baughan as Sweeney Todd. Directed by George Dewhurst, it was described as "a comedy burlesque stage play" and first screened for the "Kinematograph Society Garden Party" of 1926, an occasional gathering of early film enthusiasts. That version now seems to be lost, but another silent film of *Sweeney Todd* in 1928 was directed by Walter West and featured prolific actor Moore Marriott. With a twisted ending—the story turns out to be a bad dream—the seventy-three-minute film was advertised as being "adapted from the famous 'Elephant and Castle' melodrama," a popular theater venue managed by English actor, Tod Slaughter (1885–1956). It was known as the presenter of popular "blood-and-thunder" melodramas starting in 1924 such as *Maria Marten; or, The Murder in the Red Barn* and, of course, *Sweeney Todd*.

In 1936 director and producer George King released a film, *Sweeney Todd, The Demon Barber*, in England. The story is framed by a barber in 1936 describing Sweeney's murderous ways to a gullible patron; at the film's end, the barber's terrified patron flees the shop with shaving cream still on his face. It was released in the United States in 1939. The film's screenplay, derived from Pitt's play, was a simplified and rather reorganized version by Frederick Hayward and H. F. Maltby. It was the first cinematic vehicle for actor Slaughter to reprise the stage role he had become famous for with countless performances at the Elephant and Castle. By that time he was the British actor best known for portraying over-the-top villains and maniacs. For two more decades he was the go-to actor to play such extreme characters. His given name was Norman Carter Slaughter, but he changed it to "Tod Slaughter," firmly connecting him to his performances as the Demon Barber, an onstage role he was reputed to have played as many as 4,000 times. He came to be known as "Europe's Horror Man" for his ghoulish overacting in films, especially the classic 1936 screen version of the tale.

Partnered with King, Slaughter played villains in numerous shocking films distributed by Ambassador Pictures including *The Crimes of Stephen Hawke* (1936), *It's Never Too Late to Mend* (1937), *The Ticket of Leave Man* (1938), *The Face at the Window* (1939) and *Crimes at the Dark House* (1940). These were swiftly and cheaply made films produced to fulfill a British government quota; most were forgettable. During the Second World War, Slaughter continued stage work in productions including *Jack the Ripper* and *Dr. Jekyll and Mr. Hyde*.

In January 1946 a half-hour radio play, *The Strange Case of the Demon Barber*, was broadcast in the United States on NBC, based on an incident in Sir Arthur Conan Doyle's Sherlock Holmes 1893 story, "The Yellow Face." With actor Basil Rathbone playing Holmes, it featured an encounter between the detective and an actor performing the role of Sweeney Todd, who identifies much too closely with his stage role. The adaptation was part of a radio series, *The New Adventures of Sherlock Holmes* (1939–46).

In 1948 selections from Lloyd's by the then century-old, serialized version of *The String of Pearls* were featured in E. S. Turner's *Boys Will Be Boys: The Story of Sweeney Todd, Deadwood Dick, Sexton Blake, Billy Bunter, Dick Barton, et al.* (Michael Joseph, 1948). The same year Stanley Ellin's short story, "Specialty of the House," appeared in *Ellery Queen's Mystery Magazine*. The story of a New York restaurant with an unsavory gourmet menu was obviously influenced by the tale of Sweeney Todd. In *London Mystery and Mythology* (Staples Press, 1952) historian William Kent examined the question, "Was Sweeney Todd a Fleet Street Barber?" In 1956 actor Stanley Holloway (who played Alfie Doolittle, Eliza's Cockney father, in the Broadway production of *My Fair Lady* that same year) recorded a popular song, "Sweeney Todd the Barber" by R. P. Weston in the tradition of a Music Hall monologue.

The Demon Barber's tale became a ballet with music by composer Malcolm Arnold (Op. 68) and choreographed by John Cranko in 1956 for the Royal Ballet's touring company. The one-act ballet premiered at the Shakespeare Memorial Theatre in Stratford with scenery and costumes by Alix Stone in the style of Victorian toy theaters. Its first London performance by the Royal Ballet happened on August 16, 1960, at the Royal Opera House, Covent Garden.

In the spring of 1962 a new musical, *The World of Sweeney Todd*, with book and lyrics by William Scott and Ken Appleby and music by Peter Satterfield was staged at the People's Theatre in Newcastle-Upon-Tyne. It was revived in 1970 and again in April 1995 by the Redditch Operatic Society at the Palace Theatre in Redditch. In June 1962 Brian Burton's *Sweeney Todd, The Barber: A Melodrama*, adapted from Pitt's Victorian version, was presented at the Crescent Theatre, Birmingham.

The appetite for such horror stories continued in 1969 with *Sweeney Todd: The Demon Barber of Fleet Street* (subtitled *A Victorian Melodrama*) by Austin Rosser, performed at the Dundee Repertory Theatre, Scotland. A violent and graphic 1970 film, *Bloodthirsty Butchers*, was created by John Borske and Andy Milligan. The same year in February the British TV anthology series, *Mystery and Imagination* (1966–70), featured as its penultimate episode a version of *Sweeney Todd* based on Pitt's original melodrama.

The Futile Search for the "Real" Sweeney

Fascination with Penny Dreadful tales such as those published by Edward Lloyd has led several enthusiastic writers to claim they have identified a real Sweeney Todd whose actual deeds were the source of such tales. were built upon. British journalist Peter Haining (1940–2007) is the foremost example of the distance one writer went to prove the existence of a historic Demon Barber. In two books—*The Mystery and Horrible Murders of Sweeney Todd, The Demon Barber of Fleet Street* (London: F. Muller, 1979) and *Sweeney Todd:*

The Real Story of the Demon Barber of Fleet Street (London: Boxtree Ltd., 1993)—Haining claimed without documentation to have spent twenty-five years researching "historic details" that he spun into an intriguing narrative. His so-called research has been totally discredited and dismissed by numerous subsequent scholars.

It appears that Haining's surmises are as fanciful as the fictional narrative that Edward Lloyd published in the 1840s. Nevertheless, the narrative he spun is worth reviewing, if for nothing more than his extensive and imaginative inventions. Haining identified Sweeney's birthdate as October 16, 1756, the child of a pair of alcoholic silk winders. He supposedly hated his parents and spent much of his childhood in the Tower of London's museum studying torture instruments that might be employed in ridding himself of his neglectful, manipulative father and mother. They seemingly disappeared during a particularly cold winter in 1768, leaving young Sweeney to his own means.

Haining claimed that two years later Sweeney was apprenticed to a cutler whose specialty was razors. At age fourteen, he was sent to the notorious Newgate Prison for five years following a conviction of petty theft. While incarcerated, Haining suggested, Sweeney was a barber's assistant, cleaning up prisoners prior to public executions. Once released at age nineteen, so Haining's chronicle goes, Sweeney set up business on a street corner and shortly after opened a shop near Hyde Park. He had a young woman as his assistant. There was no record of marriage, but Sweeney referred to her as his wife and took out much of his rage on her.

Stating that Sweeney was accused of a murder in 1784, Haining linked him to the previously cited item from *the Annual Register*, in which the killer is unnamed. A young drunk boasts of having had "certain favours the night before," and is rewarded by a barber cutting his throat, believing the "fine girl" to be his wife. Haining stated that the anonymous barber leased a space for his shop—perhaps at 186 Fleet Street, adjacent to St. Dunstan's Church—and began his grisly murder spree. The crime-infested neighborhood was, without a doubt, an obvious setting for gruesome behavior by a man who promoted his services as "a barber and a surgeon," providing frequent extraction services for people suffering from dental pain.

Given this unnamed barber's vicious and argumentative personality, Haining concluded that he committed another murder in April 1785 and proceeded to slash the throats of other dissolute characters who possessed valuable items he coveted, products of their own ill-gotten gain. He extrapolated that Sweeney disposed of his victims' bodies in the crypt beneath St. Dunstan's Church.

Haining identified this barber as Sweeney Todd and suggested that he met Mrs. Lovett, a young baker, recently widowed. Together they concocted a plan to use flesh and organs from the departed as filling for her meat pies. But the bones and other remains deposited in the crypt under St. Dunstan's began to emanate a nauseating odor, resulting in a police investigation. Haining reported that Sweeney was sent to Newgate Prison, and Mrs. Lovett poisoned herself.

Haining reported that Sweeney's acts resulted in a sensational trial—of which there is no record—followed by a quick verdict. He claimed that *The Newgate Calendar* reported, "All eyes were turned upon the most dastardly criminal of the age, Sweeney Todd, who stood in the dock glaring at the foreman of the jury." According to Haining, Sweeney at age forty-six, was publicly hanged on January 25, 1802, observed by a tumultuous crowd of thousands. Haining's entire account has been discredited. Other more serious researchers have found no historical records to substantiate any of his claims. That being said, over the nineteenth and twentieth centuries many such fictional details seeped into and gave credibility to the legend of Sweeney Todd that began to circulate in the 1840s.

New Blood into an Old Play

In 1968 young actor Christopher Bond, age twenty-three, was working at the Victoria Theatre in Stoke-on-Trent, England. The company had box office success two years earlier with a nineteenth-century melodrama, so a similar production was announced of another work: *Sweeney Todd*. "We thought that if the script needed doctoring we could sort it out in rehearsals," Bond recalled in 1990. "Due to a series of cock-ups, we didn't get hold of a copy of the play until two weeks before rehearsals were due to begin, and on the page the show was crude, repetitive, and simplistic—hardly any plot and less character development."¹² That script was George Dibdin Pitt's from 1847, certainly not the kind of play that would entertain twentieth-century audiences.

Bond was an aspiring writer, so he volunteered to take a stab at making the melodrama into a more contemporary work. "It would retain the title, the razors, the pies, and the trick chair and be delivered in a week's time." He met the opening night deadline, and in the process made much more out of the story, significantly elevating Pitt's crass script by changing Sweeney's motivation. No longer was he a stone-cold murderer who cut his customers' throats in order to rob them. Instead, Bond concocted a back story about an honest man cheated out of his wife and livelihood by a corrupt judge and his unscrupulous beadle. Bond imagined Sweeney convicted of a crime he did not commit and transported to a penal colony in Australia then returned London for vengeance rather than greed.

In adapting the nineteenth-century melodrama Bond enhanced the story in numerous ways, borrowing from Thomas Middleton's *The Revenger's Tragedy* (1606) and Alexander Dumas's *The Count of Monte Christo* (1844). He also threw in

> elements of pastiche Shakespeare in a sort of blankish verse for Sweeney, the Judge, and the lovers to talk; borrowed the name of the author of *The Prisoner of Zenda* [Anthony Hope wrote the adventure tale in 1894] for my sailor boy; remembered some market patter I'd learnt as a child; and adapted the wit and wisdom of Brenda, who ran the greengrocer's shop opposite my house, for Mrs. Lovett's ruminations upon life, death and the state of her sex life.¹³

Bond's use of unrhymed iambic pentameter for the upper-class characters resembled Shakespeare's use of such language to reinforce certain noble characters in his plays. Bond wrote the role of Tobias Ragg for himself.

His object was "to add to the chair and the pies an exciting story, characters that are large but real, and situations that, given a mad world not unlike our own, are believable." Maxwell Shaw, who staged the premiere of Bond's script wrote, "When I first read this version by C. G. Bond, I was immediately aware of the fact that he had written, not only an entirely new play based on the original idea, but one with a real plot, characters, genuine comedy situations and, above all, something to say."[14]

Bond's morbidly delightful stew of storytelling was enjoyed by audiences, and his script did well at a series of regional theaters before landing at Joan Littleton's Stratford East stage in London where Sondheim saw a performance in 1973. "I had heard of Sweeney Todd," Sondheim told an interviewer in 1979,[15] "because I am an Anglophile, but I had never seen or read anything about him. So I thought it would be fun to see the play, and I just had a wonderful time."

Stratford East was a truly blue-collar theater, adjacent to a pub and raucous drinkers. They brought their beers into the auditorium, where the informal atmosphere encouraged noisy crowds that sang and clinked steins and booed, hissed, and threw food at villainous characters. Sondheim loved the production and the atmosphere: "It had a combination of charm and creepiness. I don't remember being particularly frightened . . . but it must have scared me somewhat."[16] Sondheim saw that Bond's potboiler script knitted together, "disparate elements that had been in existence rather dully for a hundred and some-odd years and made them into a first-rate play."[17]

The revisions added psychological depth and narrative texture to the play's characters. Bond made Sweeney the victim of cruel injustice by the immoral Judge Turpin (a character not present in Pitt's theatrical adaptation) who used false charges to transport Sweeney to Australia and take advantage of Lucy, Sweeney's innocent wife, assumed to be dead when the barber returned to London years later. Bond created a new story for Johanna, transforming her into Sweeney's daughter, adopted as the Judge's ward, with lascivious intentions. Sweeney became a man literally hell-bent on revenge, and Mrs. Lovett restored his straight razors, which she had kept since he was sent away fifteen years earlier. No longer was Sweeney a vile, rapacious man murdering for personal gain. Instead, when he missed an opportunity to extinguish the Judge, he experienced a psychotic break and became mass murderer, a man who was both wronged and a monster.

Bond established a delicate balance for Todd, creating a tragic character but keeping the play's tone balanced between drama with heightened language and simultaneously lighter with some tongue-in-cheek humor. His adaptation, still fundamentally a melodrama, edged closer to tragedy.

In particular, greed no longer drove Sweeney's murders. Instead, he was obsessed with revenge. Fueled by Judge Turpin's unjust treatment and the vicious rape of Sweeney's sweet wife Lucy plus the immoral cultivation of their beautiful daughter Johanna, the barber teetered on the brink of madness. This powerful psychological impetus pushed Sweeney completely over the edge as his fury shifted to all mankind. He had been a good man, but naïveté was his downfall, and his regrets impelled him toward the tale's inevitable bloody denouement.

Bond's use of more elegant language made Sweeney's tale all the more sophisticated. He injected a degree of social commentary regarding the harsh industrial nineteenth century and the way people with power, such as Judge Turpin, thought nothing of using and disposing of people of lower status. Society's harsh treatment gave the Demon Barber all the more reason to believe that his crimes against others were fitting and appropriate retribution for the miseries he had experienced. That's considerably more sophisticated than the typical Victorian melodramatic tale in Pitt's play. In fact, Bond's elevation of Sweeney's story pointed toward a full-blown tragedy, culminating in his ignorant murder of his own addled life.

Sondheim Steps In

After seeing the production of Bond's play, Sondheim immediately thought of adapting it into a serious Broadway musical. The following day he had lunch with British director John Dexter, a theater veteran who had staged *Do I Hear a Waltz?* (1965), a musical that Sondheim provided lyrics to a score by Richard Rodgers, an unhappy experience that Sondheim preferred to forget. But Dexter also staged productions for New York City's Metropolitan Opera, and he had more than once encouraged Sondheim to write a through-composed, operatic piece. When he told Dexter that he felt *Sweeney Todd* could be transformed into "an operatic piece," Dexter responded warmly. "He said it would be perfect," Sondheim recalled.[18] He seldom had an inspiration for a show, ideas more frequently advanced by playwrights. But this one truly appealed to his love of melodrama, horror, and farce.

Sondheim ambitiously imagined taking the Bond's script to a significantly higher level, further transforming the story elements the playwright had conceived: "It immediately struck me as material for a musical horror story, one which would not be sung-through, but which would be held together by ceaseless underscoring that would keep an audience in suspense and maybe even scare the hell out of them."[19] With Dexter's encouragement, Sondheim set out almost immediately to acquire the rights to Bond's script.

As it turned out, a pair of Broadway producers—Richard Barr (who produced Edward Albee's *Who's Afraid of Virginia Woolf*, Mart Crowley's *The Boys in the Band* and works by Samuel Beckett, Terrence McNally, and John Guare) and Charles Woodward (who co-produced *The Boys in the Band* and a dozen other Broadway shows)—got there first, optioning Bond's play for a New York production expanded with barroom songs. Once they learned of Sondheim's expressed interest, Barr and Woodward asked Bond if he would be willing to have Sondheim involved.

Flora Roberts, Sondheim's agent, stepped in to represent him. He was her longest-running client, dating back to his early days as a professional in the mid-1950s. She had reinforced Oscar Hammerstein's encouragement of Sondheim to join *West Side Story*'s creative team as its lyricist, even though his eagerness to compose made him reticent. She seconded the notion that work with high-profile professionals such as Leonard Bernstein, Jerome Robbins, and Arthur Laurents with Broadway experience would enhance his career. As one of Sondheim's mentors, Roberts often made firm, insightful recommendations regarding details his subsequent shows, including *Company* and *A Little Night Music*.

Roberts took in a performance at Stratford East. "The show was playing in this wonderful East End theater," she recalled, "and they had a piano player in the lobby and people drinking beer and eating meat pies . . . It was such a fun atmosphere, very colorful. And I immediately saw why Steve was excited."[20] She stepped in and took control of the negotiations.

Roberts met with the playwright, who did not require much convincing since he was already aware of Sondheim's reputation. Their paths had actually crossed a few years earlier when Bond formed a favorable impression. "What struck me most forcibly was his complete lack of bullshit. 'What a lovely bloke,' I remember thinking. 'What's he doing working in the theater?'"[21]

The imposing and persistent Roberts handled all the negotiations with Bond and the producers. "I remember being terrified of her," Bond wrote in his introduction to *Sweeney Todd*'s libretto, adding, "I still am. She reminded me of a cross between Mae West and Lady Bracknell. She was extremely direct and straightforward." Sondheim honored Roberts's efforts on his behalf by dedicating *Sweeney Todd* to her and her sister Janet. One outcome of the negotiations: Bond is credited in the libretto and recognized on the first page of all theater programs for productions of *Sweeney Todd*: "From an adaptation by Christopher Bond."

Given the show's subsequent Broadway success, Bond had nothing but praise for Sondheim. "I find it difficult to write about someone whom I admire so much without it sounding soppy; suffice it to say that since I've become familiar with his work I find it difficult to sit through a show that isn't by Stephen Sondheim without wishing that it was."[22] Writing his 1990 introduction to *Sweeney Todd*'s libretto, Bond mentioned that he had directed four productions of Sondheim's musical rendition "and seen a further six or seven productions around the world."

3

First Blood on Broadway
Sweeney Todd, 1979

By the time contractual matters were settled with playwright Christopher Bond, Sondheim was deeply absorbed in completing another show, *Pacific Overtures*, which opened on January 11, 1976. He and Hal Prince were also engaged in another time-consuming project, Prince's cinematic rendition of their 1973 show *A Little Night Music*. Sondheim was reworking several songs from that show for the movie. Starring beautiful film actress Elizabeth Taylor and stage actor Len Cariou, who received a Tony nomination for his Broadway performance as Fredrik Egerman in *Night Music*'s original production (and who would be cast subsequently as the original Sweeney Todd), the film was a box office disappointment following its release in March 1978. Sondheim was of the opinion that it should not have been made.

In the interim, *Sweeney Todd* producers Richard Barr and Charles Woodward recruited additional investors to support the show's production. New partners were the Producer Circle Company: Robert Fryer, managing director of the Ahmanson Theatre in Los Angeles; heiress Mary Lea Johnson; and Martin Richards, a leading casting agent. Fryer and Richards had backed Kander and Ebb's *Chicago* in 1975. Michigan philanthropists Dean and Judy Manos also invested in the production.[1] For the first time in a decade of working with Sondheim, Hal Prince was not involved as a producer.

With the rights in hand and the producers eager to get started, Sondheim's initial plan was to personally adapt Bond's script into a libretto while also writing the score and the lyrics. Late in the summer of 1976, an item in the *New York Times* said he was finally at work on *Sweeney Todd*.² The production was anticipated to open in California early in 1977 in advance of a Broadway transfer during the summer or fall. Producer Charles Woodward commented, "It does not try to scare you. It's a comic musical." That was not Sondheim's plan.

A year later he had made little progress, although he had convinced Hal Prince to direct the show. While no longer serving as a producer, Prince had fully embarked on his directing career, and he and Sondheim had collaborated on a winning series of

Figure 3.1 *Director Hal Prince was initially hesitant to direct* Sweeney Todd. *Once he was persuaded by Sondheim, he gave it an epic production. Photofest.*

shows during the 1970s (Figure 3.1). But he was not initially enthusiastic about *Sweeney Todd*. On their previous collaborations—*Company, Follies, A Little Night Music* and *Pacific Overtures*—Prince and Sondheim came to a quick agreement about a concept for each production.

"*Sweeney* was the one show I was reluctant about," Prince recalled. "I really did not know what that play was."³ Sondheim believed the focus should be on the issue of obsession, "the annihilating power of vindictive revenge." His instinct had been to make the production small, dark, intimate, and frightening.

Prince had a very different idea. He saw Sweeney's story as one of people driven to desperation by the dehumanizing impact of the Industrial Revolution on British society.⁴ They finally came together around the joint notion that Sweeney was a victim of the class struggle and an oppressive society. Accordingly, Prince's epic interpretation held sway for the show's initial Broadway production in the immense, relatively new 1,933-seat Uris Theatre, the largest of any regularly used Broadway theater. (Today it is known as the Gershwin, the longtime home of *Wicked* beginning in 2003.)

"What I wanted to write was a horror movie," Sondheim later explained. "The whole point of the thing is that it's a background score for a horror film, which is what I intended to do and what it is."[5] Once he recognized that he did not know how to reduce the script and understood that the intricate plot demanded more attention than he could provide, he went back to Prince.

"I was bogged down, and Hal came to my rescue, suggesting British playwright Hugh Wheeler should come on board," Sondheim said. Wheeler had written the erudite book of Sondheim and Prince's romantic and successful *A Little Night Music* and had helped with the libretto for *Pacific Overtures*. On September 16, 1977, the *New York Times* reported that Sondheim had stepped away from writing the show's book, and Wheeler would develop *Sweeney Todd*'s script. Only then did Sondheim begin to work seriously on the score.[6]

Wheeler took on the task of reducing Bond's dense, forty-six-page script to allow room for Sondheim's music. He was enthusiastic about the project. "It's a wonderful story," he said,

> and I thought Bond's version slightly better than the others. But from my point of view, even his version was that absolutely unreal, old melodrama where you boo the villain . . . whenever Sweeney would come in, the audience would hiss and throw hot dogs. The version we wanted to do was a whole tone that was so difficult to get. We wanted to make it as nearly as we could into a sort of tragedy.[7]

The show's eventual credits listed "Book by Hugh Wheeler" in addition to "From an adaptation by Christopher Bond."

A further complication slowed *Sweeney Todd*'s eventual arrival on Broadway. Backers did not quickly come forward as added production expenses were projected to exceed $1 million. Sondheim participated in more than a dozen auditions, but the gruesome tale failed to bring people with deep pockets on board. Producers Woodward and Barr resorted to an unusual strategy: they placed an ad in the *New York Times* in March 1978: "New Stephen Sondheim Musical Open for Investment." More than 1,500 interested parties responded, generating $225,000 from backers across the United States and abroad.[8] Interested parties could invest as little as $1,800 in a work in progress that featured a quartet of esteemed Broadway talents—Sondheim and Prince, plus award-winning actors Angela Lansbury and Len Cariou. That eventually convinced 271 people to step up, a record number for the time, to complete the production's $900,000 capitalization plus 10 percent budgeted for cost overruns. It was enough to close the gap for the production's nearly million-dollar budget, extremely high for a Broadway show in the late 1970s.

Variety commented, "That's a huge number of backers for a legit production, especially in the present-day climate in which larger institutional investments are common. It's thought to be a record number of backers for a Broadway show."[9] Many investors signed on, even those dubious about the show's potential. Quite a few were surprised by its relatively positive reception.[10] The original production, which opened on March 1, 1979, lost money, not an unusual outcome for a Broadway show. *Sweeney Todd* had repaid 59 percent of its investment by the time it closed in June 1980 after 557 performances.

Of course, the fact that it won eight of its nine Tony nominations—including Best Musical, Best Score, Best Book, Best Direction, Best Actor, and Best Actress—helped solidify the show as one to be admired, even if the subject seemed unlikely for a Broadway musical. Ultimate profitability took eleven years.[11] Of course, over time those original backers had bragging rights regarding their support for a remarkable work, increasingly called a masterpiece. Perhaps that was a greater return than any monetary reward.

Sondheim termed his show "A Musical Thriller." It surely was not the "comic musical" that producer Woodward proclaimed in 1977. So just what was *Sweeney Todd*? Asked to categorize it, Sondheim suggested "a dark operetta." But he added that for him it really was "a movie for the stage."[12] The music he created included twenty-five distinct songs but, in fact, nearly 80 percent of the show was either sung or underscored. Sondheim's melodies played constantly behind the action, especially leitmotifs (repetitive musical themes) that linked characters, themes, and events.

Prince's immense physical production was not what Sondheim had envisioned. He imagined staging the story it in a small, dark, spooky theater in a way that would terrify audiences. He wanted it to be as black as a coffin that would encompass entering audiences, offering theatergoers no chance to get settled before the lights went out. He intended the grisly story of a serial killer and meat pies to be relentless, and he composed a complex, emotive score to ramp up the disturbing atmosphere.

Prince had persuaded Sondheim that the show needed to be expanded in epic ways, a majestic, musical condemnation of dehumanized society crushed by the Industrial Revolution. It did that, to be sure, but woven through it also was a macabre sense of dark humor injected by Sondheim and book writer Wheeler. Angela Lansbury, who originated the role of the amoral baker Nellie Lovett, said, "We're playing the lowest comedy you can imagine in the highest comedy manner."[13]

Hal Prince's Creative Team

Prince's award-winning shows throughout the 1970s were created by a dream team of designers, led by the brilliant Boris Aronson, who created Tony Award-winning sets for *Company*, *Follies*, and *A Little Night Music*. He retired in 1976 after *Pacific Overtures*. In 1979 Prince needed to recruit a new generation of talent. For *Sweeney Todd*, he assembled a production team that included a veteran book writer and a new collection of designers and other professionals.

Hugh Wheeler (Book Writer). In 1973 playwright, screenwriter and novelist Wheeler collaborated with Prince and Sondheim to adapt Ingmar Bergman's screenplay for *Smiles of a Summer Night* (1955) into the script for *A Little Night Music*. In 1977, Sondheim confessed to be stymied in his effort to adapt Bond's concise melodramatic script. Prince knew he could rely on Wheeler, who excelled at distilling complex stories into straightforward narratives. After *Night Music*, Wheeler had revised the libretto for Leonard Bernstein's *Candide* for Prince's 1974 revival as a one-act hit. It won the Tony Award for Best Book of a Musical and ensured that *Candide* would be remembered as one of the decade's greatest productions. Prince knew Wheeler was the right collaborator to partner again with Sondheim (Figure 3.2).

Figure 3.2 *When Sondheim decided to step back from writing the book for Sweeney Todd, playwright and novelist Hugh Wheeler was recruited to adapt Christopher Bond's play. Photofest.*

Wheeler contributed some valuable ideas, and the only thing about the collaboration that irritated Sondheim was that, "Hugh, being Hugh," as he said, "removed Bond's fine dialogue in favor of his own; Sondheim made sure to go back to the original play when he wrote the songs."[14] Wheeler admired Bond's script and thought it had improved on its melodramatic roots, but he firmly believed it still required further dramatic elevation. "I wrote it as a play, but I encouraged Steve to cannibalize it and make it nearly all music."[15]

That was an important course of action. Sondheim and Wheeler's rendition hewed closely to Bond's first act. But as the Broadway production developed, story elements were added that were not derived from Bond's version, and they required songs for key moments. Most notably, "The Ballad of Sweeney Todd" became Sondheim's musical device to remind audiences of the ominous threat posed by the murderous barber. Additional memorable numbers not rooted in Bond's script were "Green Finch and Linnet Bird," "Johanna," "Pretty Women," "Epiphany," "A Little Priest," and "Not While I'm Around."[16]

"Hugh's major contribution to *Sweeney Todd* was structural," Sondheim told a Chicago interviewer. "It had to do with the pacing of the love story. Also, a couple of spoken jokes in 'A Little Priest' are his."[17] Wheeler was British and had a profound understanding of the Victorian era and the legend of Sweeney Todd. So he brought significant insight to the show's finished book. Here is a synopsis of Wheeler's book:

Synopsis of Wheeler's Book with Sondheim's Songs

Prologue

Accompanied by sepulchral organ music and a jarring factory whistle, the story opens with the citizens of London, a kind of Greek chorus, who invite the audience to witness the gruesome story of the "Demon Barber" ("The Ballad of Sweeney Todd").

Act 1

Anthony Hope, a young sailor, and Sweeney Todd, an escaped prisoner, arrive at the London docks in 1846 after a long sea voyage during which Anthony rescued Sweeney from a shipwreck. Anthony is happy to return to London, but Sweeney, while grateful to the young man for saving his life, is full of grim irony ("No Place Like London"). A ragged Beggar Woman pleads for money and offers sexual favors before they send her away. Sweeney tells Anthony that an immoral judge wrongfully ordered him transported to Australia on petty charges so as to be able to steal Sweeney's wife ("The Barber and His Wife"). He hopes to reestablish his barber business on Fleet Street.

Sweeney enters Mrs. Nellie Lovett's disgusting, unsanitary pie shop. She offers him a sample of her wares, acknowledging its lack of appeal ("The Worst Pies in London"). He asks about renting her upstairs room. She tells him it had been vacant and unwanted since the barber Benjamin Barker was sent to Australia by the evil Judge Turpin, who coveted and seduced Lucy, his pretty young wife. Mrs. Lovett says Turpin and Beadle Bamford, the judge's court assistant, got her drunk and raped her during a masked ball ("Poor Thing"). Sweeney's anguish at hearing this tale reveals his true identity as Benjamin Barker to Mrs. Lovett. She tells him Lucy swallowed poison, and the Judge took custody of their daughter Johanna as his ward. Todd swears vengeance. Mrs. Lovett has stored Sweeney's razors since his departure; he is manically thrilled to hold them again ("My Friends").

Anthony sees Johanna in a high window at Judge Turpin's mansion when she calls out to a bird seller ("Green Finch and Linnet Bird"). He instantly falls in love ("Ah, Miss"). The Beggar Woman warns him about trespassing, but Anthony is smitten and buys a bird for Johanna ("Johanna"). Turpin orders him away, and the beadle strangles the bird.

The flamboyant barber Signor Adolfo Pirelli hawks a miracle hair elixir to a noisy crowd. Toby, a young boy serving as Pirelli's simpleminded assistant, beats a drum and sings to attract attention ("Pirelli's Miracle Elixir") to the fraudulent product. Sweeney and Mrs. Lovett discredit Pirelli and his elixir, and people demand refunds. Sweeney beats the ostentatious Pirelli in a shaving contest, establishing his professional credentials ("The Contest") then begins methodically to plot his revenge ("The Ballad of Sweeney Todd").

At home, Turpin spies on and lusts after his innocent ward ("Johanna"), Sweeney's daughter, and plans to marry her. Sweeney is impatient for the Judge's arrival, while Mrs. Lovett restrains him ("Wait"). Anthony pleads with Sweeney to help him free Johanna. Pirelli reveals himself as Daniel O'Higgins, "a down and out Irish lad" and Barker's onetime apprentice. He threatens to expose Sweeney's true identity. They fight and Sweeney kills him, stuffing his body in a trunk ("Pirelli's Death").

Anthony proposes to Johanna ("Kiss Me"). Beadle Bamford urges Turpin to be better groomed to appeal to his intended ("Ladies in Their Sensitivities"), suggesting a visit to Sweeney's barber shop. Turpin goes there, and Sweeney prepares to slit his throat, savoring the moment before his revenge, while the Judge lasciviously imagines his future with Johanna ("Pretty Women"). Anthony bursts in and reveals his planned elopement before he realizes Sweeney's customer is the judge, who furiously storms out. Enraged at the missed opportunity, Sweeney's loathing explodes to all mankind, pledging to murder indiscriminately ("Epiphany"). Mrs. Lovett proposes a gruesome plan to use his victims' finely ground flesh to fill her meat pies. Sweeney admires her genius, and they celebrate the possibilities with extreme black humor ("A Little Priest").

Act 2

Mrs. Lovett's pies have become spectacularly popular ("God, That's Good!"). Sweeney's elaborate barber chair arrives, designed to drop victims down a chute into the bakehouse where a grinding machine awaits. Sweeney's pace of murder accelerates. Anthony learns Judge Turpin has locked Johanna away in Fogg's Lunatic Asylum to keep her from him. Mrs. Lovett tries to calm Sweeney with her dream of a vacation and married life ("By the Sea"). The Beggar Woman is alarmed by strange odors and smoke from the bakehouse.

Sweeney helps Anthony pose as a wigmaker to gain entrance to Fogg's Lunatic Asylum where inmates' hair is shorn and sold (Wigmaker Sequence). The barber sends a message to Turpin suggesting that Johanna will soon be hidden at his shop ("The Letter").

Toby, apprenticed by Mrs. Lovett since Pirelli's mysterious disappearance, is suspicious of Sweeney and frets about Mrs. Lovett's safety ("Not While I'm Around"). When Toby recognizes Pirelli's money purse, he realizes she is complicit in the barber's disappearance. She takes him to the cellar to teach him to grind the meat, then locks him in.

Beadle Bamford arrives to investigate complaints about foul smells. He persists in waiting for the absent Sweeney while he plays Mrs. Lovett's harmonium and sings call-and-response tunes ("Parlor Songs") that the imprisoned Toby answers. Mrs. Lovett sends the beadle upstairs to Sweeney for a free shave, and the barber quickly dispatches him. When his body comes down the chute to the bakehouse, Toby's fears are confirmed.

Anthony's rescue plan breaks down at the lunatic asylum; Johanna takes his gun and kills Jonas Fogg, the asylum's director ("City on Fire"). The lunatics run through the streets, creating pandemonium, and the lovers flee to the barbershop with her disguised as a sailor. She hides in Sweeney's trunk while Anthony leaves to hire a coach to escape London. The Beggar Woman shows up and warns Sweeney about Mrs. Lovett. With impetuous haste, he murders the Beggar Woman and sends her down the chute.

Sweeney's letter has convinced Turpin that Johanna is safe and longs to be reunited. When the Judge arrives, Sweeney offers a shave, then reveals himself to be Benjamin Barker and slashes the Judge's throat ("The Judge's Return").

Johanna emerges from the trunk and narrowly escapes Sweeney's wrath. He descends to the bakehouse where Mrs. Lovett is trying to finish off the nearly dead Judge. Sweeney is horrified to realize that the Beggar Woman is his onetime wife Lucy and that Mrs. Lovett has deceived him. He feigns forgiveness, embracing her, then pushes her into her own oven. He cradles Lucy's body. Toby, his hair gone white from shock, fear, and the mayhem he has witnessed, comes from behind Sweeney with the razor and slices the barber's throat. Constables, Anthony, and Johanna arrive and see the carnage.

Epilogue

The citizens of London and characters of the story sing a warning that revenge begets revenge. Sweeney rises from the grave, glares at the audience malevolently, then slams the oven door ("The Ballad of Sweeney Todd").

Prince assembled a team of designers to create *Sweeney Todd*'s frightening physical portrait of London populated by the denizens of decaying Fleet Street. Others shaped the music that would provide the show's unnerving atmosphere and tone.

Eugene Lee (Scenic Designer). Prince recruited Lee, an inventive academic designer, to create the monumental set for *Sweeney Todd*. The Wisconsin native trained at the Art Institute of Chicago, Carnegie Mellon University and Yale School of Drama. In 1967 he became the resident designer at Trinity

Repertory Theatre in Providence, Rhode Island, a position he held throughout his life. Nevertheless, he often worked beyond Providence. He designed Prince's environmental production of Bernstein's *Candide*, a surprise hit in 1974 for Brooklyn's Chelsea Theater Center. It moved to the Broadway Theatre later that year as a revival and won a 1974 Tony Award for Best Scenic Design. TV producer Lorne Michaels saw that production and in 1975 hired Lee as the production designer for his new NBC comedy show, *Saturday Night Live*, a role he filled until his death in 2023.

For *Sweeney Todd*, Prince booked the huge Uris Theatre. It had a 65-foot proscenium arch and an 80-foot-wide stage, but he was eager to make it feel cramped and unpleasant. He said, "The story . . . calls for a community of dirt-poor people of all ages—where better to set such a collection than the jail of a factory?"[18] Prince envisioned a Victorian structure with a vaulted, gritty glass roof covered in soot, "so filthy that the sun could not make its way to the 'slaves' below."[19] The factory became his visual metaphor for the impact of the Industrial Revolution on the downtrodden, impoverished residents of London.

Lee filled the theater's gigantic space with pieces of an abandoned iron foundry he located in Rhode Island and purchased for $25,000. The massive structure was dismantled and moved to New York City for reassembly. It became a picture frame for Sweeney's story, including a soot-covered glass roof. The grimy factory interior was backed by a cyclorama of an unpopulated London street. It looked like "a gigantic machine, part prison, part factory, part cathedral."[20] Asked what the factory manufactured, Prince typically responded—with a smile—"a musical called *Sweeney Todd*."[21] (See Figure 3.3.)

Figure 3.3 *Scenic designer Eugene Lee's immense set for Sweeney Todd's original 1979 production featured girders, catwalks, and grimy overhead windows from an abandoned Rhode Island iron foundry purchased for $25,000 and moved to New York City. Photo by Van Williams.*

Prince described elements of Lee's scenic design.

> We put a cube in the middle of the factory. From the stage level, stairs led to Sweeney Todd's barbershop at the top of the cube with Sweeney's trick chair, and each side of it presented a different view: Mrs. Lovett's pie shop, her parlor, the cellar of Sweeney's barbershop (where his dispatched victims landed), and a flight of stairs. Strewn almost randomly around the stage were machines and parts of machines. Some pieces were disguised as platforms to accommodate a scene,[22]

such as the stage for Sweeney's shaving contest with Pirelli.

The sides of the stage were filled with stairways and platforms. Some moving parts didn't have any real function other than to create the feeling of faceless industry. The rear wall of corrugated tin could be raised to reveal a painted drop of nineteenth-century London. Altogether, these elements created the production's epic and foreboding landscape. Critic Jack Kroll wrote, "It showed the Industrial Revolution as something that had dwarfed and degraded whatever it touched."[23] Lee was recognized with the 1979 Tony Award for Scenic Design.

Actor Len Cariou recalled "during the first New York preview we were having a terrible time with the set. The barber shop was directly above the pie shop, and the whole thing was supposed to be made of aluminum so that it could be pushed around, but they had made it out of steel. It weighed a ton, and nobody could move it."[24]

The weight of the factory's metal roof was another challenging factor: it could not be supported by the Uris Theatre's overhead theatrical rigging. "An engineer was brought in, and massive four-inch holes were drilled through the walls of the theatre and into the office building next door to secure the roof to the other building's foundation with rods, earthquake shields, and washers and nuts the size of a fist."[25]

Even with those provisions, the skeletal two-ton catwalk overhead, often populated with chorus members playing hopeless citizens of London, gave everyone a major scare. During an early preview, it fell while Lansbury and Cariou were onstage, barely missing them. Cariou recalled, "It came down slowly—otherwise we would have both been dead. It could never have crashed to the floor because they had safety mechanisms in place. There were only the two of us onstage at that point, Angela and I, in the scene toward the end where we're searching for Toby in the bake house." Cariou heard an unexpected noise and realized the catwalk was descending. "So I ran over and grabbed Angela. She looked at me strangely, and I pulled her downstage."[26]

"As it was falling," Cariou added, "I noticed that Paul Gemignani was mesmerized by this thing. He just stared and kept on conducting. So this huge thing just crumpled onto the stage, and I swear to God, Angela's next line that she sang was 'Nothing's gonna harm you.'" The show had to be stopped so the crew could drag the catwalk to the rear of the stage. The stage manager called for them to repeat the previous scene. "So Angela and I came out onstage, and I turned to the audience and said, 'Take two.'"[27]

The show opened with a silk banner hung above the stage featuring caricaturist George Cruikshank's 1840 illustration of the "British Beehive" above the stage on a silk banner. The illustrator frequently provided images for novels by his friend Charles Dickens. His beehive depicted the oppressive social pecking order, a graphic representation of Victorian England's hierarchical society. Based on economist Adam Smith's eighteenth-century theory that social status and identity were determined by people's means of production, it underscored a cruel, inescapable reality.

For *Sweeney Todd*, Prince and Lee saw Cruikshank's image as an ironic statement about industry and harmony that, in fact, provided virtually no possibility to climb the social ladder. From the royal family at the top of the hive through layers of privileged people such as judges, professionals, and institutions, spiraling down to tradesmen and laborers, it illustrated how government, religion, and social mores lorded over, dominated, and abused everyday people. Sweeney and Mrs. Lovett were have-nots with little chance to rise without resorting to extreme measures.

As the show began, the banner was torn down by two chorus members who were digging a grave. Its removal triggered a deafening factory whistle, a prelude to Sweeney rising from the grave. That jarring sound effect repeated each time a victim was dispatched. Prince at first auditioned a factory gong. Then the idea of the whistle emerged, and various volume levels were tested "until it was almost unbearable. Audiences found it excruciating, but we loved to torture them." Prince noted that, while no subsequent revivals were set in a factory, "all have found the factory whistle irresistible."[28]

The factory set was so massive that it would have been both challenging and prohibitively expensive to move it to Boston for a tryout such as the one Prince and Sondheim had employed when they tested *Follies* there in 1971. It was, in fact, by far the largest physical production of any of Prince and Sondheim's collaborations. No out-of-town trial run meant the cast and crew of *Sweeney Todd* had just four-and-a-half weeks of rehearsals and nineteen previews, starting on February 6, 1979, before it opened on March 1.

"*Sweeney* opened cold on Broadway with a minimum number of previews," Prince remembered. "I had had such a successful experience with *Evita* in London that I persuaded everyone to take that chance. It worked this time."[29]

Franne Lee (Costume Designer). She partnered with her then husband Eugene for *Candide* (1974 Tony), for *Saturday Night Live* (she created costumes for the Coneheads, the Blues Brothers and the Killer Bees) until 1980, and eventually for *Sweeney Todd*, for which she won the 1979 Tony for Best Costume Design. She crafted the exaggerated designs for the production's Victorian costumes. She repeated a story that Prince had said he was reluctant to take on the project, despite her urging. "He told me, 'You're crazy, absolutely crazy! You can't do a musical about people eating people.'" She responded, "Why not?"[30]

Along the way, she did whatever was necessary to give the costumes the appropriate detailing, and she often did it on the cheap. At the first preview, the creative team decided that Mrs. Lovett's raggedy pullover worn by Angela Lansbury was not dirty enough. Franne splattered it with a plate of leftover spaghetti. "Right before I went on the stage," Lansbury later recalled, "the sweater came up to me, all dried up and stinking of Romano cheese and tomato sauce and old meat. And I nearly threw up. I couldn't believe she'd done this to me. I was absolutely outraged. I had to do that performance with that smell."[31] It was eventually replaced.

Larry Fuller (Choreographer & Movement Coordinator). Fuller began his Broadway career as a dancer in *Carousel* (1957), *The Music Man* (1957) and *Funny Girl* (1964). In the 1970s he took on musical staging responsibilities for *On the Twentieth Century* (1978) and *Sweeney Todd*; he received a Drama Desk nomination for the latter. Subsequently he choreographed Hal

Prince's production of *Evita* (1979), for which he earned Tony and Drama Desk nominations. He was the replacement choreographer for Prince and Sondheim's ill-fated production of *Merrily We Roll Along* (1981). He directed and choreographed the first European productions of *Candide*, *Girl Crazy* and *On the Town*, and four German productions of *West Side Story*.

Ken Billington (Lighting Designer). Billington spent the early years of his career (1967–72) as an assistant to veteran designer Tharon Musser, considered by many to be the dean of American lighting design. Over her long career Musser designed lighting for 150 shows. She worked with Prince on several Sondheim productions—*Follies* (her first Tony), *A Little Night Music* and *Pacific Overtures*—as well as *Candide* and *A Chorus Line*. Billington liked to say that he attended "Musser University."

He was nearly as prolific as his mentor. In 1973, he began to work frequently with Prince on shows, including a 1976 revival of *Fiddler on the Roof*. Billington's first engagement on a Sondheim show was in 1977 for Prince's staging of *Side by Side by Sondheim*. Following their collaboration in 1978 for *On the Twentieth Century*, Prince hired him for *Sweeney*'s creative team. Billington worked closely with Eugene Lee and Prince to create lighting for the show's moody, grim texture, and the dark, oppressive atmosphere of factory set and seedy Fleet Street. Across his long career he earned nine Tony nominations, including one for *Sweeney Todd*. He subsequently won a Tony in 1997 for the debut of the long-running revival of *Chicago*. In 2015, he was inducted into the Theater Hall of Fame. He was the principal lighting designer for Radio City Music Hall from 1979 to 2004, where he designed the renowned Christmas and Easter spectaculars.

Jonathan Tunick (Orchestrator). Sondheim worked closely with this energetic, hardworking, and creative professional for all of his productions with Hal Prince—*Company* (1970), *Follies* (1971), *A Little Night Music* (1973), *The Frogs* (1974) and *Pacific Overtures* (1976)—and especially for *Sweeney Todd*, converting Sondheim's piano score into fully constructed orchestrations for the show's twenty-seven musicians. The remarkably adept Tunick assembled these orchestrations in twenty-four days, not just the twenty-five songs that Sondheim had composed but also its almost constant underscoring. Sondheim termed Tunick's feat "remarkable."[32] His original orchestration for

Sweeney Todd is the one that Music Theatre International still licenses for productions after more than forty years.

The size of the Uris Theatre meant that the show's orchestral support needed to be as large as possible. When the idea of using a factory gong seemed insufficient, Sondheim approved using a genuine Victorian-era factory whistle. It was so loud at first that it had to be moved far back to keep from hurting the ears of everyone in the theater.[33]

Despite not having an out-of-town tryout, *Sweeney Todd*'s preview period was largely trouble free. Sondheim observed, "I think the show may hold a Broadway record. It was in such good shape musically from the very first preview that we never had an orchestra call. Every show, including *West Side Story*—which had opened in great, great shape—had one. Except for *Sweeney*."[34]

Paul Gemignani (Music Director & Conductor). The prolific conductor was a veteran of Sondheim shows including *Follies* (1971), *A Little Night Music* (1973), and *Pacific Overtures* (1976). In addition to *Sweeney Todd*'s original production, Gemignani conducted its first London production (1979-82), the Royal Opera House production in London (2003) and the accompaniment for Tim Burton's cinematic version (2000.) His musical leadership also enhanced subsequent Sondheim productions—*Merrily We Roll Along* (1981), *Sunday in the Park with George* (1984), *Into the Woods* (1987, 2002), *Assassins* (1990, 2004), *Passion* (1994) and *The Frogs* (2004). Across his lengthy and remarkable career, he music directed more than three dozen Broadway productions, including *Dreamgirls* (1982), *The Rink* (1984), *Jerome Robbins' Broadway* (1989), *Big: The Musical* (1996) and *Kiss Me, Kate* (1999 revival).

Gemignani was the music director and conductor for most of the memorable Sondheim revues and concerts: *Side by Side by Sondheim* (1977), *A Stephen Sondheim Evening* (1983), *Follies in Concert* (1985), *Sondheim: A Celebration at Carnegie Hall* (1992), and a concert production of *Anyone Can Whistle* (1995). In 1989, he received a special Drama Desk Award for his work as a musical director and his commitment to the theater. He also received the 2001 Special Tony Award for Lifetime Achievement. In 2010 he was inducted into the American Theatre Hall of Fame.

As *Sweeney Todd*'s music director, Gemignani was in charge of the action of the eighteen chorus members. "The hardest thing to work out was the chorus," he said,

> because it was so complicated, and they were on the stage every five minutes. My biggest job was to try to get variety in who was singing . . . in harmonization. I literally memorized the color of everybody's voice and then when I came up to another section of the "Ballad of Sweeney Todd," I'd completely turn it upside down, and we never used the same person twice for solo lines. So over the course of the evening, the same tune sounded just a little different, each time you heard it.[35]

Actor Len Cariou called Gemignani

> the Jolly Green Giant. . . . He is an incredible musician, with a great sense of fun, and a great sense of the dramatic. The first time he saw the score for "Epiphany," during a break on a rehearsal day, he came into the rehearsal room and came over to me and said, "You are not going to believe what I've just seen. You are going to shit yourself." It was absolutely brilliant.[36]

Gemignani said *Sweeney Todd* was a challenge to conduct.

> Needless to say, it was a very depressing piece to play. It was very difficult from the standpoint of being so concentrated. The first month I did that show, I thought I was going to die. I'd get to the end of the first act and think, "I can't do the second act. I haven't got the energy for it." I don't think any of us realized how intense it was going to be until we started performances. One of the things I really feel about Steve's work is that, as you go on, it's getting harder and harder. It isn't only the music, but the intensity and the concentration levels of the characters and the score are getting greater.[37]

Gemignani had the responsibility of sounding the shrieking factory whistle, an effect that became an iconic feature. In typical shows, sound effects are triggered by the stage manager, following cues in the score. Gemignani argued that this could hinder the close timing required to have Sweeney's murders dramatically underscored musically. Instead,

They ran a hose from the whistle, through the top of the lighting grid, down through and across the floor, and down into the pit, to where a button was installed at Paul's feet. When the time came for the whistle, he would step on the button, sending the signal to the whistle to ring out through the theater at the exact right moment to startle the audience.[38]

Cast and Characters

Prince said *Sweeney Todd* called for "big, classical, bravura acting,"[39,40] so he and Sondheim assembled a stellar cast who came with the larger-than-life talent necessary to carry off the production (Figure 3.4).

Len Cariou (Sweeney Todd). The versatile Canadian actor played Fredrik Egerman in Sondheim's *A Little Night Music* original production in 1973, the indecisive Swedish attorney with a virginal wife and a former paramour waiting in the wings. His serious theater training and a career at the Stratford Shakespeare Festival in Ontario and other classic stages meant he had a broad range and considerable experience.

In 1976, he was the director of the Manitoba Theater Center in Winnipeg, his hometown. His season included Sondheim and George Furth's *Company*. He reached out to Prince to see if the stage manager's book from that show's original 1970 Broadway production might be available for him to see. While they were talking, Prince said, "Oh, by the way, Steve has written a musical for you. . . . It's called *Sweeney Todd: The Demon Barber of Fleet Street*. Hugh Wheeler is writing the book. I'll send you the outline." Cariou initially worried, "How are they going to make a musical out of that?"[41] In fact, his first take

Figure 3.4 *The triumphant Act I finale, "A Little Priest," featured Angela Lansbury's Mrs. Lovett and Len Cariou's Sweeney Todd with their "weapons" raised in this iconic image. Photofest.*

when he read the show's outline that Prince sent was, "Holy shit. They've lost their minds."[42]

But Cariou was genuinely intrigued and had confidence in the talents of Prince and Sondheim. "I thought, 'If Stephen writes a really romantic score for this, it could work. The guy's a genius, so he must know what he's doing.'"[43] Cariou had a film shoot conflict that meant he would miss the first week of *Sweeney Todd* rehearsals. He asked Prince, "Do you think Steve would give me music so that I'm not behind the eight ball when I get there, and I can work on it while I'm in Canada?"[44] Sondheim was fine with that and invited Cariou to his home. "There we are in the composing room and he's nervous. I'm the one who's supposed to be nervous. He was just nervous, fidgety. He said, 'Excuse me,' and he leaves the room. He comes back with a joint, and he lights it, takes a couple of tokes, offers some to me."[45]

Sondheim asked the actor if he knew the Catholic Mass for the Dead. Cariou responded, "Steve, I'm a Catholic, French Irish." Sondheim hummed a melody. "I don't get it," Cariou responded. Sondheim clarified, "That's 'Dies Irae' backwards." Cariou exclaimed, "Oh, you're a sick fuck, aren't you?" Then Sondheim played "The Barber and His Wife." Cariou said, "I was in tears. It took me about two weeks not to cry when I sang that. It still does that to me." Finally, Sondheim shared "A Little Priest." Cariou: "I'm on the floor! That was some afternoon." It was the beginning of another memorable collaborative relationship between composer and actor.

Cariou was excited by the music Sondheim was composing. But he was shocked at some of the lyrics: "At the end of my opening number when the character sings about the world 'filled with people who are filled with shit' . . . I mean, theatrically speaking, I thought it was superb . . . but I thought, 'Well, we aren't endearing [audiences] to us, are we?'"[46]

Nevertheless, Cariou was in awe of the developing score.

> It seemed to me that this was brilliant stuff. Whether the audience would get it or not was another matter, but I knew it was a fucking masterpiece. . . . I remember the very first time I did the "Epiphany" at the rehearsal studio, with just a piano and the with the lyrics in my hand. Judy Prince [Hal's wife] was at the rehearsal, and when it was over, she came to me and said, "That is the most exciting thing I've ever heard in my life."[47]

Once rehearsals began, Cariou was working closely with Angela Lansbury as Mrs. Lovett. They had met previously but never worked together. "There was instant rapport there."[48] He also said, "Most of our time was spent discovering just how to walk that tightrope between broad farce and melodrama."[49] They carefully monitored one another.

> We were really proud that we didn't go [over the top]. I said, "We've got to be really careful that we don't, or it'll turn into rat shit." We had to be conscious of it. We kept each other in check. We were pretty proud of toeing that line for that whole year. And I think Hal was astounded by the consistency of it. I know Stephen was.[50]

Although there were some people walking out at intermission during the first preview, Cariou was gratified by the ovation at the end.

> We took our bows and congratulated one another, and I go to my dressing room. Steve is standing outside the dressing room, and he says, "They understood it! They fucking understood it!" And we had a great hug. He was just beside himself. I said, "Now if we can get the Goddamn set to work, we'll be all right." But that was pretty joyous.[51]

Cariou's Sweeney rose from the grave in the show's opening moments, died gruesomely in the final scene, and frighteningly rose from the grave again for the finale. From start to finish he was made up to resemble a grotesque cadaver, pale skin and dark, deep-set eyes. His role and performance were often called operatic. Actor Ken Jennings, who played Tobias Ragg, recalled: "Len was great. He was stern, though. He'd scare you. And you really thought he was going to kill you. He really did. He got so into it. You thought he was going to slit your throat onstage. It was terrifying."[52]

His performance received many comments from critics. The *New York Times*' Richard Eder wrote,

> Sweeney, played by Len Cariou, appears from a hole in the ground. He is lit throughout like a corpse. Mr. Cariou, his eyes sad and distracted, his hair parted foppishly in the middle, dresses and carries himself like a seedy failure; but a failure illuminated by a vision. Mr. Cariou is to some degree the prisoner of his anguish; he slits throats with lordly abstraction but his

role as deranged visionary doesn't give him much variety. He is such a strong actor, and such a fine singer, though, that he makes up for it with a kind of glow.[53]

Cariou was diagnosed with strep throat just before the cast recording was made. His physician told him that vocal rest was in order. Cariou's response: "As long as I'm alive, nobody is going to sing the songs because I can sing them."[54]

Playing a murderous sociopath was an arduous task for Cariou, to be sure, but today he does his best to put it in context with other major roles he's played. Just before he originated the part of the Demon Barber, he starred in a production of *King Lear*. "It changes everything, playing a role like that. And playing a role like Sweeney changes everything, too."[55]

He was immensely proud to have been part of *Sweeney Todd*'s original production. "You know something is right from the get-go. And it was very satisfying to know that we were right. This thing is a piece of genius. And I had a lot to do with that."[56]

Angela Lansbury (Mrs. Nellie Lovett). Sondheim was familiar with Lansbury's skills as an actor: in her first Broadway role, she played Cora Hoover Hooper, the unethical, power-mad "Mayoress" in his and Arthur Laurents's musical *Anyone Can Whistle* (1964), a disappointing nine-performance Broadway failure. Her previous career had largely been in movies, and she had little experience as a singer or a stage actor. But they sensed that she had what was needed for a complicated comic role, and she was a bright spot in what was an extremely avant-garde show that was unloved by audiences and panned by critics. *Whistle* did make an original cast recording that certified Lansbury as a promising musical theater performer. *Anyone Can Whistle* established her lifelong friendship with Sondheim.

Lansbury's extensive cinematic career had begun in the 1940s. Fifty years later she became known to many television viewers as amateur detective Jessica Fletcher in the series *Murder, She Wrote* (1984–96). She is one of the few performers who have received all four "EGOT" awards—Emmy, Grammy, Oscar, and Tony.

Musical theater composer Jerry Herman saw one of her *Anyone Can Whistle* performances and sought her out to play the title role in *Mame* (1966), his musical adaptation of the 1955 novel *Auntie Mame*. (Rosalind Russell had played the role in a 1958 nonmusical film, but she declined to star in the musical.) *Mame* was Lansbury's first leading role, and it firmly established her as a musical theater star, winning the 1966 Tony for Best Actress in a Musical. She received her second Tony 1969 playing Countess Aurelia in another Jerry Herman show, *Dear World*, adapted from Jean Giraudoux's play *The Madwoman of Chaillot* (1945).

In 1973, she starred in an award-winning London production of *Gypsy*, playing the daunting role of Rose, the hard-driving stage mother. Sondheim had written the lyrics for Ethel Merman in 1959, with songs by composer Jule Styne. When the London production transferred to Broadway, Lansbury won her third Best Actress Tony, inhabiting the role as thoroughly as she had *Mame*. (Later she was the voice of Mrs. Potts in the animated *Beauty and the Beast*, 1991).

Lansbury's performance as Mrs. Lovett in *Sweeney Todd* resulted in her fourth Tony. In 2009, she won a Supporting Actress Tony when she played the daffy Madame Arcati in a Broadway revival of Noël Coward's classic 1941 comedy *Blithe Spirit*. In 2022, she received the Tony's Lifetime Achievement Tony Award. She died in 2022 at the age of ninety-six.

Although she was a London native, Lansbury was not deeply familiar with the story of *Sweeney Todd*. She was in her kitchen in Ireland when she received a wire from Prince and Sondheim asking her to consider the role. Back in 1964 when Sondheim recruited her for *Anyone Can Whistle*, she thought that show was "nuts, crackers" when she first read its script.[57] By 1978 she had much more experience. Taking on *Sweeney Todd*'s notorious, lovelorn baker seemed worth considering, especially since it meant another opportunity to work with Sondheim, whom she deeply admired.

Nevertheless, she came to New York City with some skepticism, since Mrs. Lovett was not the show's title role.

> I went and listened to the score with Stephen. He played me "The Worst Pies in London" and I thought it was so damned funny. It just killed me. He did it all. He kept slapping the piano for the dough. He kept getting the lyrics all mixed up. I was immediately terribly interested. How could I not be? And I was interested because Hugh Wheeler who I knew from the movie *Something for Everyone*, was going to be the book writer. Hugh was such an

inventive and clever writer. He understood the British and Cockney humor. I knew his dialogue would be tremendously good, and it was.

Lansbury was quickly won over. "It became clear to me that the part was a key role, and it also represented the only relief in the whole piece. It had the kind of comedic moments which appealed to me because I knew I understood the background of the piece really well."[58] Lansbury's grandfather, George Lansbury, was a British politician, a socialist who led the Labour Party from 1932 to 1935. As a member of Parliament he represented his home borough, the working-class neighborhood of Poplar.

That neighborhood's proximity to Fleet Street meant that, as a child, young Angela was often exposed to "the common people, the have-nots," as she described them in a 1981 conversation with radio interviewer Studs Terkel. Her grandfather's home was "open to everyone," she recalled, a fact that enabled her to know people much like the desperate denizens of Fleet Street in *Sweeney Todd*. "I know who they are, and I can empathize with them. I hope I have inherited my grandfather's understanding of people, a feeling of warmth and affection for the human race."[59]

When Terkel asked how she interpreted the role of Mrs. Lovett, Lansbury answered frankly,

> I look upon her as a woman who is pushed to the utmost extreme to exist in the world. I think that living on the edge of society with one foot in the gutter, facing starvation daily, when the proposition enters her mind that she will have a great deal of easy raw material at her fingertips . . . here she is faced with an easy supply, and she doesn't hesitate to suggest to Mr. Todd that they should make good use of it and bolster the family business. She's simply a woman of expedience. I think she recognizes a good thing.[60]

The British Music Hall tradition that Lansbury knew from her childhood was another key component in her performance.

> The class that Mrs. Lovett was made of is taken from many, many little songs and little glimpses that one has had—little things and dances that I do that come from British pantomime—and an awful lot of that shtick, as we call it in the business, I actually learned as a child, or rather I simply

absorbed it, whatever you see in life, you put it away as a child. I saw a lot of the variety shows in London.[61]

Lansbury's Cockney roots gave her an advantage in playing Mrs. Lovett.

> The Cockney mentality is quite something unto itself. I knew a lot of Cockney people in my time. I did use a woman I had known as a kid, when I was ten or eleven. She worked for us. Her name was Beattie, and she was from the East End of London. She had this kind of sluttish aspect and an unbelievable accent that you could cut with a knife. She was such a lovable, engaging, fat woman that we just adored her, my sister and I. The characters I have portrayed are often rooted in my memory of people I have known or have had dealings with. Sometimes I do it without even being aware that that's who I'm using for a muse. Luckily that is something which comes easily to me. I just pluck from the places I've observed or seen. Beattie is a lot of Mrs. Lovett, I'll tell you that.[62]

Lansbury also explained how acting freed her from any inhibitions she might have had. "I can be released on stage to do all kinds of things that I couldn't conceive of in my everyday life. I can feel free to do absolutely anything, play any kind of character." Early in her career she was frequently cast as "bitter, nasty women. I don't want to play any more bitter, nasty women! I've had enough of that."[63] Nellie Lovett might have been an amoral, but she was certainly neither bitter nor nasty—she was *Sweeney Todd*'s comic relief. Theater commentator Ethan Mordden defined the show as "a compound of discrepancies."[64] Lansbury's take on Nellie Lovett was completely musical comedy, balanced against Cariou's serious, obsessive Sweeney Todd.

For Sondheim, having Lansbury in the role made the task of writing songs for her more straightforward. "It wasn't a matter of writing for Angela Lansbury, it was a matter of writing for Angela Lansbury as Mrs. Lovett."[65] Sweeney and Mrs. Lovett's partnership was refined by Christopher Bond in his adaptation of the play. In earlier versions of the story, Mrs. Lovett was little more than a selfish opportunist. In Bond's play and subsequently in Wheeler and Sondheim's musical, her love for Sweeney became a driving force. She had, after all, stored his valuable razors for fifteen years when she could have sold them to support her meager income from baking "the worst pies in London."

Lansbury put her formidable stamp on Nellie Lovett, giving the role a remarkable vitality that has colored subsequent acting performances. In his *New York Times* review, Richard Eder wrote,

> Her songs, many of them rapid patter songs with awkward musical intervals; and having to be sung while doing five or ten other things at once, are awesomely difficult, and she does them awesomely well. Her voice is a visible voice; you can follow it amid any confusion; it is not piercing but piping. Her face is a comic face; her eyes revolve three times to announce the arrival of an idea; but there is a blue sadness blinking behind them.

In many ways, she became the production's most memorable star, delivering a performance for the ages (Figure 3.5).[66]

Figure 3.5 *Angela Lansbury won a 1979 Tony Award as Mrs. Lovett. She was the original production's most memorable star, and her performance defined the role for many who followed. Photofest.*

Lansbury's sense of humor as a performer was subtle but frequent. While singing "The Worst Pies in London," she began to make tiny balls of dough. In the blackout following the song, she'd fling them at conductor Paul Gemignani. He couldn't figure out where they were coming from. "What started as a one-off incident started happening once every two weeks, then twice a week, until eventually he was hit ten performances in a row. At his wit's end, Paul scoured around his podium after performances, and one day he found a tiny dough ball." When he brought several remnants to her dressing room, she played "the innocent child" and then laughed gleefully.[67]

Victor Garber, who played Anthony Hope, fondly recalled working with Lansbury.

> Not only was Angela definitive as Mrs. Lovett, she taught me what it was to lead a company and what it was to be the star of a show. She was extraordinary. . . . Angela made it a point to be the den mother and take care of people. She's very much from the old school of a company mentality, and she made everyone feel they were an integral part of the show and took care of people. I marveled at her professionalism, her brilliance and her warmth.[68]

Actor Ken Jennings remembered the memorable night of Cariou and Lansbury's final performances and curtain call at the Uris Theatre in February 1980.

> They each signed a year's contract, so they had the same closing night, and it was amazing what that evening was like . . . we had begun [the show] with Len and Angela. The loss, the experience, it was more even than a theatrical experience, more like a religious experience. They were like the priest and priestess who were leaving us. . . . To think that these two, these leaders, these members of the clergy, were leaving. There was such a pride. We were so honored to have had the experience.[69]

For their final curtain call,

> Len came out that great metal door in the back of the stage and ran down to the lip of the stage and with arms in the air like a runner who had finished a race, and he reached the lip of the stage with the audience cheering for him. He suddenly rolled around and took his first bow to us. That broke us. We began to cheer like crazy.

He asked the ensemble to come down, and they all began milling. "Angela hadn't even come out yet. The door opened upstage, and the crowd began . . . parting in the center of the stage, and Angela just eventually came through us and these enormous cheers from the darkness of the house."[70]

Cariou and Lansbury embraced at center stage. "We began backing away from them," Jennings remembered.

We knew it was their moment. Len began, saying "Don't go away! Stay!" . . . There they were, Len and Angela standing and embracing center stage with this long white spotlight piercing down through the darkness of the house from way at the top of the back of the house. This long shaft of light falling in a pool on center stage with them embracing and suddenly the ensemble began to toss their roses into that white light from the darkness. I remember that sight, those two people standing in that pool of light with the red flowers sort of dancing in the light around them and falling to their feet and the roar of the crowd that surrounded them. It went on so long, eventually the house lights came up, and there we were, all of us. . . . It was one of the most thrilling moments I've ever had in the theater. Probably the most thrilling.[71]

On March 4, 1980, Dorothy Loudon and George Hearn took over the roles of Mrs. Lovett and Sweeney Todd, which they performed until the production finished its Broadway run on June 29, 1980.

Ken Jennings (Tobias Rigg). At the age of thirty-one, the youthful-looking actor played Toby, the charlatan barber Pirelli's fifteen-year-old apprentice later adopted by Mrs. Lovett as an assistant in her pie shop. His hawking of Pirelli's "miracle elixir" to grow hair and his earnest duet with Lansbury for "Not While I'm Around" are two of the most memorable musical performances to be heard on the original cast recording. He received the 1979 Drama Desk Award for Outstanding Featured Actor in a Musical. His subsequent Broadway credits included *Side Show* (1997) and *Urinetown* (2001).

Jennings developed Toby's character by considering the boy's background and "seeing what the text says about the character and, of course, paying attention to how the director guides. Also, really careful study of text and continual concentration and delving more and more into the overtones or reverberations that one picks up from the text. Trying to dig deeper and deeper, trying to overturn stones in the actor's personality."[72]

Jennings recalled that rehearsing with Sondheim present was intimidating. "I couldn't look at the area of the room in which he was sitting." Despite his anxiety, he said, "He was always friendly, and we had nice conversations," but Jennings was uneasy about talking with the composer and lyricist:

I was always sure that I was going to use a word improperly. I was going to use the word "laconic" or "lugubrious" mistakenly, and I thought, "Oh God, I'm going to feel so embarrassed in a few minutes." . . . I was always aware that I was in the presence of this master of language. I was tongue-tied, in awe of him.[73]

He enjoyed working with Hal Prince and found him easy to talk to. "I found that he'd tailor his approach to the actor." He recalled that he and Merle Louise were the only two actors who did not wear body microphones. "We were only picked up by other people's mics and foot mics. So the size of the theater had an impact because one had to be aware of projection."[74]

Victor Garber (Anthony Hope). As a handsome 29-year-old, Garber originated the role of the romantic, naïve young sailor who rescued Sweeney at sea and subsequently fell in love with the beautiful Johanna. The Canadian-born and -trained actor played Jesus in a 1972 Toronto production of *Godspell*; he made his feature film debut in 1973 in the same role. Garber moved to New York City after hearing the original cast recording of Sondheim's 1964 show, *Anyone Can Whistle* (featuring Angela Lansbury), which convinced him to be a Broadway performer.

As part of his audition process for *Sweeney Todd*, he was invited to Sondheim's home. "He played 'Johanna' for me. I had to learn the song, and I don't really read music, so I taped it on a little cassette recorder I'd brought. I went home and learned the song, and I came back and sang it for him." Sondheim cried when Garber sang the song. The role was his.[75]

Once he was cast, he and other actors went to Prince's home where Sondheim played and sang the score.

> That was one of the most thrilling nights I've ever had. I remember it well because it was the first time I'd heard the whole score, not just "Johanna." I knew then that I was part of something unique. It was pretty obvious. And just being in the presence of Len Cariou and Angela Lansbury—it was unbelievable to me to me. I still can't believe it.[76]

Garber left the production after six months.

> I felt I couldn't play this juvenile anymore. "Johanna" is arguably one of the greatest songs ever written for the musical theater, and I was so fortunate and blessed to sing it.... To me [Anthony] was always a real person. I think that's why they cast me in the role, because that's what they knew I would bring to it.[77]

He's received four Tony nominations for various Broadway performances in *Deathtrap* (1978), *Little Me* (1982), *Lend Me a Tenor* (1989), and a revival of *Damn Yankees* (1994). He became a familiar face to television viewers on the series *Alias* (2001–2006) as Sydney Bristow, an international spy; he received three Primetime Emmys. He also appeared in guest roles on several TV series and as numerous characters in critically acclaimed movies such as *Sleepless in Seattle* (1993), *Titanic* (1997), *Legally Blond* (2001), and *Dark Waters* (2019).

Sarah Rice (Johanna). In her first and only Broadway performance, the operatic soprano played Sweeney's beautiful daughter, held captive by the lecherous Judge Turpin. Her audition involved five callbacks before she was offered the role. What clinched it, she remembered years later, was singing the aria "Steel Me, Sweet Thief" from Menotti's opera *The Old Maid and the Thief*. "Mary Lea Johnson, one of the producers, was there. Apparently I made her cry, and she said, 'That's the one you have to hire.'"[78] Rice's lilting soprano voice was perfect for the challenging number, "Green Finch and Linnet Bird."

Asked if she had been directed to play Johanna as a character in a melodrama or more realistically, Rice said, "The direction that Hal Prince gave us was that he wanted it very out front—not quite melodramatic, but very presentational. My original wig went all the way down to the floor, but the first time I tried it on, Stephen Sondheim said, 'Sarah, you look like a depraved Dolly Parton.' So they cut it down."[79]

Rice played Johanna

> as a ray of hope in the midst of this unremitting grayness. Terrible things start to happen to her as an adult, but she's basically a survivor. And you have

to remember, when she sees all that carnage in the basement at the end, she has no idea who these people are, that they're her father and mother. And no one is going to tell her.... When you play Johanna, you have to play her story, which is very different from the whole story. It's interesting to think about what happens to Anthony and Johanna afterwards. What do they go off and do? Does she become a desperate housewife? I've always wondered about that.[80]

Rice performed as The Girl in the long-running Off-Broadway production of Tom Jones and Harvey Schmidt's *The Fantasticks* and in various operas around the world. She was recognized with a 1979 Theatre World Award for her performance in *Sweeney Todd*. She became well-known for her solo cabaret performances, winning a 2010 Bistro Award and a 2011 MAC Award (Female Vocalist). She died in 2024.

Merle Louise (The Beggar Woman). Already a versatile Broadway performer when she was chosen for the daunting *Sweeney Todd* role of the crazed Beggar Woman, Merle Louise was known to Sondheim from her Broadway debut as one of *Gypsy*'s Hollywood Blondes and later as "Dainty June" (1959) in that show's original production and national tour. She also worked with Sondheim and Prince in *Company*, playing Susan, a sort of Southern belle. In *Sweeney* she was a woman who was startlingly and tragically the sad remainder of Lucy, Benjamin Barker's beloved wife, despoiled by the vile Judge Turpin.

Although Prince encouraged her to audition for the adolescent Johanna; Louise was initially reticent, feeling she was too mature for the role. Prince asked her about the Beggar Woman. She was surprised and a bit miffed. "39? half-crazed? I said, 'I don't look 39 onstage,'" although she was forty-five at the time. But Prince hounded her. "My agent thought I was all wrong for it, but she made arrangements for an audition."[81]

She tried every excuse in the book to get out of it, including a scheduled vacation to Florida. Once there, she spent more time practicing in her hotel bathroom than heading to the beach. She worked up "the shortest Italian aria I knew, 'O mio babbino, caro'" from Puccini's *Gianni Schicchi*. Back in New York, despite being nervous, she auditioned. "It went fine. They called me back, that surprised me. And I got the part, I couldn't believe it. I just sat down on the bed and cried!"[82]

As she thought more about the role, she felt that the Beggar Woman had definitely experienced "some great trauma, something deep inside and birdlike, which was a description which I thought was kind of interesting. It made her fragile. I put that birdlike quality into the reading when I did it. I think that is what was needed. It became a real personal experience for me." She came up with the idea of carrying a stuffed rag doll, perhaps a distant memory of the child she lost. "Hal liked that idea," and she carried the doll throughout the show's run.[83]

After *Sweeney Todd*, Louise was cast in the original production of *Into the Woods*, as Cinderella's Mother and Red Riding Hood's Grandmother. She is the only actor to have appeared in four original Sondheim productions. Later in her career she was in the original Broadway productions of Jerry Herman and Harvey Fierstein's *La Cage aux Folles* (1983), Kander and Ebb's *Kiss of the Spider Woman* (1993) and Elton John's *Billy Elliott the Musical* (2008). Louise died in 2025 at the age of ninety.

Edmund Lyndeck (Judge Turpin). He was the sadomasochistic Judge Turpin on Broadway and for *Sweeney Todd*'s first national tour, as well as the 1980 TV broadcast and a production in 1994 at the North Shore Music Theatre. He made his Broadway debut as John Witherspoon in the original production of Sherman Edwards and Peter Stone's *1776* in 1969. He originated the role of Cinderella's father in Sondheim and James Lapine's *Into the Woods* (1986) and played that show's Mysterious Man in later performances. He was Scrooge in the Pittsburgh Civic Light Opera's production of a musical version of *A Christmas Carol* for many years between 1992 to 2007. Lyndeck died in 2015 at the age of ninety.

Joaquin Romaguera (Adolfo Pirelli). An operatic tenor, he created the comic role of the scheming barber Pirelli. He became Sweeney's first victim after losing a shaving contest and trying to blackmail the barber to whom he had been apprenticed years earlier. Romaguera performed with the New York City Opera from the 1960s to the 1980s. His final stage performance in 2000 was as Magaldi in Andrew Lloyd Webber's *Evita* with Broadway Sacramento. He died in 2023.

Jack Erick Williams (Beadle Bamford). The American actor and composer is particularly remembered for his performance in *Sweeney Todd* as the beadle, Judge Turpin's fawning henchman. He made his Broadway debut in the Lincoln Center revival of Kurt Weill's *Threepenny Opera* in 1976. Sondheim wrote some challenging countertenor vocal lines for the beadle with Williams's remarkable voice in mind. Despite several well-received Broadway performances, Williams considered himself principally a composer.

The Ensemble. The chorus of *Sweeney Todd*'s original production was populated by eighteen actors: Duane Bodin, Walter Charles, Carole Doscher, Nancy Eaton, Mary-Pat Green, Cris Groenendaal, Skip Harris, Marthe Ihde, Betsy Joslyn, Nancy Killmer, Frank Kopyc, Spain Logue, Craig Lucas, Pamela McLernon, Duane Morris, Richard Warren Pugh, and Maggie Task. The swings were Heather B. Withers and Robert Hendersen

Sondheim's score required an operatic sound from its theater chorus. Operatic performers were typically not trained as actors, and musical theater actors were, in most cases, not operatically trained. Conductor Paul Gemignani worked closely with casting director Joanna Merlin to locate New York City's best trained voices who also possessed acting skills, especially two *basso profundo* talents to deliver on the rich sound Sondheim had in mind.

The chorus framed the action as the wretched citizens of London who came and went from the stage to perform "The Ballad of Sweeney Todd" for scene transitions and to underscore the melodramatic nature of Sweeney's terrifying swath of murders. Prince said,

> I worried about how to deal with the ensemble. I knew I needed to give them something to elevate their contribution, so I encouraged each one to create a character. "You are prisoners in a factory and collectively driven to cannibalism." I told them, "You never see the sun because of the soot that covers the roof of the factory. You must decide, individually, whether

or not you are married, whether you have any children. Make up a history for your character. You don't have to tell me what you have decided, but you have to make specific choices for yourselves." One of the ensemble said she had seen an illustration of a young woman wearing a heavy iron brace from thigh to ankle and asked me if I would mind if she wore one. It was exactly the kind of thinking I wanted to stimulate in each member of the ensemble. The entire chorus created lives for their characters, backstories that enriched what was onstage throughout the show.[84]

Chorus members Cris Groenendaal and Betsy Joslyn eventually stepped into the romantic roles of Anthony Hope and Johanna for the latter part of the original production's Broadway run; they also played those characters on *Sweeney Todd*'s first national tour. Chorus member Craig Lucas learned that Sondheim had a lot of songs that had been cut from previous shows. He asked if he might use some of them to create a show, *Marry Me a Little* (1981), that he performed with Suzanne Henry. Lucas went on to establish a career as a Broadway book writer, especially for the Tony Award-winning *Light in the Piazza* (2005) with composer Adam Guettel.

An Iconic Bloody Image

Given *Sweeney Todd*'s unusual story, the art for advertising and posters was an essential choice. Frank Verlizzo was the senior art director at J. Walter Thompson Entertainment in 1979. The agency went all out to make its artwork presentation for the show's advertising an eye-popping event, and Verlizzo applied his imagination to creating a memorable image.

Several artists and designers developed concepts. Verlizzo said, "The final favorites came down to another artist's silhouette graphic of headless figures of Mrs. Lovett and Sweeney Todd, and my drawing—stylistically based upon woodcuts of the period."[85] Sondheim and Prince were immediately drawn to Verlizzo's version, especially his hand-drawn, bloody lettering for the title. His tiny, trademarked signature, "FRAVER," floated in a pool of blood just beyond Sweeney's left foot.

"My initial sketches of Mrs. Lovett," Verlizzo explained, "were based on a combination of costume designer Franne Lee's concepts and illustrator John Tenniel's vision of the Queen of Hearts from *Alice in Wonderland* (1865). All that changed when I was informed that Angela Lansbury would not be wearing 'padding' as depicted in the costume renderings. I revised my design to reflect a svelte-waisted Mrs. Lovett character."[86] (See Figure 3.6.)

Verlizzo recalled discussing how much blood would be acceptable in the artwork. The *New York Times* and other publications in 1979 had strict guidelines about certain visuals, especially blood. "The ad agency wanted much less blood," he said, "but Mr. Sondheim eventually won the day."[87]

Figure 3.6 *Frank Verlizzo's poster art for Sweeney Todd's original Broadway production was inspired by nineteenth-century woodcuts.* © FRAVER.

Reviews and Reactions: A Show Not Afraid to Draw Blood

Following its opening on March 1, 1979, *Sweeney Todd* received initially mixed reviews. A few speculated as to whether it was a Broadway musical or an opera. Others were confounded by the moral issues raised by a story about vengeance, murder, rape, and cannibalism. But Sondheim's score was universally praised, as was Prince's direction. Over time, the show has been acknowledged as Sondheim's masterpiece—but that judgment did not come wholeheartedly or immediately.

Sondheim once cited Lillian Hellman's theory that audiences prefer stories about nice people solving pleasant problems. Referencing Rodgers and Hammerstein's *The Sound of Music*, he suggested that many Golden Age musicals offered easy solutions to challenges. "Can I get away from the Nazis and be a nun and still marry the richest man in the country?"[88] *Sweeney Todd* was about unsavory people performing vile acts, and that's what several of the production's first critics reacted to. Their opinions had a negative box office impact.

For the influential *New York Times*, Richard Eder wrote a respectful but mixed review, opening with this: "The musical and dramatic achievements of Stephen Sondheim's black and bloody *Sweeney Todd* are so numerous and so clamorous that they trample and jam each other in that invisible but finite doorway that connects a stage and its audience, doing themselves some harm in the process." And yet, he quickly went on to say, "There is very little in *Sweeney Todd* that is not, in one way or another, a display of extraordinary talent." He stated, "There is more of artistic, energy, creative personality, and plain excitement in *Sweeney Todd*, which opened last night at the enormous Uris Theater and made it seem like a cottage, than in a dozen average musicals. . . . Mr. Sondheim has composed an endlessly inventive, highly expressive score that works indivisibly from his brilliant and abrasive lyrics."[89]

Eder was impressed with the leading performances. "Sweeney, played by Len Cariou, appears from a hole in the ground. He is lit throughout as a corpse. Mr. Cariou, his eyes sad and distracted, his hair parted foppishly in the middle, dresses and carries himself like a seedy failure, but a failure illuminated by a vision." Eder had even more praise for Angela Lansbury, who "has more opportunities as Mrs. Lovett, and she makes towering use of them. Her initial number in which she sings of selling the worst pies in London, while pounding dough and making purposefully flailing gestures as a pinwheel, is a triumph."

Eder praised other performers: "Victor Garber is most attractive as Anthony, Ken Jennings is strong and touching as Tobias, a hapless apprentice, and Jack Eric Williams is funny and sings beautifully as the villainous Beadle."

But he followed with a reservation: "There is very little in *Sweeney Todd* that is not, in one way or another, a display of extraordinary talent. What keeps all its brilliance from coming together as a major work of art is a kind of confusion of purpose." Eder suggested that the show's "crudity of the characters and their actions . . . is given too much artistic power. The music, beautiful as it is, succeeds in a sense, in making an intensity that is unacceptable." He concluded, "These are defects, vital ones, but they are the failures of an extraordinary, fascinating, and often ravishingly lovely effort."[90] Eder's commentary was truly a mixed review.

Eder was not the only one with reservations. A week later, again in the *New York Times*, Walter Kerr issued another negative assessment. "I am afraid that what *Sweeney Todd* most wants to be is impressive" was his gloomy opening sentence. He concluded his review suggesting,

> We are without a perspective from which to view the mayhem, then, and can only sit back and admire the earnestness and the efficiency with which director Prince, composer Sondheim, librettist Hugh Wheeler, and—most especially—designers Eugene and Franne Lee have worked. The turntables spin, bodies are popped into an oven, we quite believe a filthy street hag when she speaks of the stench and the strange fire in the sky over London. We are plainly in the hands of intelligent and talented people possessed of a complex, macabre, assiduously offbeat vision. Unhappily, that vision remains a private and personal one. We haven't been lured into sharing it.[91]

Writing for the *Wall Street Journal*, Edwin Wilson was more positively impressed, even if he felt some people would be offended by *Sweeney Todd*.

> No matter how divided audiences are on the new musical . . . and they are like to be sharply divided—few will be able to deny its enormous impact. It comes across as forcefully as any musical in recent history. . . . There are times, especially at the climax, when the audience's emotions are flooded by sights and sounds so powerful that the effect is one usually achieved only by opera. Whether for the controversy of its subject matter or the artistry of its presentation, *Sweeney Todd* will be talked about for a long time to come.[92]

Others delivered praise. The eminent critic Clive Barnes, writing for the *New York Post*, exclaimed, "*Sweeney Todd* is not just next month's cocktail party conversation—it will be talked about for years. This is sensationally entertaining theatre. Simply great." He added, "[Sondheim] has finally created what he has been aiming for in most of his later works, a genuine-folk opera."[93]

In *Newsweek* magazine, Jack Kroll offered a mixed review. "*Sweeney Todd* is brilliant, even sensationally so," he wrote,

> but its effect is very much a barrage of brilliancies, like flares fired aloft that dazzle and fade into something cold and dark.... Sondheim has been inching closer and closer to pure opera, and *Sweeney Todd* is the closest he's come yet.... The problem is one of concept and unity: *Sweeney Todd* wants to make the same fusion of popular and high culture that Brecht and Weill made in *The Threepenny Opera*. But the fusion is never really made.[94]

Suggesting wryly that "*Sweeney Todd* is one giant step for vegetarianism," *Time* magazine's T. E. Kalem disparaged the venue. "Broadway's Uris Theater is the worst place to hear [Sondheim's] intricately clever lyrics. As a tractor factory, the cavernous Uris might pass muster, but as a theater, no." He went on to say,

> Irony is Sondheim's razor, and its cutting edge is equally present in bittersweet ballads ("Pretty Women," "Johanna") or in "A Little Priest," an antic account of what kinds of pies the varying professions taste like ("Here's a politician so oily/ It's served with a doily").... As Sweeney, Cariou performs with epic ashen gravity like a scion of the House of Usher summoned forth by Poe. Quite wonderful and totally different is Lansbury's Mrs. Lovett, a blowsy pragmatist as wickedly succulent as one of her pies.

Kalem also offered a mixed remark about Prince's staging: "Within a broodingly ominous ironclad set, [he] directs his accomplished forces with the flash, flourish and panache of a Broadway Patton. But to what end? Nature abhors a moral vacuum, and no sophistication of style can fill it."[95]

The negative opinions did not prevail. Slightly less than two decades later, theater critic Peter Marks wrote a tribute to Sondheim for the *New York Times*. He summed up his take on the composer as a "Home-Grown Musical Master" this way:

> The entire production, directed by Mr. Sondheim's longtime collaborator, Harold Prince, and designed by Eugene Lee to resemble a Victorian house

of horrors, seemed perfumed with the sickly sweet odor of a slow-acting, poisonous gas. That was a key to its artistic success. Here was a musical that was not afraid to draw blood. Even lighthearted moments were underscored in the discordant tones of deep distress: an overwhelming sense of doom engulfed the audience the moment the lights went down. Though it won eight Tony Awards, including best musical, *Sweeney Todd* was not a hit on the order of mega-musicals like *Cats* and *The Phantom of the Opera* that would follow in the 1980s, the Andrew Lloyd Webber Decade for Broadway. *Sweeney* closed after 557 performances. But for me and, I suspect, many other theatergoers, that production is an abiding cultural landmark. It was a theater experience that had the power to make you swoon, as fixed in the memory as any Broadway playhouse is anchored to midtown bedrock.[96]

Writing about the 1989 revival of *Sweeney Todd* at Broadway's Circle in the Square, *New York Times* critic Frank Rich said, "No one writes more passionately for the musical theater than Stephen Sondheim. It's the nature of those passions that makes frightened audiences want to shunt them aside by dismissing them as 'intellectual.' Mr. Sondheim fearlessly explores psychic caverns where civilized people are not dying to go."[97]

Awards

Sweeney Todd was by no means a blockbuster: its Broadway run in 1979 and 1980 was just shy of 18 months (557 performances). Its London transfer was onstage less than five months (157 performances), which disappointed Sondheim. He said the reception in England was "particularly disheartening... since I had written the show as a love letter to London, a city I treasure above all except for New York."[98]

But the original production was expansively recognized with just about every possible Broadway theater award. Nominated for nine 1979 Tony Awards, it took home eight, including Best Musical Book (Wheeler), Best Original Score (Music and/or Lyrics) Written for the Theatre (Sondheim), Best Actor in a Musical (Cariou), Best Actress in a Musical (Lansbury), Best Director (Prince), Best Scenic Design (Eugene Lee), and Best Costume Design

(Franne Lee). Ken Billington's lighting design was nominated but did not win. (Ironically, that Tony went to a show by Paul Giovanni called *The Crucifer of Blood*.).

The New York Drama Critics Circle added nine awards: Best Production of a Musical, Best Musical Score (Sondheim), Best Lyrics for a Musical (Sondheim), Best Book for a Musical (Wheeler), Best Actress in a Musical (Lansbury), Best Actor in a Musical (Cariou), Best Featured Actor in a Musical (Ken Jennings), Best Costume Design (Franne Lee), and Best Scenic Design (Eugene Lee). From the Drama Desk came another eight awards: Outstanding Music (Sondheim), Outstanding Lyrics (Sondheim), Outstanding Book (Wheeler), Outstanding Actress in a Musical (Lansbury), Outstanding Actor in a Musical (Cariou), Outstanding Featured Actress in a Musical (Merle Louise), and Outstanding Featured Actor in a Musical (Ken Jennings). The Outer Critics Circle Award for Best Musical also went to the production. The production's cast recording won the 1979 Grammy for Best Original Cast Show Album and a second Grammy for Best Engineered Recording, Classical for Thomas Z. Shepard.

Within a few years, *Sweeney Todd* became what theater chronicler Martin Gottfried called "a repertory hit, a staple of opera companies around the world, and an acknowledged classic. Had he composed nothing else, this would have established Sondheim as a giant of the American stage."[99] Lansbury suggested that early audiences that had been put off by the unusual subject matter "were told to pull up their socks, open their eyes and their ears, and receive this extraordinary piece of work and give it the attention it deserved. And thank goodness they did . . . because, you know, sometimes you just have to educate an audience."[100]

Eventually the show's morality—or immorality—was accepted as part of a thrillingly scary tale in many of the ways Sondheim had intended and desired. Most agreed that "the score was Sondheim's most romantic, and the production was a triumph of Prince's directing skills."[101] Sondheim especially appreciated an assessment by composer Jule Styne, with whom he'd collaborated to create *Gypsy* twenty years earlier: "I think the most unbelievable job of music writing, and I say this with deep reverence and envy . . . is *Sweeney Todd*."[102]

Sondheim was grateful for Sweeney's eventual success. He believed that it proved "if you give an audience a good story, especially an extravagant one, they'll accept it with pleasure, no matter how bizarre and idiosyncratic it may be."[103]

National Tour

Once *Sweeney* opened, Prince moved on to direct his next production: Andrew Lloyd Webber's *Evita*. He invited Gemignani to go to Los Angeles to conduct that production's out-of-town tryout, but Gemignani was unwilling. "He loved *Sweeney*, and to abandon Len and Angela just as they were settling into the run felt like a betrayal of what they had built from the ground up. Hal acquiesced, Paul stayed with *Sweeney Todd* for the rest of its Broadway run, and he was put in charge of setting up the touring company."[104]

Gemignani chose Jim Coleman to be the tour conductor. They had worked together on a 1976 touring production of *A Little Night Music*. Lansbury, who continued as Mrs. Lovett on the tour, was nervous about working with a new conductor. But Coleman thoroughly prepared for the task, haunting the Broadway orchestra pit and learning the score inside out. He actually conducted the New York company for a week, his Broadway debut.

The first national tour of *Sweeney Todd* began on October 23, 1980, at the Kennedy Center Opera House in Washington, D.C. Subsequent stops were in Philadelphia (Miller Theatre), Boston (Wang Theatre at the Boch Center), Chicago (Arie Crown Theater), San Francisco (Golden Gate Theatre), and Los Angeles where it concluded on September 20, 1981, at the Dorothy Chandler Pavilion. For the tour, George Hearn took over the role of Sweeney opposite Lansbury. Joining her from the original Broadway cast were Edmund Lyndeck as Judge Turpin, Calvin Remsberg (who had replaced Jack Erick Williams) as Beadle Bamford, and Ken Jennings as Tobias Ragg.

Broadway chorus members Cris Groenendaal and Betsy Joslyn continued as Anthony Hope and Johanna. Angelina Réaux began the tour as the Beggar Woman; she was replaced by Pamela McLernon, then by Sara Woods. Spain Logue, an original chorus member from Broadway, played the Birdseller. New to the show were Sal Mistretta as Adolfo Pirelli and Michael Kalinyen as

Jonas Fogg. Other members of the touring company were Skip Harris, Mary Johansen, James Edward Justiss, Steven Kosinski, Duane Morris, Meredith Rawlins, Stuart Redfield, Michael Rockne, Clark Sayre, Laury Tatz, Joyce Tomanec, and Maryrose Wood. Edmund John Koury and Colleen McNamara were the swings.

The tour did not fare especially well, as reported in a piece by Alan Rich, "Sweeney Agonistes."[105,106] His subtitle gave the gist: "With *Sweeney Todd*, Stephen Sondheim moved the American musical a big step forward. Alas, California audiences refused to follow." Lansbury's contract ended on September 20, 1981. It had been reported that she was willing to continue another four weeks, but there was little demand for tickets. The same thing had happened in San Francisco during the tour's penultimate stop, where it closed down four weeks ahead of schedule.

Rich offered his opinion that it was the show's music that made it a hard sell at the time. It's "the greater problem: astonishingly varied, little of it in the neat rhythmic and phrase structures that encourage an audience to toe tap. Its artistic units are not single songs or production numbers but large and tensely conducted scenes whose length sometimes challenges the attention span audience are used to exerting at a stage musical."[107] He gave credit to director Hal Prince:

> It can't be easy working with a creative genius dedicated to doing violence to every pat definition in the book. *Sweeney Todd* slashed away at definitions and categories as gleefully as Sweeney slashed away at the throats of his victims. The audience around me at the Music Center squirmed and groaned and chattered from one row to the next, thus hiding their confusion at what they had been duped into seeing. They had come for a Big Mac and had been handed a plate of caviar.[108]

Rich expressed his opinion that the tour was better than the original Broadway production, "deprived, at no loss, of the ponderous ironworks that constituted the set at the Uris and deprived also of a couple of useless songs that had slowed down some scenes. The cast here was altogether superior, with the Sweeney, George Hearn, a far more interesting foil to Angela

Lansbury's loopy virtuosity than Len Cariou, and a considerably better pair of juveniles than in New York."[109]

The touring production, with Lansbury and Hearn in the key roles, was taped before an audience at the Dorothy Chandler Pavilion in Los Angeles near the end of the tour, produced by Ellen M. Krass, Archer King, and Bonnie Burns. Terry Hughes directed the television production, which included additional taping in an empty theater. It was first televised on The Entertainment Channel on cable television on September 12, 1982. It subsequently aired nationwide in 1984 on the PBS television series *Great Performances*, for which it received three Emmy Awards: Outstanding Directing in a Variety or Music Program (Terry Hughes), Outstanding Individual Performance in a Variety or Music Program (George Hearn as Sweeney Todd), and Outstanding Videotape Editing for a Limited Series or a Special (Jimmy B. Frazier). Angela Lansbury was nominated in the same category as George Hearn. Initially released on VHS in 1984, in 2004 the video became available on DVD from Warner Home Video.

4

Blood on the Big Screen
Tim Burton's Horror Musical, 2007

Over the years Stephen Sondheim's musicals recreated as movies often received mixed reviews. Although the 1961 film of *West Side Story*, directed by Robert Wise and Jerome Robbins, won ten of the eleven Academy Awards for which it was nominated, Sondheim was not proud of it. He found it unbelievable on screen: "When I see a gang of juvenile delinquents dancing down a real street, Broadway, in color coordinated sneakers, with color coordinated wash on the line behind them, I'm not scared."[1] That movie's actors' voices were dubbed by better singers, a customary practice in the 1950s and 1960s, but one that made *West Side Story* a bit too polished.

Gypsy, a show with lyrics by Sondheim, became a 1962 movie directed by Mervyn LeRoy with Rosalind Russell playing domineering stage mother Rose with Lisa Kirk's voice dubbed in to sing Sondheim's lyrics originally written for Ethel Merman. The 1966 movie of *A Funny Thing Happened on the Way to the Forum* continued to be a vehicle for the show's Broadway stars Zero Mostel and Jack Gilford, but director Richard Lester and his screenwriters fiddled with Burt Shevelove and Larry Gelbart's expertly plotted book, cut almost half of Sondheim's score, and spent more time on pure slapstick.

In 1976, Sondheim did not agree with Hal Prince's decision to turn *A Little Night Music* into a movie. But Prince forged ahead, and Sondheim, out of loyalty to his friend, agreed to rewrite some lyrics. Three years before Len Cariou was cast as Sweeney Todd, he reprised his Tony Award-winning stage performance as *Night Music*'s stodgy lawyer Fredrik Egerman. But Prince miscast Elizabeth Taylor as the actress Desirée Armfeldt, and his foray into film directing was misguided. Famed *New Yorker* film critic Pauline Kael wrote, "The picture has been made as if Harold Prince had never *seen* a movie before."[2] The film was a box office disaster.

With a lifelong love of film, Sondheim had strong opinions. "I liked theater, but I *loved* movies, and movies of every kind: dramas, comedies, short subjects and especially trailers—everything in fact except musicals, with the exception of *The Wizard of Oz*, I either tolerated if I enjoyed the songs or I was bored by if I didn't."[3] For him, film and theater were distinctly different. He saw theater as an artificial medium that makes it easy to suspend disbelief when characters begin to sing. Film, he believed, was something else altogether. "It's a reportorial medium, two-dimensional and fixed, however poetically shot and gracefully edited it may be. Characters singing on-screen . . . tend to lose credibility immediately, and usually seem faintly ridiculous."[4]

Between his general diffidence and the many missteps of films based on his shows—not to mention *Sweeney Todd*'s grisly story—there was almost no expectation that any filmmaker would step up to make a movie of Sondheim's "musical thriller." But in 2006, the production company DreamWorks announced plans were underway for a cinematic adaptation.

It would be helmed by Sam Mendes, the respected British stage and film director. He was the force behind London's Donmar Warehouse, a studio performance space that became known for several productions of Sondheim's musicals. (The theater's very first production was *Assassins* in 1992.) Mendes directed his first film in 1999, the Academy Award-winning *American Beauty*, starring Kevin Spacey. During its filming, Mendes also worked with Sondheim and writer John Weidman on workshops in 1999 for their musical initially called *Wise Guys*. (It evolved into *Bounce* in 2003 and finally into *Road Show* in 2008.)

Screenwriter John Logan initially partnered with Mendes. But when the director's intended *Sweeney Todd* casting failed to come together, Mendes stepped away in 2006 for other opportunities. Macabre director Tim Burton came on board, and Logan quickly shared the extensive research he had assembled for Mendes. He and Burton began a productive collaboration. They both loved Sondheim's original Broadway show, and they intended to honor it with a serious cinematic adaptation.

Love at First Bloody Sight

In fact, the 1979 stage production by Hal Prince of Sondheim and Hugh Wheeler's musical adaptation of the melodramatic tale was an inspiration for both John Logan and Tim Burton. At age eighteen, Logan saw *Sweeney Todd*'s final Broadway preview in March 1979; he returned twice for performances during the show's original Broadway run. He became obsessed with it, as did Burton, who saw several performances of the show's London premiere in 1980.

Logan earned a theater degree from Northwestern University in 1983, then undertook a playwriting career in Chicago. He often focused on disturbed criminal minds. His first play, *Never the Sinner* (1985), was about an infamous child murder case from 1924 focused on killers Nathan Leopold and Richard Loeb; he also wrote *Hauptmann* (1991), a play about the kidnapper who murdered Charles Lindbergh's infant son in 1932. His career expanded into screenwriting in the 1990s with major feature films such as Ridley Scott's *Gladiator* (2000), *Star Trek: Nemesis* (2002) and Martin Scorsese's *The Aviator* (2004) about Howard Hughes. By the time of the *Sweeney Todd* project, Logan had earned Academy Award nominations for his screenplays for *Gladiator* and *The Aviator*.

After working on Burton's film of *Sweeney Todd*, Logan's successful writing career continued with the Tony Award-winning play *Red* (2010, about painter Mark Rothko) and films such as Scorsese's *Hugo* (2011) and a pair of James Bond films, *Skyfall* (2012) and *Spectre* (2015). From 2014 to 2016 he created and wrote the horror drama television series *Penny Dreadful*, rooted in the same lurid nineteenth-century materials that spawned *Sweeney Todd*.

In 2002, when Logan learned that DreamWorks planned to make a screen adaptation of *Sweeney Todd*, he pursued it energetically. Based on his youthful enthusiasm for the Broadway production, he said, "I went after it like a rabid dog. 'It is my destiny to write that,' I said to myself. 'I know every note of the score. I'm one of those Sondheim Trekkies.'" He researched Victorian entertainment and crime and put together a lengthy background document for Sam Mendes, saying, "'Here's the world of *Sweeney Todd*.' In a movie, characters have to have a tactile response to the world they're living in; there's no illusion in a stage play."[5]

In a 2007 interview Logan said, "I've never done a movie adaptation of a stage show before, so I didn't know what to expect going into it. . . . But I think you had to understand the language of theater and the language of movies to begin that difficult, treacherous transformation. I can't imagine anyone who wasn't respectful of theatrical traditions approaching *Sweeney Todd*."[6]

A Musical Horror Movie: Burton in Charge

In 1980, Tim Burton, then a 22-year-old student living in London, saw a poster promoting *Sweeney Todd*'s London premiere. He was intrigued and captivated; more than forty years later he still calls it his favorite musical. Like Logan, he went back to see it more than once. In fact, years later in 1997 Burton had a desultory conversation with Sondheim about his interest in making a film of *Sweeney Todd*. But he moved on to other projects, and nothing came of it for another nine years.

Burton, a California native, attended the California Institute of the Arts after graduating from high school in 1976. He studied animation at CalArts and made some short films, including *Stalk of the Celery Monster*, which led to a job with Walt Disney Productions. He worked as an animator, storyboard artist, graphic designer, art director, and concept artist, but never comfortably fit into the Disney regimen. While there he made *Frankenweenie* (1984), a live-action short film about a boy who tries to reanimate his dog after it's run over by a car. Disney fired him for making a film too dark for children. However, it also attracted Paul Reubens who chose Burton to direct his oddball comedy *Pee-Wee's Big Adventure* (1984).

Burton's dark, offbeat films included *Beetlejuice* (1988) and the 1989 superhero film *Batman* starring Michael Keaton as the title character and Jack Nicholson as the Joker. Thanks to a substantial marketing budget, *Batman* was a box office hit (grossing $250 million in the United States and $400 million worldwide) and earned critical acclaim for Burton and his stars. His first film with Johnny Depp was the oddly imaginative *Edward Scissorhands* (1990). In 1992 Burton's sequel, *Batman Returns*, was another financial success.

Burton wrote the original story for the stop-motion animated *Nightmare Before Christmas* (1993) which he produced but did not direct. He worked again with Depp on *Ed Wood* (1994) and *Sleepy Hollow* (1999). After *Planet of the Apes* (2001, with a cast including Helena Bonham Carter) and *Big Fish* (2003), Burton and Depp teamed again for *Charlie and the Chocolate Factory* (2005) and the animated *Corpse Bride* (2005). In 2006, he turned to *Sweeney Todd, The Demon Barber of Fleet Street*.

Given the grisly nature of the tale of Sweeney Todd, Burton's reputation for goth culture and fantasy made him a logical choice to take on the film project after Mendes stepped away. Burton was certain that movie adaptation could tell the *Sweeney Todd*'s story in a way not possible onstage.

> In the stage version, you were far away from the characters. Here we can get up close and look in their eyes and kind of feel the pain and feel the loss and feel the longing. I feel I took advantage of that opportunity, to just kind of make it a bit more of a tragic romance, in a different way than you could get onstage.[7]

Burton believed Sondheim's music enabled deeper insights into Sweeney's tormented mind. "Because Sweeney is such an internal character," he explained, "one of the only times you get a chance to know what he's feeling is through song—it's his internal monologue."[8] What's more, Burton's notion of Sweeney was that he was more than a victim or a cold-blooded murderer: in fact, Burton envisioned the Demon Barber as a misunderstood artist, with razors—not unlike Edward Scissorhands in his 1990 film about another frightening, misperceived character.

A Haunted, Black-and-White Look

Burton had a strong and precise sense of what he wanted the film to look like. He assembled a production team to create *Sweeney Todd*'s memorable visuals. He planned to use digital manipulation only sparingly. "Obviously you can do almost anything [digitally]. But we kind of kept the green screen to a minimum," Burton explained later. "Color manipulation is left to a minimum, too." His team was Dante Ferretti as the production designer, Colleen Atwood doing wardrobe, and Dariusz Wolski as the director of photography. But he wanted the set to be stylized version of Victorian London. "We just felt it was important to have the actors be in the environment, even down to the color scheme."[9]

Ferretti, a veteran Italian production designer, had worked extensively with the legendary Italian film director Federico Fellini on a half dozen films, as well as with Martin Scorsese on *The Age of Innocence* (1993), *Casino* (1995), *Jundun* (1997), *Gangs of New York* (2002), and *The Aviator* (2004).

Burton did not want a historic replica of nineteenth-century London. Instead, he shared with Ferretti a DVD of *Son of Frankenstein*, Rowland V. Lee's 1939 horror movie and said he envisioned something resembling this work from an earlier era. He imagined *Sweeney Todd* as a kind of fable, so he sought to make it in the style of the 1930s *Frankenstein* movies. "They didn't go: 'The Romanian Mountains 1740.'" Burton explained. "By not doing that, there's a certain amount of fable aspect that feels important to the piece. This is one you want to keep in that fantasy London world."[10]

Based on Burton's concept Ferretti's design was "like black-and-white in color, just a few colors, don't put in too many colors, it will be desaturated in the post-production." He crafted more than a dozen full sets that were built at England's Pinewood Studios. His repurposed each of them with modest changes. A huge street scene doubled as St. Dunstan's Market for the shaving contest with Pirelli. With movable walls and interchangeable store fronts, the marketplace could be transformed into Fleet Street. Ferretti also built Sweeney's second-floor barber shop, Mrs. Lovett's bakehouse, and Judge Turpin's ballroom where Sweeney's innocent wife was raped. (That was the only set with bright red accent colors.)[11]

Logan said,

> There's something miraculous when, as a writer you write INT. PIE SHOP and then you see what Dante and Tim have created. In the screenplay I said the barber shop looked haunted, and that's what I think every square inch of this world looks like—haunted. It's creepy. They are very unsettling sets to walk through because they're dark and they have strange, broken angles. . . . They're frightening sets, which is appropriate because it's a horror movie.[12]

Burton wanted to avoid digital manipulation as much as possible. He felt the actors responded better when surrounded by historic details. "Being on a set helps me, it helps the actors, it helps everybody," Burton said. Helena Bonham Carter, who played Mrs. Lovett, felt strongly that working in front of a green screen was a drain. "There's something about being suspended in the space," she said. "The green makes you feel sick and very disembodied."[13]

Ferretti's designs exceeded expectations according to producer Richard D. Zanuck. "It's extraordinary what he's done. You're going to feel like you're in London at that time period and, obviously, we have set extensions that are done digitally so you'll get the feeling it's a big outdoor picture."[14] The movie opens with Sweeney and Anthony on a ship coming up the Thames River to the London harbor, passing a digital image of Tower Bridge. (It appears to be under construction; in fact, it wasn't built until 1886, years later than Burton had in mind for the story.)

In the *New York Times*, film critic A. O. Scott wrote, "Dante Ferretti's production design . . . can make even daylight look sinister."[15] He won the 2008 Academy Award for production design. Critic Terry Teachout called the sets "flamboyantly operatic" and described them as "a Gothic caricature of Victorian London, and the film's grim palette, in which the only bright color is the spurting red blood of the victims whose throats the revenge-crazed Sweeney slashes with his razor."[16]

Costume designer Colleen Atwood opted for a plain, understated and austere look to for Sweeney's attire. "It's a very simple character," she pointed out. "He basically has two different looks, except for in Mrs. Lovett's fantasy numbers." That meant a long leather overcoat and a waistcoat made from an antique bed sheet that was dyed, distressed, and cut into shape. Atwood gave him a kind of holster for his razors, and his boots had hobnails.[17]

The first idea for the barber Pirelli was that he would be fat. But when tall and imposing Sacha Baron Cohen was cast, the vision changed, and he was dressed more as a stylish toreador, wearing bright-blue suit with skintight pants. Cohen asked Atwood "to insert manhood-enhancing material into his tight trousers."[18]

Burton chose the Polish-born cinematographer Dariusz Wolski to handle the camerawork. He had worked with Depp on the three *Pirates of the Caribbean* films. Wolski saw that Burton and Depp shared a minimal approach for this project. "They both love silent cinema," he pointed out, "Buster Keaton, Charlie Chaplin. They both love acting through gestures, looks, more than dialogue. I mean, dialogue has to be in the film, but a lot of times a look, the angle of the camera, an expression on the face is way more powerful than words."[19]

Wolski also said that Burton and Depp were like "creatures of the night." He found ways to make the shadows under Depp's eyes as dark as possible. As he did with Ferretti, Burton showed Wolski several old horror films. "We both like film noir. We like old black-and-white movies. So that was the general approach, to make it very moody, very dark, a lot of contrast, very graphic." That matched up well with Feretti's stark, monochromatic sets. Wolksi used lighting that gave the flavor of photographs of old London. "We tried to make the film look like an old movie with contemporary technology—a modern way of making an old-fashioned film."[20]

In postproduction Wolski stripped out even more color. "What we're doing in this film," he said, "is a combination of make-up, wardrobe, set design and me treating the film, pulling the color out. We're trying to make this movie almost black and white, except for some faded colors, here and there. And blood."[21] The monochromatic look truly made the fearsome spurts of arterial blood spectacular and frightening.

Gallons of Blood

Special effects supervisor Joss Williams was the man behind all the blood. Burton recalled seeing a lot of blood the 1980 London stage production: "The blood is part of the story."[22] In fact, Burton said, "We went for the Monty Python approach [spurting, almost comic blood effects] rather than the realistic approach." He believed that some productions tried to soften the gory splatter, but that caused it to lose its impact.[23]

Some critics were turned off by the spurting blood, but no one claimed it was inappropriate. Williams said, "We made maybe 60, 70 gallons of blood for our tests. And for filming purposes we had a stock of probably 20 or 30 gallons for ourselves. We gave the props department some 20 gallons for dressing, and the prosthetics department, I think, probably 20 or 30 gallons. That's quite a lot."[24]

Neal Scanlan, the film's prosthetics supervisor, used hydraulic tubes and hand-pushed pumps to make the blood spurt as the actors' latex throat overlays were slashed. "The effects in this film are very gory," he said. "However, what we're trying to do is push the boundaries to make it slightly ludicrous, and by doing that you take the audience away from the feeling that this is real." Their goal was to strike a balance between old horror films and the passionate performances of Depp and other actors.[25]

Nevertheless, the gallons of blood shed ensured an R-rating for *Sweeney Todd*, unusual for a movie musical. From the very beginning, producer Richard D. Zanuck and Burton told the studio to expect blood: "You can't be politically correct with this because it's a story about a serial killer, and they cook people in pies. Don't try and soften it." He believed it was not overly graphic but characterized it as a part of the movie's color scheme. Burton's contract stated that *Sweeney Todd* would be an R-rated film. Zanuck said, "There was no way of doing this properly as a PG-13."[26]

Logan and Burton Do Some Slashing

Burton and Logan also had to address numerous pragmatic issues, particularly the standard two-hour length of most successful feature films: stage productions of *Sweeney Todd* typically run close to three hours. Noting the number of chorus scenes and the amount of recitative—singing that adopts the rhythm and delivery of ordinary speech, a musical practice familiar to operagoers—Logan knew these elements would not translate well into a movie. "Movies are really about close-ups," he said. "They're about characters whispering to you, not about characters singing at you or toward you. I knew that a major focus for me was going to be about making it a psychologically driven film. And making it about one single story—and that meant making Sweeney's story very straightforward."[27]

The necessary changes that Burton and Logan undertook with the film adaptation were done in close collaboration with Sondheim. "Mr. Sondheim not only approved every change, as his contract required, but also did the musical reworking himself," Burton said. "Though he was at first shocked by the suggested elimination of 'The Ballad of Sweeney,' Mr. Sondheim said that when he put on his 'movie-buff hat,' he 'completely agreed,' because it would hold up the action."[28]

Sondheim said, "You've got to be ruthless. . . . A song like 'Kiss Me' has its delights onstage if it's played well, because it's funny and silly." He also envisioned it as being suspenseful, anticipating the possible discovery of the lovers by Judge Turpin. "But that's just not how the sequence in the movie is written, and if you don't have that, then you're stuck in the parlor with the lovers singing and singing and singing and singing--and . . . there's no point."[29]

Sondheim explained that a show onstage is for audiences sitting and listening to a song that's several minutes long—"Because that's the convention, and you can enjoy it because it's taking a moment and expanding on it. . . . But on the screen . . . I want the story to be told, and I want it to go swiftly. So that meant we had to excise certain parts of songs and excise certain songs."[30]

Sondheim observed that virtually everyone who translated a stage musical to film—including his shows made into movies—failed to grasp the differences between the mediums. He knew remaking his theatrical production of *Sweeney Todd* into a movie would be risky and involve major surgery. "I'm hoping people will just forget what they know and enjoy the movie or not. But if they go in counting the things that are missing, they're going to be distracted."[31]

Perhaps the film's most startling departure was the removal of "The Ballad of Sweeney Todd," the song that memorably launched the storytelling. But it simply was not cinematic. Its melody remains beneath the movie's opening credits, but the jarring choral delivery from the stage production is gone. Logan and Burton explored several approaches. "But it's not sung by the major characters, and it is not emotionally motivated by their journeys through the story," Logan pointed out. "I tried ghosts singing it, I tried the people of London singing it, but it never really worked . . . it was always going to be an artificial construct."[32]

Sondheim told an audience at a screening in December 2007, "This is not a film of a musical, it's a movie based on a musical."[33] That's an important distinction. Another example is the action within Sweeney's song "Epiphany." Onstage Sweeney turns and menaces the audience. In the film, Depp as Sweeney is suddenly on a London street, accosting unreactive passersby. "That was a surprise, and I thought it was brilliant. It was just as scary," Sondheim said. "But what Tim did in the movie is something you can't do on the stage."[34]

Sondheim and Burton worked together closely. "Tim is a perfect fit," Sondheim said. "In many ways, it's his simplest, most direct film, and you can see that he's telling a story he likes." Burton appreciated Sondheim's engagement in the process: "What I respect and feel grateful for is that Stephen can let the story go—he understood that it's not a stage thing, it's a movie."[35]

Shaping a Horror Movie Score

Music coordinator Mike Higham played a key role in shaping Sondheim's score for Burton's narrative and Logan's screenplay. They previously collaborated on *Corpse Bride* in 2005.

> Tim gave me a very early version of the [*Sweeney Todd*] script and had me go through it and look at the structure of the songs, how long they were, was there anything repeated in the songs that was repeated in the dialogue after, to see whether there was a flow in the music, and make sure it didn't feel too repetitive or too long.[36]

Higham dissected Sondheim's songs line-by-line, verse-by-verse, using the original Broadway cast recording to edit versions of songs and work out how long each number could be. Some numbers were dropped completely, "but Tim still liked sections of them, so I musically lifted some of those to put them into the same incarnations of other songs. We tried to mix and match to get the best of everything."[37]

The actors pre-recorded their vocal tracks. Higham was responsible for overseeing all of their lip-synching and administering Burton's last-minute musical changes. If the director felt that four bars needed to be removed from a song, Higham could do that easily with the digital recordings. "We can slow things down, speed things up. So if Tim suddenly feels like one part needs to be slower, I can do that."[38]

Higham told an interviewer that Burton routinely chose to convey thoughts as concisely and economically as possible. "He can say three words, and he completely sums up what his vision is." For *Sweeney*, Higham said, Burton's words were, "I want the music almost not to stop."[39]

The masters behind the film's score were Sondheim's longtime collaborators, orchestrator Jonathan Tunick and conductor Paul Gemignani, both members of the creative team for the original Broadway production that had twenty-six musicians squeezed into a cramped orchestra pit. For the movie's soundtrack, Tunick enlarged the orchestra to seventy-eight musicians for expansive studio recording sessions made before filming began.

Higham explained that for the big screen a fuller, larger orchestral sound was essential.

> We added 30 violins, some more horns, a tuba, just to give it a big, fatter, wider sound. Tim likes simple melodies and darkness, and when you take the melodies away from some of the songs, the underscoring between dialogue, it's very simple, it's very dark, and having extra strings makes it feel wide, and it sort of glues to the picture a bit better.[40]

New York Times music critic Anthony Tommasini observed, "The actors benefit enormously from the inventive work of Mr. Sondheim's longtime orchestrator. . . . Adapting his original orchestrations, Mr. Tunick has created a soundtrack that has old-fashioned Hollywood film plushness. Yet there is still so much color and detail in his scoring that the orchestra sounds like a pit band for a classic Sondheim show."[41]

Tommasini added,

> Mr. Tunick has transformed . . . choral numbers into lush, sweeping orchestral transitions that run through the film. In one way, though, this change brings the work closer to Mr. Sondheim's original inspiration: the British melodrama. In that once-popular theatrical genre of mysteries and melodramas, an ominous orchestra would churn away in the pit almost continually during the play.[42]

With the enlarged orchestral support, balance needed to be maintained between voices and musical accompaniment. That was the task of conductor Paul Gemignani. His charge was all the more complicated since most of the actors cast by Burton were inexperienced singers. Gemignani pointed out,

> Those actors couldn't sing it in the theater eight times per week, but that's not the point. We could have pushed them to sing theatrically; but singers should sing where they speak and feel comfortable. If we had big operatic singers or singing actors like Len [Cariou] and Angela [Lansbury] performing like they did onstage, it would have looked and sounded stupid. In a movie, it's all internalized.[43]

Burton had further thoughts about the movie's music. "On Broadway you're sitting in an audience and a song ends with a 'ta-da,' cue for applause," he explained.

> You don't want to do that in a movie. But you also want it to build up to what it's supposed to build up to. On one level you say you're doing a silent movie, so there's a certain amount of acting style which you might say is a bit broad. But at the same time you try and cut out completely any Broadway kind of singing, although there's a couple of moments. So it was a weird dynamic to find. Being broad like you might be in a silent movie or an old horror movie without being too Broadway.[44]

Screenwriter Logan was totally in synch with Burton regarding the storytelling. He said that *Sweeney Todd* is, "in the classical dramatic sense, a blood tragedy. Obviously it pays homage to Grand Guignol, it pays homage to the Penny Dreadfuls of Victorian London. But it's important to say that the blood in *Sweeney Todd* is not sadistic, it is not unnecessary." Logan contended that blood is a key part of the world of the story. "The truth of this is people are being killed. This central character is motivated with so much desire and passion that he has to kill people with his hands, and the blood gets on his hands and his face, and he is coated with it—figuratively and literally."[45]

Filling Memorable Roles with Inexperience

None of Burton's prior movies were musicals, of course, so Sondheim's numerous fans were wary of how he would handle the film. When he cast Johnny Depp, a star of several Burton films, as Sweeney, and Helena Bonham Carter, then Burton's domestic partner, as Mrs. Lovett, doubters became more vociferous about inexperienced singers (Figure 4.1). The common wisdom that Burton would shape his adaptation as a "horror musical" did not allay those concerns. When it was revealed that the movie's final cut was under two hours—113 minutes versus the three hours needed for most stage productions of *Sweeney Todd*—rumors about drastic changes ran rampant. Would this be another Sondheim film project that failed to live up to the original?

Figure 4.1 *Director Tim Burton's 2007 cinematic adaptation of* Sweeney Todd *featured a pair of veteran film stars—Johnny Depp and Helena Bonham Carter. Neither one had ever sung onscreen. Photofest./ DreamWorks LLC and Warner Bros.*

Burton and Depp had frequently collaborated, so it was no surprise that he was chosen for the leading role. The director certainly knew that Depp made his film debut in the very first of Wes Craven's *Nightmare on Elm Street* films in 1984, playing Glen Lantz, who suffers a bloody demise at the hands of Freddy Krueger. After their initial collaboration on *Edward Scissorhands* (1990), the actor and director became frequent partners—for *Ed Wood* (1994), *Sleepy Hollow* (1999), *Charlie and the Chocolate Factory* (2005), and *Corpse Bride* (2005).

But casting Depp in the leading role of a musical was a surprise. As a teen, Depp played bass guitar in a band, The Kids, but never sang professionally. Depp was a recognizable worldwide movie star for his performances as Captain Jack Sparrow in Disney's *Pirates of the Caribbean* series, *The Curse of the Black Pearl* (2003), and *Dead Man's Chest* (2006). Speaking with a flawless Cockney accent (the same one he used to play Sweeney), Depp played the colorful but ethical pirate Sparrow, with further flavors inspired by the Rolling Stones guitarist Keith Richards, a pair of antic, mischievous cartoon characters—Bugs Bunny and Pepé Le Pew—and a touch of Groucho Marx.

Despite his cinematic renown, Depp's inexperience as a singer provoked considerable concern. Screenwriter Logan pointed out,

> Normally Sweeney is sung by a bass-baritone, and he's presented as a lumpen proletariat, someone with a very large physical presence. Johnny's not that. He's slender, he's elegant, he's sexy, and yes, he's a tenor. What I think he brings to the role is sort of this Byronic quality; there's something tormented and anguished and poetic about his Sweeney Todd that is wildly appropriate.[46]

Although fans fretted about Depp's singing, Sondheim was not concerned. He told Depp that his acting was more important. "I think he was probably saying that to make me feel better about what I was about to attempt."[47] But it proved to be a successful decision, and Sondheim remained enthusiastic: "Johnny's performance is extraordinary," Sondheim offered. "Sweeney's desire for revenge and the simmering anger and hurt he feels carry the story forward, and Johnny finds the most remarkable variety within that narrow set of emotions. The intensity is at a boil all the time, and he never drops it."[48]

Depp's key to playing Sweeney was to think of him not as a killer but as someone brutally and unjustly treated, similar to Burton's sense of the character. "Sweeney is obviously a dark figure, but quite sensitive," Depp said.

"He has experienced something traumatic in his life, a grave injustice. I always saw him as a victim [and] a little slow. Not dumb, just a half-step behind. The rug was pulled out from under his perfect life. The only reason he came back was to eliminate the people who had done him wrong."[49]

Depp wanted to show that Sweeney suffered from

> something tragic . . . this guy [had] been dealt such a horrible blow. His family has essentially been stolen from him, and he's sent away for 15 years to some hellhole. The way we looked at it is that essentially the guy died. The only way his heart has continued to beat is to go and avenge that hideous wrong that has been dealt to him. That makes him, to me, a very sad character.[50]

Rather than take singing lessons, Depp reached out to his friend of thirty years, Bruce Witkin, singer and bass player with The Kids, the band Depp was part of in his teens. They went into Witkin's Los Angeles studio to record some demos. Depp told Witkin he wouldn't play Sweeney unless his old friend helped him. "I think instead of going in front of somebody with a piano and doing vocal warm-ups or whatever," Witkin observed, "he just wanted to go in with a friend that would be honest with him and say if he sucked or if he was great, and whether he should do it or he shouldn't."[51,52]

The first number that Depp undertook was "My Friends," when Sweeney is reunited with his razors. "That was, basically, the first song I ever sang in my life. It was pretty weird and scary." After their recording session, Witkin joked, "The bad news is you're going to have to do this." They made a demo cassette that impressed Burton, producer Richard Zanuck, Sondheim, and others. Everyone was relieved since production had already begun. Depp's demos proved he was up to the task.

Witkin remained involved with the movie as the producer of Johnny's voice throughout the shoot. "Johnny's voice is a little raspy, in the sense that it's not operatic, it's not Broadway. I think he's got a little mixture of Shane MacGowan [lead singer of the Pogues, a punk band] and David Bowie, going on with the accent and the rasp." Witkin called it a "human" sound, imperfect and perhaps better for movies. Since the film was shot with the actors lip-synching to recordings, Depp relied on Witkin to watch for any missed cues, misplaced words, or fluffed lines. (Higham kept an eye on Bonham Carter and the other singing cast members.)[53]

Tommasini, the *New York Times* music critic, was impressed with Depp's performance.

> As a devotée of Stephen Sondheim's musicals and a big Johnny Depp fan, I was surprised, intrigued and very dubious when I first heard that Mr. Depp would play the title role in Tim Burton's film . . . [but] his performance as captured on screen is stunning in every dimension: dramatically, psychologically, physically and, yes, vocally. . . . [He] takes a film actor's approach to singing. His voice does not have much heft or power. Don't expect him to play the role onstage. But in the film he can almost whisper many lines. . . . The effect is chilling. . . . Beyond his good pitch and phrasing, the expressive colorings of his singing are crucial to the portrayal. Beneath this Sweeney's vacant, sullen exterior is a man consumed with a murderous rage that threatens to burst forth every time he slowly takes a breath and is poised to speak. Yet when he sings, his voice crackles and breaks with sadness.[54]

Writing for *Rolling Stone*, critic Peter Travers exclaimed, "Depp is simply stupendous. He's not Pavarotti and doesn't try to be, but his light [voice] has clarity, timbre, and emotive power. Depp erases the line between singing and acting, fusing them into something that keeps the movie blazing."[55]

Depp's tormented, anguished, and indeed poetic performance was largely praised, despite his vocal inexperience. His edgy tenor voice heightened Sweeney's tragic and romantic persona. Depp's good looks at age forty-three, even as a violent, vengeful character, gave him undeniable sex appeal. An added benefit to the film's success: Depp's involvement surely ensured strong box office for the "horror musical."

As a teen Helena Bonham Carter loved musicals, especially several by Stephen Sondheim. At thirteen, she even gave herself a Mrs. Lovett hairdo with twisted topknots. "The funny thing is," she recalled, "I didn't quite realize I was doing it until one of my friends told me recently, 'Well, we used to call you Mrs. Lovett, don't you remember?' I was a strange child."[56]

She was first noticed as sweet Lucy Honeychurch in *A Room with a View* (1985) and the title role in *Lady Jane* (1986), playing England's ill-fated, sixteenth-century "Nine Days' Queen." Early in her career her "corset" roles pigeon-holed her as a young, virginal Englishwoman. In 1997, she earned a best actress Academy Award nomination as strong-willed Kate Croy in *The Wings of the Dove*, based on a novel by Henry James. After that, she took on acting choices that would change her image. She portrayed dark, often quirky women in movies such as *Mary Shelley's Frankenstein* (1994), *Fight Club* (1999), and a virtuous chimpanzee in *Planet of the Apes* (2001), the latter directed by Tim Burton. They struck up a romantic relationship, and he cast her in a series of his films, including *Big Fish* (2003), *Corpse Bride* (2005), and *Charlie and the Chocolate Factory* (2005).

She and Burton were four years into their long-term though unwed relationship when he took on the *Sweeney Todd* project. (They separated amicably in 2014.) "He was always very proper whenever he wanted me to be in a film," Bonham Carter remembered.

> He said, "I want you to try out for Mrs. Lovett, but it's not up to me. It's Stephen, insisting, quite rightly, on casting." So I went to a singing teacher and practiced and practiced, and then I auditioned. Frankly, my voice wasn't great, and I had to re-audition for Stephen. Then I did get it, and it was my dream come true. When Tim told me, he burst into tears.[57]

In all, Bonham Carter had nine auditions before she was finally hired. Sondheim watched tapes of multiple candidates. Before he chose her, he didn't know she was Burton's choice. According to producer Richard Zanuck, Sondheim said, "I think she is far and away the best. Not voice-wise, because there were some really skilled singers, but voice and personality and look and everything [combined], she was Mrs. Lovett."[58]

As he was with Depp, Sondheim was more impressed by Bonham Carter's acting and less concerned with her singing. She did not attempt to mimic Angela Lansbury's blowsy music hall character. In fact, her performance is almost as internalized and intense as Depp's Sweeney. "Which is right for the movie," Sondheim pointed out, "but not how I'd cast it onstage."[59]

Bonham Carter aspired to make Mrs. Lovett sexy and sensual and felt she should be the same age as Sweeney. "I think Sondheim always saw her as older than him and a sort of maternal figure. I wanted her to have a side that was a bit of a slut, frankly. I even thought she makes her living by being a prostitute, which was pretty common in Victorian times. But Sondheim didn't like that idea at all."[60] Nevertheless, Bonham Carter believed Mrs. Lovett had the potential to be anything and everything, and she played her accordingly. "She's a tough, pragmatic survivor, but she's as vital and zestful as Sweeney is sensitive and depressive and introverted. And she's completely delusional."[61]

To prepare for Mrs. Lovett's complex first song "The Worst Pies in London"—performed while assembling a meat pie in her unsanitary shop, flicking off dust and insects—Bonham Carter took some lessons from Katherine Tidy, a period pie maker and home economist.

> I made a few pies so at least I understood the whole chemistry of making a pie--shortcrust pastry, the meat, what kind of pies they were. . . . It's hard work. In film you have to do everything exactly the same because of continuity, every single thing, on the same lyric. I'm quite good at multi-tasking, but "Worst Pies" is like the Olympics of multi-tasking.[62]

Bonham Carter had a clear-eyed grasp of the role. "I saw her as totally amoral, full of zest and full of life. . . . She's very canny, and a wannabe middle-class person. But the main thing that motors her, the main thing that defines Mrs. Lovett, is that she's tragically in love with somebody who doesn't love her back."[63]

The actress learned she was pregnant with her second child the day the filming of "A Little Priest" happened. During Mrs. Lovett's waltz with Sweeney at the end of that number, she was spinning and barely able to avoid throwing up. "My daughter is called Nellie Burton," Bonham Carter chuckled, "so she can thank Mrs. Lovett for her first name."[64]

Bonham Carter received a Golden Globe best actress nomination for her performance as Mrs. Lovett. She also received a best actress recognition from the 2007 *Evening Standard* British Film Awards. After *Sweeney Todd* she appeared in three more films by Burton: *Alice in Wonderland* (2010), *Dark Shadows* (2012), and *Alice Through the Looking Glass* (2016). She also played the evil witch Bellatrix Lestrange in the final four *Harry Potter* films (2007–2011). In *The King's Speech* (2010), she portrayed Elizabeth, the steady, faithful wife of King George VI, earning an Academy Award supporting actress nomination. In seasons three and four of the streaming series *The Crown* (2019–20), she was an older incarnation of Princess Margaret, sister of Queen Elizabeth II.

Alan Rickman, known for his performances as several villainous characters, beginning as Hans Gruber in *Die Hard* (1988) and especially as Severus Snape in the eight *Harry Potter* films (2001–2011), was an obvious choice for the despicable, nefarious Judge Turpin who banished Sweeney to Australia on a false charge to clear the way for his designs on Sweeney's young wife. Even though, like Depp and Bonham Carter, he had no experience as a singer, Rickman was a spot-on choice with his deep, sinister voice. *New York Times* music critic Anthony Tommasini wrote that he gave "a harrowingly understated portrayal of the evil Judge Turpin, which comes through in his literate, dry and menacing singing."[65]

Rickman attended John Doyle's 2005 actor-musician Broadway revival of *Sweeney Todd*. "The difference in theater is it's very much about the singing. When you see Patti LuPone playing Mrs. Lovett, you're kind of pinned to your seat by the force of her presence onstage. But on film, you have to have something completely other."[66] He enjoyed being part of Burton's cast: "It was great to do the movie because I was working with great film makers and great actors and a great script with great music, so it was more than fun—it was a privilege."[67]

The particular thrill for Rickman was working with the composer.

The greatness of Sondheim . . . is that he has the lyrics in his mind, he's got the character in his mind, and you've got to match all of them. But they're all there if you work at it and listen to it and hand yourself over to it. It's a bit like Shakespeare. It tells you how to say it if you obey the punctuation. And breathe. Great writing's done it for you.[68]

Rickman died in 2016.

To play the flamboyant barber Adolfo Pirelli, Burton chose Sacha Baron Cohen, a similarly extravagant actor, who received extensive notice in 2006 as a comic pseudo-documentarian in *Borat: Cultural Learnings of America for Make Benefit Glorious Nation of Kazakhstan*. Producer Richard Zanuck said Baron Cohen was hired before he had become well-known for his zany film performance. He was not an actor Burton initially envisioned for the role. "We met him for the first time in a recording studio," Zanuck said. "He told us he's always loved this show, and that he had sung early on in his life in choirs, so we asked him to step into the booth." For his audition Baron Cohen sang several songs from *Fiddler on the Roof*.[69]

At 6–5 Baron Cohen gave a memorable performance as the charlatan barber. His costume included anatomically graphic, royal blue spandex pants. Sondheim observed,

> He's a really sleazy Pirelli, which we've never had before on the stage. And he is sinister, too. It was a great pleasure to see him die. Pirelli has always been played by a tenor. Sacha is a baritone, but he was able to have the flavor of a tenor. The whole idea was a take-off on an Italian tenor singing, a man showing off his voice. It's wonderful that Sacha sings it all in that baritone voice and then on the last note, he goes way into the stratosphere . . . into this pretentious falsetto. That was really funny.

Sondheim added, "I also loved that he used the Italian flag as a bib. That was not my idea—it was his. I wish I had thought of it."[70]

Logan noted that Pirelli is a very schizophrenic part, starting with *Sweeney Todd*'s

> most entertaining song . . . "The Contest," where literally he is putting on a show for the people of St. Dunstan's Market and then has a challenge with Sweeney. Later he has a completely private scene with Todd where that mask comes off and the jovial Italian persona that he's projected completely disappears to be replaced by a ruthless, ice-cold blackmailer. There's not a bigger transition in the movie . . . when he's not playing the character Pirelli, he is so ice-cold and so frightening that you truly realize what a gifted actor [Baron Cohen] is.[71]

Versatile British character actor Timothy Spall was enlisted to play the creepy, fawning Beadle Banford who enabled Judge Turpin's depraved behavior. One of Britain's most respected film, TV, and stage actors, he played the villainous Peter Pettigrew in five of the *Harry Potter* films (2004–2010). Spall called the Beadle "a nasty piece of work, really. He's a small-time parish official who has authority because he has ingratiated himself to the Judge. He's sort of Turpin's bodyguard and henchman. He's a procurer of various things, seemly and unseemly. Also, he's pretty violent. He's not very nice!"[72]

Laura Michelle Kelly, who played innocent and luminous Lucy Barker and then the bedraggled, demented Beggar Woman who Lucy became, was the film's only professional singer. She had stage experience in a series of productions on London's West End: as Sophie in *Mamma Mia* (2002); as Eliza Doolittle in *My Fair Lady* at the National's Theatre Royal Drury Lane (2003); and as *Mary Poppins* (2004), winning the Olivier Award for Best Actress in a Musical. (She repeated that role on Broadway from 2009 to 2011.) She also played Galadriel in the London musical stage adaptation of *The Lord of the Rings* (2007).

Kelly was impressed with Depp's and Bonham Carter's singing.

> Everyone's so confident. It helps to be able to express a lyric as opposed to singing it with no meaning, and they've taken to it like ducks to water. Most people find Sondheim the hardest thing to sing, what with the tempos and the changes and the lyrical melodies; all of them are difficult. Watching Helena and Johnny, I'm amazed. Some people try for years to do what they're doing naturally.[73]

According to Higham, when Kelly played the Beggar Woman, the character was "weird and needed to sort of sing, speak, sing, speak, so many times she comes out of dialogue and goes into song, [meaning] it needed to be so of the moment." While most of Burton's cast lip-synced their songs, he had Kelly perform live.[74]

Two relatively unknown young actors made breathless film debuts as the story's innocent adolescent lovers. Jayne Wisener, just nineteen when *Sweeney Todd* was filmed, played Sweeney's daughter Johanna and beautifully sang Sondheim's complex aria, "Green Finch and Linnet Bird," a metaphor for her sheltered existence in the clutches of Judge Turpin. As Anthony Hope, the naïve young sailor who rescued Sweeney and fell hopelessly in love with Johanna, Jamie Campbell Bower, age eighteen, ardently delivered the beautiful song "Johanna" the moment he saw Wisener's visage in an upper window of the judge's home. Bower's audition was almost accidental: he was seeking recommendations for a drama school when Laura Michelle Kelly passed his name along to *Sweeney Todd*'s casting director.

Edward Sanders, a thirteen-year-old child performer from Sussex, was an unexpected choice for the role of young Tobias Ragg. (Onstage Toby is generally played by a youthful 20–30-year-old.) Sanders told an interviewer he was more interested in music than in acting. He had three months of auditions before the role was offered. "That was amazing," he said. "It was a big shock as I'd only done small productions at school before, so acting was never really my thing."[75] He colorfully sang the jaunty promotional song "Pirelli's Miracle Elixir," and then, as Mrs. Lovett's devoted shop assistant, he earnestly performed "Not While I'm Around" evincing genuine, childlike emotion. He was nominated for "best young actor" by the British Film Critics Choice Awards. Writing for *The Sondheim Review*, Michael Portantiere called Sanders "innocence personified as poor Toby, adding greatly to the effect of one of the finest stage-to-film transfers of all time."[76]

Movie Soundtrack

Sweeney Todd's soundtrack recording was issued in December 2007 as two separate CDs. "Highlights" has seventeen tracks (55:21 minutes), while the "Deluxe Compact Disc" (71:50 minutes) has three additional tracks and several others that are significantly longer than they are on the "Highlights" recording. The "Deluxe" package comes with an eighty-page booklet containing lyrics and numerous production photos.

The recording was produced by the film's music supervisor Mike Higham using the performances orchestrated by Jonathan Tunick and conducted by Paul Gemignani at Air Lyndhurst Studios in London. The expanded orchestral ensemble—with seventy-eight players—sounds great, but the inexperienced voices of Johnny Depp, Helena Bonham Carter, and the others, while suitable for the movie, don't deliver a truly satisfying audio experience for fans of Sondheim's lyrics. It's not likely that anyone who admires the show's the original cast recording of *Sweeney Todd* with the voices of Angela Lansbury and Len Cariou will be satisfied with the movie's soundtrack.

Burton wrote a brief note for the booklet that's part of the "Deluxe" package. "Of all musicals," he wrote, "*Sweeney Todd* is my favorite." He added,

> We tried to capture the essence and spirit of the Stephen Sondheim musical while at the same time creating something different for the film version. What makes these recordings so unique is that they are performed by actors who for the most part had no formal musical training. I believe this gives the songs a different dimension than any previous version.

There is no arguing with that claim. In fact, the soundtrack sold more than 400,000 copies in the United States and the United Kingdom.

Critical Reactions: Bloody Good

The review aggregation website Rotten Tomatoes gave *Sweeney Todd: The Demon Barber of Fleet Street* an 86 percent positive "Tomatometer" rating, based on reviews by 233 critics. The audience score of 81 percent was based on more than 250,000 ratings by everyday moviegoers.

Many critics gave the film and Tim Burton high marks, both for its ambition and its execution. According to Roger Ebert in the *Chicago Sun-Times*,

> The bloodiest musical in stage history . . . now becomes the bloodiest in film history, and it isn't a jolly romp, either, but a dark revenge tragedy with heartbreak, mayhem and bloody good meat pies. . . . To an unusual degree, *Sweeney Todd* works on a quasi-realistic level and not as a musical fantasy. That's not to say we're to take it as fact, but that we can at least accept it on its own terms without the movie winking at us. It combines some of Tim Burton's favorite elements: The fantastic, the ghoulish, the bizarre, the unspeakable, the romantic and, in Johnny Depp, he has an actor he has worked with since *Edward Scissorhands* and finds a perfect instrument.[77]

New York Times film critic A. O. Scott suggested that Burton and Sondheim were well suited collaborators for this film.

And so it should not be surprising that *Sweeney Todd: The Demon Barber of Fleet Street*, Mr. Burton's film adaptation of Mr. Sondheim's musical, is as dark and terrifying as any motion picture in recent memory. . . . *Sweeney* is as much a horror film as a musical: It is cruel in its effects and radical in its misanthropy, expressing a breathtakingly, rigorously pessimistic view of human nature. It is also something close to a masterpiece, a work of extreme—I am tempted to say evil—genius.[78]

Peter Marks wrote an enthusiastic review for the *Washington Post*.

Admirers of Stephen Sondheim who have long wondered whether a film of distinction would ever be made from one of his stage musicals can put aside their skepticism: Tim Burton has accomplished it in his ravishing *Sweeney Todd*. With oceans of gore, streams of luscious musicality and a performance by Johnny Depp redolent of malevolence and magnetism, Burton brings Sondheim's 1979 musical to the screen with a bravura visual style thrillingly in touch with the timelessly depraved delights of Grand Guignol. . . . The added marvel is that the director has crafted a version of a stage musical that honors the source without being slavishly devoted to it. By excising choral numbers and highlighting the sorrow inside the sordidness of Sondheim's wit-infused score, Burton invites us into a more intimate communion with horrible yet hummable aspects of human nature.[79]

National Public Radio commentator Bob Mondello recommended the film, saying,

In Tim Burton's splendid adaptation of the Stephen Sondheim-Hugh Wheeler musical . . . blood flows both freely and imaginatively. Happily, so do melody and feeling. Depp's snarling, vengeance-crazed Sweeney Todd is a wonder, and Helena Bonham Carter's Mrs. Lovett wields her rolling pin deftly. Both look as if they comb their hair with garden rakes and roll in flour before they head out in the morning, to greet a London that Burton films in sooty grays with the occasional blood-red highlight. . . . In short, the movie may substitute Grand Guignol for laughs at times, but it's spectacularly stylized—each throat-slashing is exceptional—persuasively sung, and imaginatively adapted for the screen."[80]

By most accounts, Burton's adaptation exceeded expectations. Of course, there were critics who condemned the actors for their untrained voices, the reduction of Sondheim's full score and the outright removal of several cherished numbers, and the amount of blood spilled. But Sondheim himself was pleased with the finished product.

Nine years after the film's release, film writer David Thomson, reviewer for the *New Republic* and the *Guardian*, contributed an essay to *The Oxford Handbook of Sondheim Studies* in which he compared Burton's movie with *Psycho*, the 1960 horror film that starred Sondheim's friend Anthony Perkins as the murderer Norman Bates. That film, Thomson suggested, "was a landmark in art or entertainment in that Alfred Hitchcock managed to make horror or slaughter into popular entertainment."[81] He was less certain that *Sweeney Todd* succeeded in that way.

Thomson suggested that "Burton and the powers behind the film decided was what a young audience would expect . . . connoisseurs of slaughter." He found Mrs. Lovett's murder, "waltzed into her own oven—the cruelest in the film." His final assessment: "The film is misguided and often unpleasant in ways that might confirm the worst fears of Sondheim's critics." Thomson's conclusion: "The thought that remains from the movie is how the ponderous and highly skilled effort of enlargement and reality has killed off this fierce game. That may be the worst murder."[82] His is a decidedly minority opinion.

Burton's movie appeared on numerous top ten film lists for 2007, with many critics giving *Sweeney Todd* their stamp of approval. It grossed over $153 million against DreamWorks' production budget of $50 million.

The two-disk DVD of Burton's film was released on April 1, 2008. (Its Blu-ray release was on October 21, 2008.) In addition to the complete 113-minute film, one disk offers a behind-the-scenes look at the collaboration between Burton, Depp, and Bonham Carter with footage from rehearsals and recording sessions. The second disk includes a feature about the historical roots of Sweeney Todd's story; a "making of" feature about the film; one about Sondheim's score; and a set of short takes about the tradition of Grand

Guignol, the film's design process and the bloody special effects, and a Moviefone unscripted interview with Burton and Depp. As of 2024, nearly two million copies of the DVD had been sold, bringing in more than $38 million in revenue.

Thomas Peyser, writing for *Style Weekly* in Richmond, Virginia, offered a collection of positive assessments. "Jubilantly grim, with its lens pitilessly focused on injustice, vengeance and gore—not to mention its songs extolling cannibalism," he wrote,

> it's the anti-Christian movie par excellence. It's also the most exhilarating, if wrenching, film adaptation of a musical in many years. . . . Burton's adaptation is faithful, but he hasn't shied away from cutting those elements more suited to the stage, most notably the musical's opening number, "The Ballad of Sweeney Todd," sung by the company in Greek chorus mode. Purists may mourn such losses, but the film is tighter for them. With powerful assists from a crack cast and production designer Dante Ferretti, whose labyrinthine London seems braced for a retributive blow from above, Burton has done that rare thing—turned a great play into a great film.[83]

Sweeney Todd was nominated for three 2008 Academy Awards. Johnny Depp was a candidate for Best Actor in a Leading Role. Costume designer Colleen Atwood was also nominated. Dante Ferretti's art direction won the film's only Oscar, for its production design. *Sweeney Todd* won the 2008 Golden Globe for Best Motion Picture—Musical or Comedy and Depp won as Best Actor—Motion Picture Musical or Comedy. Since its release, the film has been widely assessed as one of the greatest musical films of the twenty-first century.

Screenwriter Logan is a staunch defender of Burton's film adaptation. "What sets *Sweeney Todd* apart from other musicals is the solid emotional core," he said.

> It's a dark but passionate story about a man who's wronged, seeks revenge and, in the process, goes mad. It's also about a woman who's in love with him but can't make a connection with him. And it's about a young girl raised by a brutal stepfather trying to find happiness. All these emotions

collide in the film, and the fact that it's heightened by music and singing makes it all the more lushly romantic.[84]

Sondheim believed moviegoers would be as pleased as he was when he watched the final cut. "I was knocked out by it . . . I was knocked out by *how* knocked out I was."[85] He extravagantly called it "the first musical that has ever transferred successfully to the screen."[86]

It certainly achieved Burton's goal of creating "both a full-bore musical and a bone-chilling, violent horror movie."[87] Peter Marks called the film "the brilliant singing splatterfest that finally gives [Sondheim] a stab at cinematic immortality."[88]

In an essay entitled "The Hollywood Musical Done Right," the esteemed theater critic Terry Teachout said, "The fact that a well-known director like Burton should have collaborated with a popular actor like Depp on a screen adaptation of the most critically acclaimed musical of the past half-century was bound to pique the interest of artists and audience members for whom the musical theater is still very much a living genre." He called Burton's adaptation of *Sweeney Todd* "the best and most artistically serious film ever to be made from a Broadway musical."[89]

5

Sweeney Swings Back . . . Again and Again

Revivals, Opera Houses, and Concerts

There's no question that the tale of Sweeney Todd has been eagerly devoured by horror seekers for the better part of two centuries, from its Penny Dreadful roots in the 1840s to the Victorian melodramatic stage, from Bond's adaptation as a twentieth-century play with psychological motivation to Sondheim and Wheeler's transformation into a musical thriller and Tim Burton's horror musical. No matter how the story is told, it appeals to a human hunger to witness terrifying behavior, not unlike modern-day rubbernecking at horrible car accidents. That versatility of form and approach has inspired numerous interpretations for subsequent productions across five decades, many fueled by Sondheim's personal willingness to allow *Sweeney Todd* to be staged in different ways.

For nearly a decade after Harold Prince's original epic Broadway production it was the standard, replicated by several opera companies in large venues. Prince's staging was impressive, to be sure, and Eugene Lee's scenic design won a 1979 Tony Award.

Prince had prevailed over Sondheim's preference for intimacy with his notion to stage *Sweeney Todd* on a grand scale to demonstrate the horrific impact of the Industrial Revolution on lower-class people. Despite that, Sondheim never gave up on his personal desire to present a tale that was intimate, dark, and scary. "When I first wrote this thing," Sondheim said in a 2005 interview, "all I wanted to do was write a horror story, a Grand Guignol piece.... I characterize all the major productions I've seen in terms of a single adjective. Hal's was epic."[1]

Prince's twenty-six-perforner 1979 Broadway, supported by a score orchestrated for twenty-six musicians, made *Sweeney Todd*'s original production of an expensive proposition. It was indeed visually and sonically impressive, but that did not ensure financial success. When the Broadway production closed after 557 performances on June 29, 1980, just 53 percent of the original investment had been recouped.

Sweeney Todd's 1980 London premiere remounted Prince's epic staging at the West End's Theatre Royal, Drury Lane. It was not a success. It replicated Lee's gigantic scenic design. The theater's 1,996 seating capacity was comparable to Broadway's Uris Theatre, with 1,933. Despite positive advance critical notice and an impressive 1979 Tony Award haul, British audiences in 1980 did not flock to the show's London premiere. It lasted for a disappointing 157 performances. According to theater historian Ken Mandelbaum, "local critics and audiences did not buy the show, failing to take to its serious, operatic treatment of a tale that was, to them, something of a childhood jest."[2] It lost most of its investment.

More affordable approaches made sense. Christopher Bond, the actor and playwright whose 1979 adaptation inspired Sondheim, staged a 1983 production of the musical at the Liverpool Playhouse, where he was the artistic director. It focused on suspense and comedy rather than the angry social conscience that Prince used. The physical and budgetary demands of scenery were certainly less.

Bond's rendition was the first of more compact approaches that made it possible for the show to reach more audiences. He subsequently became the artistic director of the intimate Half Moon Theatre in East London with ninety seats. In 1985 he again staged *Sweeney Todd* to positive reviews, with several critics preferring his small-scale version to the show's London premiere at Drury Lane.

Reducing the size of the show to sharpen and intensify the storytelling was director Declan Donnellan's goal when he staged *Sweeney Todd* in 1993 at the

Royal National Theatre's 400-seat Cottesloe Theatre in London. (Today it's the Dorfman.) He "emphasized . . . the chamber-opera aspect of the piece, the sense that we are all trapped in Todd's barber shop above the ovens of Mrs. Lovett's human bakery."[3] This was much more in line with Sondheim's original notion. Referencing Prince's Broadway production, Sondheim said, "Declan Donnellan's production was done in the Cottesloe . . . and it was much scarier. The orchestra was a great deal smaller, but the audience was more intimately involved."[4] Comparing Donnellan's production to Prince's epic staging, Sondheim called it "exactly the reverse, it was very intimate."[5]

British critic Sheridan Morley wrote that Donnellan made it clear that the show "can survive and thrive on the grand scale as well as on the minimalist: this production is not better or worse than the original, it is just very different, the difference being that between a landscape and a close-up."[6]

At the Cottesloe, Julia McKenzie dazzled audiences and critics with a definitive portrait of Mrs. Lovett, and the production ran for four-and-a-half months. It then transferred to the Lyttelton Theatre with 890 seats, offered in rep from December 16, 1993, to June 1, 1994. The production's year-long run won over London critics who had dismissed the 1980 London transfer, and audiences followed suit. Sondheim deeply admired it, calling Donnellan "the best director in London." He told the director that this production was exactly as he had imagined it.[7]

Accordingly, other creators of theater saw that *Sweeney Todd* could be successful across a broad spectrum of venues—from 60 seats to nearly 2,000. This opened the door for a surprising array of concepts, including actors accompanying themselves musically and imaginative immersive approaches in tiny spaces such as a London pie shop. Sondheim approved of an adaptation of the show for high schools. These diverse productions have demonstrated the innate power and versatility of the musical.

Nevertheless, large-scale revivals of *Sweeney Todd* have also continued in New York and London, on the stages of America's regional theaters and at major opera houses in Europe, the United States, and Australia. Additionally, several producers presented concert versions of the show supported by major orchestras and featuring well-known singers and actors in the leading roles.

Meanwhile other directors found ways to produce *Sweeney Todd* more economically—using smaller casts and reduced orchestras. The show's impact was seldom diminished. Cast and concert recordings expanded familiarity with Sondheim's score and overcame much of the initial resistance to the horrific story. As the show's fame spread and critical consensus coalesced, *Sweeney Todd* was increasingly called Sondheim's masterpiece.

This chapter describes some of *Sweeney Todd*'s most important subsequent productions, concerts, and revivals.

London Turns Its Back on Sweeney Todd

Theatre Royal, Drury Lane (November 15–July 2, 1980, 157 performances). London's first *Sweeney Todd* remounted the original Broadway production, staged again by Hal Prince. Actor Denis Quilley was cast as Sweeney and won the 1980 Olivier Award for Best Actor in a Musical. When he collected his award he said, prophetically, that the show would come back in some form for a longer run. Sheila Hancock, another British stage veteran, was Mrs. Lovett. Her portrayal was described by one critic as having "caught the love-story element perfectly."[8]

Although the production won that season's Olivier for Best New Musical, in general, critics were unenthusiastic. Their negative reviews resulted in a short run, just 157 performances. "*Sweeney Todd* was a resounding commercial failure . . . in the West End," Sondheim wrote in *Finishing the Hat*. He found its negative reception "particularly disheartening . . . to me, since I had written the show as my love letter to London, a city I treasure above all others except for New York."[9] Some observers found that a strange way to characterize the tale of a murderous barber and an amoral baker.

Houston Grand Opera (June 14–24, 1984). Given Sondheim's initial thoughts to create an operatic retelling of Sweeney's story, it was no surprise when it became an opera house production for the first time by Houston Grand Opera, one of America's most respected companies. Prince again directed, with John DeMain conducting ten performances in the summer of 1984. The cast featured American baritone Timothy Nolen as Sweeney and mezzo-soprano Joyce Castle, a Texas native, was Mrs. Lovett.

Prince's production was remounted by *New York City Opera* at the Lincoln Center for the Performing Arts' New York State Theater (October 11– November 18, 1984; thirteen performances) where General Director Beverly Sills had championed it. For this engagement, conductor Paul Gemignani, who led the original 1979 Broadway orchestra, was on the podium. Nolen returned as Sweeney; Rosalind Elias, the longtime Metropolitan Opera mezzo-soprano, played Mrs. Lovett in her New York City Opera debut.[10] Cris Groenendaal, who replaced Victor Garber as Anthony Hope in 1979 on Broadway and in the touring production, again stepped into the role of the besotted young lover.

The production was panned by *New York Times*' Donal Henahan, who complained of "unsympathetic orchestration and an eccentric amplification." He described Nolen and Elias as "a rather quaint, if kinky, London couple whose particular commercial activities were not worth shuddering over." Henahan described the sets as "imaginative enough, given their overuse of pseudo-Brechtian cliches such as visible lighting technicians and costumed stagehands. The scenery consists largely of pipe structures that are wheeled about to become stairways of houses, bridges and the like, with backdrops of industrial buildings to suggest the grimy milieu."[11]

Twenty years later *Sweeney Todd* returned to New York City Opera (March 5–28, 2004) for sixteen performances, again employing Prince's staging. Arthur Masella was the stage director, and George Manahan conducted. Timothy Nolen was involved again, alternating in the role of Sweeney with City Opera regular Mark Delavan. West End musical theater diva Elaine Paige played Mrs. Lovett. She brought her "splendid singing and high-wattage stage presence to the role . . . [making her] a worthy successor to the one-and-only Angela Lansbury; she's a brilliant musical comedian for whom the wide vocal and emotional range of the part is triumphantly met."[12]

Soprano Sarah Coburn was Johanna, matched with Keith Phares as Anthony. Keith Jameson played Toby, Judith Blazer delivered an agonized Beggar Woman, and Walter Charles was creepy as Judge Turpin. Critical reception was not much warmer than it had been in 1984: "Voices were amplified, but at the [New York] State Theater indistinctness was simply made louder," wrote Bernard Holland in the *New York Times*. He added, "Mr. Delavan's sure, booming voice, which seemed for some reason more amplified than that of his colleagues, made a case for *Sweeney*'s operatic side."[13] For *The Sondheim Review*, Sean Patrick Flahaven wrote, "The physical production is terrific, and the musical forces are large, but the time allotted to acting and musical preparation for the performers was obviously not enough."[14]

National Theatre, Drury Lane (May 1, 1985, thirteen performances). London's first *Sweeney Todd* revival was staged by playwright Christopher Bond, the actor who crafted the script that inspired Sondheim. Earlier in the year, Bond had staged it in an intimate production in Liverpool. It was the first time for a production to demonstrate that a grand scale was not a necessity for *Sweeney Todd* to work. Leon Greene played Sweeney; Gillian Hanna was Mrs. Lovett.

"Teeny Todd" Makes a Big Impression

York Theatre Company (March 31–April 29, 1989, twenty-four performances). Just nine years after the Broadway production closed, the ninety-nine-seat York Theatre Company mounted an imaginative Off-Off-Broadway revival, staged by director Susan H. Schulman. It happened in the basement gymnasium of the former Church of the Heavenly Rest on New York's Upper East Side. Bob Gunton performed the role of Sweeney with a ragged baritone and incandescent rage. Beth Fowler was a more vulnerable Mrs. Lovett than Angela Lansbury. A three-piece band using synthesizers accompanied the performance. The instruments provided "textural subtleties [that] range from birdsong to snare drum. And the colder, pricklier electronic textures that frequently sound like pipe organ and harpsichord eerily complement the play's fiendish imagery of glinting, lethal razor blades."[15] (See Figure 5.1.)

Figure 5.1 *Bob Gunton played Sweeney Todd opposite Beth Fowler as Mrs. Lovett in the show's intimate "Teeny Todd" 1989 Broadway revival, staged by Susan H. Schulman. Photofest.*

The floor of the playing area was painted to resemble a cobblestone street, and the audience was seated on both sides. At one end of the street was the pie shop and the barber's parlor; Judge Turpin's home was at the opposite end. According to reviewer Stephen Holden, it "happily proves the show can be just as well done as a small chamber opera. In some ways it even benefits from the more intimate scale"[16]—very much as Sondheim preferred.

About two weeks after York's *Sweeney* began, *New York Times* critic Frank Rich referred to it as "an altogether extraordinary production."[17] In an essay, he observed that, with Schulman directing, it was likely the first time a woman had staged the show, and that perspective changed it considerably. He called Beth Fowler's portrait of Mrs. Lovett "more pathetic and conniving, more lost in vague and doomed romantic fantasies about Sweeney Todd than obsessed with making a killing in the meat-pie racket,"[18] as Lansbury's original performance had characterized her. Rich suggested that SuEllen Estey's performance as the Beggar Woman was also elevated, rendering "a suffering woman . . . beneath the rags and derelict's makeup."[19] He noted that "The audience at the York is held spellbound, and in my experience that wasn't always the case at the Uris."[20] Rich concluded with the hope that the York's limited run could be extended.

His plea was answered when the production transferred to *Circle in the Square* (September 15, 1989–February 25, 1990, 189 performances), a theater in the basement of the building that housed the Uris, where the original *Sweeney* had been staged. (The large theater was renamed the Gershwin in 1983.) Schulman's production was nominated for four Tony Awards—Schulman for Best Director of a Musical, Gunton for Best Actor in a Musical, Fowler for Best Actress in a Musical, and as Best Revival of a Musical. It garnered no wins, but it's the production that spawned the satirical title "Teeny Todd," coined by *Forbidden Broadway*.

D.C. Theater Begins Its Commitment to Sondheim

Signature Theatre in Arlington, Virginia, just outside of Washington, D.C., surely holds the record for the most productions of *Sweeney Todd*. Staged by Eric Schaeffer, it was Signature's inaugural production in 1991, with a cast of eighteen and a fifteen-piece orchestra in an intimate space with seating for just ninety people at the Gunston Middle School. Donna Migliaccio, who co-founded Signature with Schaeffer, played Mrs. Lovett, and Michael Forrest was Sweeney. The production earned five Helen Hayes Awards (Outstanding Resident Production of a Musical, Schaeffer for Best Director, Outstanding Actress for Migliaccio, Lou Stancari for Best Set Design and Outstanding Actor for Pedro Porro as Anthony Hope). That recognition launched Signature's reputation as an outstanding producer of shows by Stephen Sondheim. It revived *Sweeney* in 1999, 2010, and 2023.

In his 1999 revival, Schaeffer again featured Migliaccio as Mrs. Lovett. Broadway regular Norm Lewis was Sweeney. "With his bruised-looking eyes and frightening inwardness, Lewis is a great Sweeney," wrote Lloyd Rose in the *Washington Post*, "and something innately gentle in him suggests the tragedy of destroyed goodness."[21] This time the show was presented in Signature's new, 136-seat theater, a former auto garage where chrome car bumpers were made. An eighteen-piece orchestra supported the production. Audiences entered through a narrow hallway that reminded one writer of a mine shaft. Lou Stancari designed another set that was "a gloomy, ramshackle array of platforms and catwalks that wrapped to three corners of Signature's black-box space."[22]

In 2007 Signature raised $16 million to build a new two-theater and office facility that became the cultural anchor of Arlington's Village at Shirlington, a shopping complex that also houses a public library. The new theater tripled the amount of performing space the company had at the garage. Schaeffer staged *Sweeney Todd* once more (February 9–April 4, 2010) in the new 266-seat space with an environmental design by James Kronzer resembling a construction site. This time the production was supported by a chamber-sized ensemble: a pianist doubling on harmonium, a cellist, a woodwind player handling flute, piccolo, clarinet, bass clarinet, oboe and English horn, and a percussionist playing numerous instruments from tom-tom to timpani to glockenspiel and washtub. Conductor Zak Sandler orchestrated the score for the musicians and conducted from the piano. Edward Gero played a crazed Sweeney, and Sherri L. Edelen as Mrs. Lovett added to the production's thrilling chemistry.

Eric Schaeffer retired in 2020, but the Sondheim/*Sweeney* tradition continued with a 2023 production (May 23–July 9, 2023), this time directed by Sarna Lapine, niece of longtime Sondheim collaborator James Lapine. Jon

Kalbfleisch was the music director, the same role he'd filled for the earlier productions. The cast included Nathaniel Stampley as Sweeney and Bryonha Maria Parham as Mrs. Lovett. *Washington Post* critic Peter Marks termed Lapine's direction "bland" and "listless," suggesting that it soft-pedaled the story's horror. "The genre is Grand Guignol, a theatrical embrace of depravity. On this occasion, unfortunately, it's only petite guignol."[23]

Signature was recognized with the American Theatre Wing's Regional Theatre Tony Award in 2009, largely for its dedication to Sondheim's works. The company annually hosts a Stephen Sondheim Award, recognizing actors and others known for work in his shows. (The annual gala event benefits the theater's artistic, education, and community outreach programs). Artists with *Sweeney Todd* connections who have been honored include Sondheim himself (the very first award in 2009), as well as others with Sondheim credentials: Angela Lansbury (2010), Patti LuPone (2012), Hal Prince (2013), orchestrator Jonathan Tunick (2014), and Audra McDonald (2019).

Intimacy Works for Declan Donnellan—and Sondheim Approves

Royal National Theatre's London revival of *Sweeney Todd* began at its Cottesloe Theatre (June 2–October 19, 1993), then transferred in repertory to the *Lyttleton Theatre* (December 16, 1993–June 1, 1994). Declan Donnellan staged it as an intimate, audience-involving production at the 400-seat Cottesloe. It won four Oliviers: Best Director, Best Actress in a Musical (Julia McKenzie), Best Actor in a Musical (Alun Armstrong) and Best Musical Revival. Denis Quilley (the original Sweeney at Drury Lane in 1980) was Judge Turpin; when the show transferred to the Lyttleton, Quilley replaced Armstrong. Early in his award-winning career Adrian Lester played Anthony Hope.

Critic Sheridan Morley, writing for the *International Herald Tribune*, said, "*Sweeney* is not another cozy Victorian ballad show: no lines of Cockney orphans chanting Bart-ish pit-a-pat lyrics, no lovable Annie-type heroines, no guarantee that when you leave the theater you will feel anything but worse. *Sweeney* is a jet-black, vicious and vitriolically brilliant musical played on the razor's edge."[24] Sondheim frequently cited Donnellan's production as scarier than Prince's original. The production was recorded by the BBC for broadcast in July 1994.

An Asian Take on the Demon Barber

East West Players (September 8–November 20, 1994) presented a low-budget *Sweeney Todd* in a ninety-nine-seat black box space in Silverlake, California, between Hollywood and downtown Los Angeles. This intimate production, directed by the Tim Dang, the company's artistic director, was another that benefited from its intense, claustrophobic staging. It was also steeped in Asian influences. The show won awards and brought national recognition to East West Players. Dang's Asian-Pacific cast was led by Orville Mendoza as Sweeney and Freda Foh Shen as Mrs. Lovett. It proved so popular that its initial run was extended by three weeks.

In 1998 East West Players moved into the 240-seat David Henry Hwang Theater in the Union Center for the Arts. The company mounted its second production of *Sweeney* there in 2006 (February 8–March 10), again staged by Dang. It was praised for its "freshness and ferocity."[25] Ronald M. Banks played Sweeney, and Marilyn Tokuda was Mrs. Lovett. Audience response again warranted an extension for the show's four-week run.

A Vote for Sweeney at a Traditional Venue

Goodspeed Opera House (April 10–June 21, 1996). At this 398-seat venue in East Haddam, Connecticut, known for reviving classic musicals, *Sweeney Todd* in 1996 became the "youngest" show ever to be produced there, just sixteen years after its original Broadway production. It was directed by Gabriel Barre. Sweeney was played by veteran Timothy Nolen, who sang role with the Houston Grand Opera and New York City Opera in 1984. A *New York Times* review said, "As a singing actor, the man is the real thing. Mr. Nolen plunges his voice into the lowest depths of loathing and lifts it to the needs of caressing lyricism."[26] Film and TV actress Barbara Marineau, a contralto, was Mrs. Lovett. "In no Broadway theater, with beyond-human over-amplification, can lyrics be heard so distinctly as at Goodspeed."[27]

Small Sweeney Has Intensity

Leicester Haymarket Theatre (November–December 1996). Director Paul Kerryson's production "solves the problem of getting . . . close-to intensity and cleanness of focus on a large stage. The stark scaffolding and the mobile gantreys that can rise and fall to create bridges, streets and balconies make clear statements with splendidly uncluttered flexibility."[28] Dave Willetts delivered a powerfully acted Sweeney. Jeanette Ranger as Mrs. Lovett was a "knock-out, both vocally and dramatically. There's a chilling comic discrepancy between her comfortably plump, maternal presence and that mental cut-out from ordinary human feeling which enables her to do anything to hold on to Sweeney and her dreams of sweet domesticity."[29] Reviewer Paul Taylor called the production "a stunning study of love warped by injustice to an obsessional vengefulness and Sondheim's likeliest passport to immortality."[30]

Kerryson's rendition of *Sweeney Todd* staging was remounted again with a pair of performances on February 12, 2000, at London's *Royal Festival Hall*, billed as the "twentieth anniversary London concert production." It was a benefit for the HIV and AIDS charity Crusaid. These London performances, with a 40-piece orchestra, were even larger than his previous environmental staging four years in Leicester.

This time Kerryson featured three American stars. Len Cariou, the show's original star, returned to the role. "He was in such robust voice once again and so full of dramatic power that it was as if twenty years hadn't passed."[31] The production also featured Judy Kaye as Mrs. Lovett, who "astutely combined the hilarious but chilling practicality of the character with real musical comedy verve." Davis Gaines was Anthony Hope (a role he had played in the Reprise! Production in Los Angeles in 1996). British performer Owen Jones (at the time playing Jean Valjean in a *Les Mis* production at London's Queen's Theatre) was cast as Pirelli and "transformed a potentially stock supporting role into a bruising study in narcissism turned nasty."[32]

A focal point of the evening was the Royal Festival Hall's organ, a truly frightening instrument, probably the largest ever used for the opening chords of *Sweeney Todd*. This staging overcame any doubters who recalled the show's disappointing 1980 London reception. Kerryson's production "reestablished the piece's credentials on the grander rather than domestic scale."[33]

Opera North (UK) based in Leeds, England, produced *Sweeney Todd* from January 17, 1998, to March 30, 1998. Directed by David McVicar, it was praised for its "sublime musicality."[34] Through the early months of 1998 it toured to Manchester, Nottingham, Newcastle-Upon-Tyne and twice in London. Steven Page played Sweeney, and Beverly Klein was Mrs. Lovett. McVicar moved his production to Sadler's Wells Opera in London (June 7–15, 2002) for nine performances.

In 2002, Alfred Hickling wrote, "David McVicar's production . . . is sinister, spectacular and not at all suitable for vegetarians." Comparing it to an earlier production, he called it "mercifully fresh, and enabling one to appreciate that this is one of Sondheim's most ambitious, fully integrated scores. . . . Conductor James Holmes and the Opera North orchestra draw out far more subtleties from this deceptively complex score than the average pit-band can muster."[35]

Actors, Not Singers

An intriguing pairing of British actors stood onstage at the Hollywood Bowl in Los Angeles on September 9, 1998: Patrick Stewart (veteran of the Royal Shakespeare Company and best known as Capt. Jean-Luc Picard on *Star Trek: The Next Generation*) and Lynn Redgrave (winner of multiple Golden Globe Awards). Several program segments assembled by conductor John Mauceri were suites from various Broadway shows, including one with material from *Sweeney Todd*. According to Richard S. Ginell for *Variety*, the pair were "two stage-savvy Thespians with just enough voice to put the music over."[36]

They were especially praised for their cutting from *Sweeney Todd*. "Sondheim's 1979 masterpiece . . . has an emotional depth and wicked humor that set it jarringly apart from the other entertainments of the night. It also received the most authentic-sounding performance, with Redgrave cast perfectly as the amoral Mrs. Lovett and Stewart a subtle, formidable Todd despite losing touch with the tunes now and then."[37]

In his memoir, *Making It So*, the unflappable Stewart confessed that just before he began performing this segment, he experienced stage fright for one of the only times in his life.³⁸ "As I stood behind a music stand while the symphony orchestra played the rousing overture to Stephen Sondheim's brilliant *Sweeney Todd* . . . it was just the two of us onstage, and as the orchestra pounded out the introductory chords of Sweeney's entrance, my heart pounded just as fast."

In a television interview in March 2017, Stewart joked that he fantasized about a production of *Sweeney Todd* with Hugh Jackman as the Demon Barber, his friend and RSC colleague Ian McKellen as Mrs. Lovett (!) and himself as the vile Judge Turpin. With a smirk, he added that as time went on he might become more serious about such casting.³⁹

TV Stars Shed Some Blood

Reprise! Broadway's Best in Concert (March 12–14, 1999, five performances). A pair of familiar faces to television viewers stepped into the roles of Sweeney and Mrs. Lovett in 1999 at the Ahmanson Theater in Los Angeles: Kelsey Grammer, TV's Frasier Crane, and Christine Baranski, known at the time as Maryanne Thorpe, Cybill Shepherd's sitcom sidekick on *Moonlighting*, but subsequently as Diane Lockhart in *The Good Wife* and *The Good Fight*. Despite the Reprise! billing, this was not a concert production. With stationary mics onstage, actors were off book, wearing makeup and costumes, with props and set pieces. Unfortunately, an inadequate amount of time for preparation made the production look "like the dress rehearsal of a highly promising but still under-rehearsed show."⁴⁰

Grammer made Sweeney more introspective, but he was not up to the vocal challenges of the score. Baranski, on the other hand, was appreciated by the audience and played the role with a welcome sense of sauciness. Another TV actor, Neil Patrick Harris (age twenty-six at the time and known then for playing *Doogie Howser, M.D.*, 1983–93) was a pleasant surprise both vocally and dramatically as Toby. Davis Gaines played Anthony Hope. The production was staged by Calvin Remsberg, who played the Beadle in *Sweeney*'s first national tour in 1980. On the evening of the first performance, March 12, Sondheim was in attendance and received an award for lifetime achievement in musical theater from ASCAP, the American Society of Composers, Authors and Publishers.

Symphonic Sweeney

A three-concert performance of *Sweeney Todd* by the New York Philharmonic (May 4–6, 2000) was staged by Lonny Price. Featuring a cast drawn from both opera and musical theater, it was presented at Lincoln Center's *Avery Fisher Hall* and conducted by Andrew Litton. The timing was in conjunction with Sondheim's seventieth birthday in March 2000. Patti LuPone was featured as Mrs. Lovett, a portrait described as "blunt, sly and vocally smooth"[41] in *The Sondheim Review*. Veteran George Hearn delivered "a shattering performance,"[42] replacing Welsh opera star bass-baritone Bryn Terfel, who had to withdraw for health reasons.

An impressive array of supporting players included Davis Gaines as Anthony, Neil Patrick Harris as Toby and Audra McDonald as the Beggar Woman. Opera singers in the cast included Heidi Grant Murphy as Johanna, Paul Plishka as a menacing Judge Turpin, John Aler as the Beadle and Stanford Olsen as Pirelli. The forty voices of the New York Choral Artists, led by choral director Grant Gershon, added heft to the concert performances. The exuberant packed house for the final evening—with Sondheim present—gave it a fifteen-minute standing ovation.

Sondheim wrote a note for the concert program:

> When the New York Philharmonic first approached me about them performing *Sweeney Todd*, I was in immediate succession stunned, proud, delighted and anxious. Although like many in the Broadway musical and opera worlds, I question arbitrary distinctions between the two (in some instances, anyway). I felt more than a little intimidated at the prospect of the score being played by one of the world's great orchestras. The excitement of the prospect prevailed, and I happily said yes.[43]

A live recording of the concert was produced by the orchestra after Deutsche Gramomophon withdrew due to budgetary concerns. The German recording company's decision also prompted PBS to step back from a planned video version for "Great Performances."[44]

When Price's staging was repeated a year later with the San Francisco Symphony (July 19–21, 2001) at *Davies Symphony Hall* with conductor

Rob Fisher, there was no hesitation about preserving the performance for a television audience. San Francisco's KQED worked with Ellen M. Krass Productions to create a live-on-tape video of the concert which aired on Halloween night 2001 on many PBS stations. It won a 2002 Emmy Award for Outstanding Classical Music-Dance Program, and Hearn received a 2002 Emmy for his performance. The video was subsequently released on DVD.

Many of the performers from New York were involved again. Stepping into major roles were Victoria Clark as the Beggar Woman, Lisa Vroman as Johanna, and Timothy Nolen as Judge Turpin. A review in *The Sondheim Review* said, "Hearn once again proved that twenty years later, he can still sing and act the hell out of his incredibly physically and vocally demanding role."[45]

During the San Francisco engagement, Lonny Price was interviewed by *The Sondheim Review*. Asked how he approached the staging, he said he scrapped the traditional concert format, instead using three levels surrounding the orchestra. "My main concern," he said, "was how to tell the story clearly and have the audience get it."[46]

The orchestral concert had one more iteration a month after its appearance in San Francisco when it received a one-night presentation at Chicago's outdoor *Ravinia Festival* (August 24, 2001) with the Chicago Symphony Orchestra, conducted again by Andrew Litton. This time Chicago musical theater performer Hollis Resnik was the Beggar Woman. This event launched a subsequent series of summer Sondheim performances at Ravinia, produced by Welz Kaufman, who had moved from the New York Philharmonic to manage the Chicago Symphony. These annual productions, each staged by Lonny Price, featured LuPone, Hearn, and McDonald, as well as Michael Cerveris.

In 2014, the New York Philharmonic teamed again with Price for a five-performance revival of *Sweeney Todd* at *Avery Fisher Hall* (March 5–8), conducted by Alan Gilbert. This time Welsh opera star Bryn Terfel, following back surgery, was able to play Sweeney. He performed opposite movie actress Emma Thompson as Mrs. Lovett. A writer for *The Sondheim Review* pointed out that the performers had "shared citizenship—the two might hail from different performance worlds, but they are unmistakably from the same isles as their characters, and this gave their scenes together an easy familiarity that helped compensate for the inevitable disconnect between the two."⁴⁷ Terfel's "rich, pitch-dark voice soared into the auditorium with an enveloping intensity"⁴⁸ wrote Charles Isherwood in the *New York Times* but his "acting wasn't always as expressive as his singing." Meanwhile, Thompson, not much known as a singer, gave a triumphant performance, "scuttling around the stage with a variety of silly walks, jabbering in a perfect Cockney accent, and singing with impressive range and assurance . . . she put a lively personal stamp on the role."⁴⁹

This time Price again demonstrated his flair for avoiding formulas in his various concert stagings, beginning with a raucous opening transition. The performers entered wearing evening attire and began to perform the prologue from folders on music stands. But after a moment or two, they ditched their books, frayed their costumes, kicked over their music stands, and even overturned a fake grand piano. The performances carried this irreverent attitude throughout, including a moment when Thompson snatched conductor Gilbert's baton.

This time around Price assembled a new cast that included Philip Quast as Judge Turpin, Erin Mackey as Johanna, Jay Armstrong as Anthony Hope, Kyle Brenn as Tobias, Jeff Blumenkrantz as the Beadle and Broadway star Christian Borle as Pirelli. Audra McDonald reprised her performance as the Beggar Woman for several performances, then Bryonha Marie Parham stepped in.

The *New York Times* declared, "Sondheim's score seems to grow more majestic each time you hear it . . . and the forward thrust of the drama as it reels into nightmare territory remains a model of musical theater writing."⁵⁰

Terfel and Thompson reprised the 2014 concert staging a year later with the English National Opera at the London Coliseum, offering thirteen performances (March 30–April 12, 2015), again staged by Lonny Price. David Charles Abell conducted. "One of the evening's delights," according to Michael Billington in the *Guardian*, was

> the way it uses whatever is to hand to evoke Sondheim's world. An upturned piano serves as a rostrum, Mrs. Lovett cooks her filthy pies on top of a kettledrum and, when the pies acquire a flesh-and-blood savor, they are served from a cymbal. Even the trunk in which the demon barber conceals his first victim has ENO clearly imprinted on the side.⁵¹

Sweeney Todd Close to Home

London's *Bridewell Theatre* located just off Fleet Street was a particularly suitable venue for this monthlong revival (June 14–July 15, 2000). The predictably enterprising theater is probably the first in England to give *Sweeney Todd* a fully environmental and immersive production. The theater's seating was removed, and the audience was moved from one part of the room to another, "as a result, even more implicated as part of the community that the show describes."[52] Staged by a young director, Richard James (born just five years after *Sweeney* debuted on Broadway) director, it worked especially well for crowd scenes such as Pirelli's barbering contest, but proved challenging when singers were distant from the production's two-man keyboard accompaniment.[53] Michael McLean delivered a powerful Sweeney; Jessica Martin was an "unusually seductive" Mrs. Lovett.[54]

Celebrating Sondheim at the Kennedy Center

During a hot Washington, D.C., summer the *Kennedy Center for the Performing Arts* presented *The Sondheim Celebration* (May–August 2002), a season-long festival tribute, producing six of his musicals. In addition to *Sweeney Todd*, the $10 million celebration, curated by Eric Schaeffer, the prolific director of Sondheim shows at Arlington's Signature Theatre, featured *Company* and *Sunday in the Park with George* in the first six-week set of rotating repertory. The second round of repertory presented *Merrily We Roll Along*, *Passion*, and *A Little Night Music*.

Sweeney Todd opened the festival, and its sixteen performances in the *Eisenhower Theater* across the event's first cycle were completely sold out. Christopher Ashley staged the production; Larry Blank was the conductor, and the leading roles were filled by Broadway star Brian Stokes Mitchell and stage and television actor Christine Baranski.

Writing for *The Sondheim Review*, Mark Eden Horowitz said there was no radical rethinking of the show, and the ambience of the 1979 original was replicated.

But there were differences. This was a funnier and sexier production. . . . Both in fine voice, Mitchell and Baranski made the demanding score sound almost too easy. . . . In general, theirs was a more human, less melodramatic duo than we usually see. This made the show less frightening on the surface, but more real, more plausible.[55]

"Together, Baranski and Mitchell are the very faces of comedy and tragedy," wrote Nelson Pressley in his *Washington Post* review, "the eternal odd couple that Sondheim brilliantly unites in this show. . . . In Mitchell and Baranski, the casting gods have truly smiled on this show, and the supporting performers (plus the vast chorus) are almost uniformly admirable."[56] Other roles were played by Hugh Panaro (Anthony), Celia Keenan-Bolger (Johanna), Mark Price (Tobias), Mary Beth Peil (Beggar Woman), Kevin Ligon (Pirelli), Walter Charles (Judge Turpin), and Ray Friedeck (Beadle).

Mitchell and Baranski were excited to play the leading roles in a high-profile event that garnered international attention. "It's very possibly my favorite musical of all time," Mitchell said in a *Sondheim Review* interview. "It's a role I've always wanted to do, but I had to wait until I was older. Now, fortunately or unfortunately, I'm old enough."[57]

Baranski also spoke to the *Sondheim Review*, noting that when she heard that *Sweeney Todd* would be part of the celebration, she wrote to Sondheim of her interest, which led to her being cast. "I have to approach every song as an acting piece," she explained. "I have so much experience as an actress, but not as a singer, and I like to think each song is not different from my acting, but an extension of my acting."[58]

"The production succeeded in being funny and frightening," Horowitz wrote, "and various gasps from the audience confirmed how shocking and surprising the show still is to the uninitiated."[59]

More Opera and Concerts

Veteran Broadway conductor Paul Gemignani was in Chicago to lead the orchestra for the *Lyric Opera of Chicago*'s first production of *Sweeney Todd* (November 18–December 22, 2002, twelve performances). Staging was by

Australian director Neil Armfield. Welsh bass-baritone Bryn Terfel took his first swing at playing the Demon Barber; alto Judith Christin, a Lyric Opera regular, was Mrs. Lovett. Nathan Gunn was Anthony and Timothy Nolen was Judge Turpin. CLO's dramaturg Roger Pines said the production was cast "exclusively with operatic singers, and they all performed brilliantly. The success that Terfel, a leading operatic bass-baritones of our time, suggests the possible directions the role can be taken vocally." The *New York Times* exclaimed, "It would be difficult to imagine a more perfect marriage of role, voice and stage personality."[60]

Terfel, who's sung on major stages in New York City, London, Vienna, and Paris, said *Sweeney Todd* was much like operatic roles he had played elsewhere. "I'm tackling this role as I would tackle Wagner, Mozart or Strauss. The rudiments are the same. You have to have wonderful diction, color, everything. It all boils down to giving a performance."[61]

Christin was in awe of *Sweeney Todd*'s score. "Every day you go in, and you hear something new, and you know how brilliantly it is all put together. Nothing is wasted, not a note, not a word. That's my biggest obligation, to be as true to the lines as I can be. Sondheim is a genius, the way the music flows and goes back and forth."[62]

Chicago-based *Sondheim Review* critic John Olson wrote,

> What the musical theater buff might not have expected in this opera house was a visually inventive interpretation that went into the darkest corners of the piece. This alone would earn it recognition as a landmark production. Australian designer Brian Thomson set the action in a world of shadow and fog, created by a system of grids, cages and curtains.[63]

Performers wore Victorian costumes, but there was no period scenery. "This *Sweeney* was much less about social inequities in 19th-century London and more about deception, madness, revenge and rage."[64] All the performers, including Terfel, were miked, a concession to musical theater that was unusual for an opera house.

A year later when Armfield's production was remounted at London's *Royal Opera House, Covent Garden* (December 15, 2003–January 14, 2004; nine performances) with a new cast, *Sweeney Todd* didn't win the effusive praise it had received in Chicago. Armfield's staging was panned by London critics, especially Thomson's scenic design.

> The set was visually plain (when it was not plain ugly), composed merely of a scaffolding grid from which hung drapes that were endlessly rearranged to define different spaces.... The cast had to work hard to animate this large vacant space, and though their voices more than filled it, their performances were frequently broader than the subtle modulations of character that are required.[65]

Thomas Allen was cast as Sweeney and Felicity Palmer played Mrs. Lovett. Rosalind Plowright was the Beggar Woman. Paul Gemignani again conducted. "When it came to the music, this production was blood-curdlingly good. Sondheim's score with Jonathan Tunick's orchestrations was gloriously performed by the Opera House orchestra."[66]

Doyle Cuts Sweeney Down to Size

British director John Doyle assembled a highly distilled, intimate production of *Sweeney Todd* in early 2004 at the *Watermill Theatre* (February 4–March 27), a small 220-seat venue in Newbury, west of London. Restricted by a limited budget and a tiny, cramped performance space, Doyle applied the "actor/musician" concept that he had used previously to reduce *Sweeney Todd* to nine actors who were also musicians, called upon to enact roles and serve as the production's orchestra. Staged and designed by Doyle, the production used reorchestrated arrangements by musical director by Sarah Travis.

Doyle framed the story in an asylum: after witnessing the carnage that concluded the barber's series of bloody murders, young Toby's mind has cracked, and he's been committed to an institution. The inmates recall and enact the tale. Rather than dripping blood from slit throats, Doyle's actors poured blood from one bucket to another and then donned bloodstained white lab coats to signify their demise. A large coffin was at center stage; Sweeney initially appeared from it, and it also served as Mrs. Lovett's pie-making table, Judge Turpin's courtroom bench, and more. Additionally, Sweeney carried a miniature coffin, a symbol of his grief, anger, and the knowledge that death that was always close at hand.

Doyle's version of the tale at the Watermill met with mixed reviews. But it gained attention and momentum through a series of weeklong engagements across England in Bath, Liverpool, Huddersfield, Exeter, Guildford, and Salford, between April 20 and May 29, 2004. As a result, it was remounted in London at the 400-seat *Whitehall Theatre* at Trafalgar Square (July 27–October 9, 2004). Next it transferred to the West End's *New Ambassadors Theatre*, with 444 seats (October 13, 2004, to February 5, 2005).

Sweeney Todd at the Watermill was not the first time Doyle had reduced a musical using this approach. Having served as the artistic director at a series of modestly funded regional theaters around the Great Britain,[67] he had staged more than 200 productions. In 1992, he undertook a version of Leonard Bernstein's *Candide* in Liverpool, a show with many characters and a complex score. "We didn't have the resources for an orchestra as well as a full cast, so I found just about the only people in the U.K. who could both perform and play it."[68] They sat at music stands to perform the score then came downstage without their instruments to perform the show's book scenes.

Over the next decade Doyle utilized this approach for a series of well-received productions including Bizet's *Carmen*, Kander and Ebb's *Cabaret*, Sondheim's *Into the Woods*, and Bock, Harnick and Stein's *Fiddler on the Roof*. He was not the first to use actor/musicians, a concept that began in the 1960s at British regional theaters. But Doyle significantly refined the technique as a complement to his overall methods of theatrical storytelling.

"My approach creates a great ensemble," Doyle said in a 2006 interview.

It gets back to what theater is all about; it gets back to why people perform. The honesty of the relationship between the actor and the audience is key: We're telling you this story. We're not pretending. We're all in the same place at the same time. We want to break through the fourth wall.... I always say, "Let's go to the beginning of the story."... It was a great challenge to me to find clarity in the story. That's my job, bottom line. That's what I do for a living. I'm a storyteller.[69]

Several British critics negatively assessed Doyle's production at first. Mark Shenton wrote,

> Turning an already tiny collection of actors into a living orchestra on top of everything else, however, might be initially intriguing, but it quickly palls (and eventually appalls), for several elementary reasons. There simply aren't enough of them, whether as actors, singers or musicians, to do full justice to the plot, let alone the score. . . . The result is that it's more like a novelty concert than a full-blooded one (in every sense), but given its severe musical limitations, it's made entirely pointless.[70]

But others were fascinated with Doyle's initial production. His hardworking actor/musicians, led by Paul Hegarty (a charismatic Sweeney), Karen Mann (a genially grotesque Mrs. Lovett who played the trumpet) and Sam Kenyon (a touching Toby) were praised, and most critics acknowledged that Sondheim's lyrics came to the forefront rather than being lost in the din of heavy orchestration. Several reviewers suggested that Doyle's approach offered revelatory insights. "After the mixed reviews that greeted the recent overblown production of this masterpiece at the Royal Opera House, John Doyle's stunningly inventive staging confirms my belief that *Sweeney Todd* works most powerfully as a claustrophobic chamber piece," wrote Charles Spencer. "When it comes to atmosphere, invention and total commitment, this *Sweeney Todd* packs a knockout punch."[71]

Doyle's actor/musician approach is exceptionally challenging for performers who must memorize the entire score and perform it simultaneously with stage movement, dialogue, and character interaction. In some scenes, action required the actors to hand off instruments or to step up to a keyboard so another performer could enact a critical moment critical. Theatergoers unfamiliar with *Sweeney Todd*'s plot had trouble following the action. But for those who knew the essence of the murderous barber's tale, it made for a show with deeper, more profound meaning, dramatically and emotionally.

One quick example from *Sweeney*: Doyle's two actors portraying the young lovers Johanna and Anthony were both cellists. Often seated side by side, their synchronized bowing underscored their attuned relationship. Separated when Johanna is sent away to Fogg's Lunatic Asylum, her skittering notes on her cello became more plaintive as Anthony sustained the melody representing his ardor.

Sondheim saw Doyle's 2004 London production and compared it to Declan Donnellan's intimate 1993 Cottesloe Theatre production, which he had highly praised. His enthusiasm for Doyle's rendition of the show was enough to attract New York producers willing to mount a new production on Broadway.

Sweeney Todd began previews in New York City at the 1,100-seat *Eugene O'Neill Theatre* on October 3, 2005, with an all-American cast. It opened on November 3, 2005. After seventeen weeks, March 21, 2006, it recouped its $3.5 million investment, a bargain for Broadway in the early twenty-first century, and a rare success for a Broadway production by Sondheim. Winning the 2006 Tony for Best Director (Doyle) and Best Orchestrations (Travis),[72] the production continued at the O'Neill until September 3, 2006, when it finished its run after 349 performances. A year later a touring production of Doyle's actor/musician rendition toured the United States for ten months (August 30, 2007–June 29, 2008) to twenty-one cities.

Doyle's stripped-down Broadway production featured two established Tony Award-winning Broadway stars—Michael Cerveris as Sweeney (accompanying the action on bass guitar) and Patti LuPone as Mrs. Lovett (playing the tuba, triangle, and glockenspiel or "orchestra bells") (Figure 5.2). Manoel Felciano was Tobias (violin, clarinet, keyboard). Cellists Benjamin Magnuson and Lauren Molina played the young lovers, Anthony and Johanna. Diana DiMarzio (clarinet) was the Beggar Woman, and versatile Donna Lynn Champlin (accordion, keyboard, flute) was Pirelli. Mark Jacoby (trumpet, orchestra bells and percussion) portrayed Judge Turpin. Alexander Gemignani

Figure 5.2 *For director John Doyle's 2006 actor/musician Broadway revival, Michael Cervers (foreground) was a sepulchral Sweeney Todd and Patti LuPone (center right) was a cynical Mrs. Lovett. The story was imagined by Manoel Felciano (far right) as an insane Tobias, suffering from the violence of the tale's bloody finale. Sara Krulwich/The New York Times/Redux.*

(keyboard, trumpet), son of *Sweeney Todd*'s original Broadway conductor Paul Gemignani, was the Beadle. Bassist John Arbo (string bassist) held together the show's driving rhythm; he also played Jonas Fogg.

Once it was running on Broadway, Doyle's version was called everything from "thrilling," "radical," and "triumphant" to "barren," "disappointing," and "eccentric." It was sometimes asserted that Doyle's reduced telling was too much of a challenge for the uninitiated to follow. Despite such naysayers, however, the production was a success. In addition to its Tony haul, the production also received the 2006 Drama Desk Award for Outstanding Revival of a Musical.

Theater historian Ken Mandelbaum expressed some apprehension about seeing the scaled-down rendition of *Sweeney* on Broadway. "But John Doyle's minimalist Brechtian staging is one of those one-offs that works. Seemingly taking place in the mind of a deranged Tobias and with the characters inmates of the asylum to which he's confined, the production is striking, chilling and effective."[73]

In 2007 prior to embarking on its national tour, a version of Doyle's Broadway production played a limited summer engagement at American Conservatory Theater in San Francisco (August 30–October 14). It was subsequently performed for audiences in twenty-one US cities and finished on June 29, 2008.

On tour David Hess played Sweeney (as well as trumpet, orchestra bells and percussion) and Judy Kaye was Mrs. Lovett (orchestra bells, percussion, and tuba), roles they had understudied on Broadway. Ben Magnuson and Lauren Molina continued their Broadway performances as the cello-playing lovers, as did Diana DiMarzio as the Beggar Woman and John Arbo as Jonas Fogg. Other members of the touring cast were Edmund Bagnell (Tobias Ragg, violin, clarinet), Keith Buterbaugh (Judge Turpin, trumpet, orchestra bells, percussion), Benjamin Eakeley (The Beadle, clarinet, keyboard, saxophone), and Katrina Yaukey (Pirelli, accordion, keyboard, flute).

David Loud served as the resident music director for both the Broadway production and the national tour. "I would run a week-long 'band camp' to get the actors in shape on their instruments. In most cases, they did have experience on the instruments they were playing in the show, but often that experience had been in high school, sometimes 20–25 years since they had picked up their clarinet or their cello or their trumpet."[74]

During his band camp, Loud would make any necessary changes needed to perform Sarah Travis's "remarkably flexible orchestration. Each company of *Sweeney Todd* ended up with its own individual roster of instruments, depending on the experience and talents of the cast, and the difficulty level of the parts could be adjusted according to the experience of the players."[75]

Arbo was an essential performer in New York and on tour. A professional bass player, he sang baritone in the ensemble and spoke Fogg's few lines as the lunatic asylum director. His most important job was

> to anchor the show rhythmically, which was essential, as there was no conductor. All changes in tempo—every *ritard* and *accelerando*, each *fermata*, all the *rubato* passages—had to be carefully planned and negotiated ahead of time, with different people being responsible for setting tempos and dictating cutoffs, depending on what instruments the actors were playing at the time and who could see who from where they were onstage.[76]

During the 2007–2008 tour, Loud traveled to various cities once or twice a month to keep the show in shape musically.

In an April 2020 feature for the *New York Times T Magazine*, Doyle's 2005 Broadway production was cited as a trendsetter that inspired streamlined productions focused on small casts of actor/musicians rather than extravagant, large-cast, big orchestra shows with lots of spectacle. The show "not only incited a new era of theatrical minimalism but encouraged a new generation of composers, directors and musicians to experiment on Broadway."[77]

Calling the production "an exuberant revival," *New York Times* writer Patricia Cohen stated, "Doyle's critical and commercial success had lasting influence: It helped persuade audiences and producers that artistic innovation was just as commanding as lavish scenery and effects, and cleared the way for shows in the same vein, many of them new works developed Off Broadway, where scarcity often prompts reinvention."[78]

Keeping It Small

Doyle's Tony Award-winning minimalist revival remounted for Broadway evoked so many fascinating responses that it's worth exploring several of them more deeply. A *New York Times* feature in August 2005 by Jesse Green pointed out that numerous upcoming productions showed signs of retrenching. The 2005–2006 season had just one commercial revival, Doyle's *Sweeney Todd*. "It features a cast of [ten] actors who all double as musicians, a creative choice that has the additional advantage of lowering the show's weekly running costs."[79] In 2005, most Broadway hits required investments of $5–$10 million and might generate $700,000 to $1 million in revenue weekly. But that was rare.

So how to produce a successful *Sweeney Todd* for audiences that might recall Prince's original staging? Doyle's response, rooted in the stringencies of a minuscule budget, worked. He stripped the show down to its essentials, recruited performers who were actors and musicians, and approached storytelling in a carefully insightful way. Based on his experience with prior productions, he knew he would have to rely on the audience's imagination. An interview in the *Sondheim Review* explained Doyle's mindset:

> When they came to see the show, the audience had to work. . . . The audience has to bring their imagination. We tell them, "You are now going to need to accept that we are telling you this story in a certain, basic, wooden-floorboard way. In order for us all to suspend our disbelief, you as an audience have to work with us."[80]

In his *New York Times* review, Ben Brantley wrote,

> This *Sweeney* never stints on the music's drama, intricacy or sheer beauty. Your ears don't just coast on a symphonic sweep. Every note and sound, whether from a plucked violin string or a tinkling triangle, seems to count fully. You become newly aware of the harmony in Mr. Sondheim's calculated

dissonance. And because the performers are the musicians, they possess total control of those watching them in a way seldom afforded actors in musicals. They own the story they tell, and their instruments become narrative tools. It is to Mr. Doyle's infinite credit that while he ingeniously incorporates the physical presence of, say, a bass fiddle into his *mise-en-scène*, 10 minutes into the show you're no longer aware of this doubling as a self-conscious conceit.[81]

In the *Washington Post*, Peter Marks pointed out that the actors doubling as musicians made for

> an evening of wonderful transparency: The music becomes indivisible from actor and character in a way you almost never experience. The players are in every sense a band, gathered to entertain, sustain a mood and tell a story, to convey every aspect of Sweeney's sorry saga.... Doyle's version might have actors tooting and strumming, yet it's truly about words, words, words.[82]

New York Times' classical music critic, Anthony Tommasini, marveled that the musicians perform "Mr. Sondheim's long and complex score from memory" and without a conductor, "a musical feat in itself. If they simply sat in place and played their instruments while singing their roles, this would be impressive enough. But they also get up and act!"[83] He also praised the work of orchestrator Sarah Travis, who

> adapted the original orchestration by Jonathan Tunick, which called for 27 players, down to a 10-person ensemble. In the process of saving money, however, she gave the score the intimacy of a chamber ensemble. ... Whatever Ms. Travis's scoring loses in strength, it gains in subtlety. Mr. Sondheim's curious contrapuntal inner voices come through vividly, which brings out the music's transfixing strangeness. Also because the balances favor the singers, Mr. Sondheim's ingenious lyrics leap off the stage at you.[84]

For the *Sondheim Review*, I wrote,

> While yearning seethes below the surface of each character, the production's overall emotional tenor is restrained. Each slashed throat is handled

ritualistically with a surging wave of red light, pouring blood from one bucket to another and the reverential donning of a splattered lab coat. By play's end, almost every actor is wearing such a garment. It's grim but gripping, almost dreamlike. Once murdered, actors assume the deadened, expressionless visages of people drained of life. And yet that restraint has a cumulative, overwhelming power.[85]

J. Wynn Rousuck suggested that the music was more likely to give audiences the creeps than "the blood-spurting razors" in Prince's original production. "Nothing stands in the way of Sondheim's score in this ingenious *Sweeney*. Though Doyle's *Sweeney* is teeny, it's the most frightening version I've ever seen."[86]

Cast members eagerly praised Doyle's methods. "I haven't done a show in ages," said Michael Cerveris, who played Sweeney on Broadway, "where we actually came together as a company and did a vocal warm-up. It was good in terms of warming the voice up. But I think it was even more important in terms of forming that ensemble feeling that is so essential to this production."[87] Interestingly, for the Broadway staging, Doyle worked without any record of his production in England. The differing musical skills of the New York actors from the British original meant many changes in orchestration.

"John was creating on his feet," Cerveris explained.

> We would stage several minutes of the show and then work several minutes of the story, and then we would go back and recap everything leading up to that. There was a huge amount of repetition, which was really useful because it drilled everything into your head. You found that you had memorized things really organically. It was in your body and was connected to what you were doing physically. It became a really organic process of learning instead of just sitting at home with your script. . . . It's all about just trying to make the story clear.[88]

Doyle repeatedly hammered home the importance of telling the story. "It's 'places for the top of the story,' not 'places for the top of the show,' for example, and when asked about blocking, the actors revealed that Doyle forbade the term."[89]

Doyle's Broadway cast responded enthusiastically to the musical demands of their roles. As the Beadle, Alexander Gemignani played keyboard and trumpet. Like several of his castmates, he had started with piano as a child, picking up the trumpet in fourth grade. He went to the University of Michigan as a trumpet major. He suggested that, while playing the trumpet in *Sweeney Todd*, he was "using air in a different way than I ever have before. My vocal cords are usually my only medium; now my breath and my breathing are totally different—they are both being focused in a different way. Playing the trumpet and playing the Beadle does make me more conscious of breathing correctly when I sing."[90] As Tobias, Manoel Felciano played violin, clarinet, and keyboard. "Playing violin in *Sweeney Todd* is the earliest way I have of expressing myself," he explained, "artistically, emotionally, whatever. To integrate that with acting is exciting—the instrument is an extension of the body."[91]

Doyle confessed he was not surprised about resistance by some observers to his actor/musician interpretation of *Sweeney Todd*.

> You'll always have people who are going to say it's wrong, people who are more fundamental about how things should be. And that's fine. Hal Prince's production . . . was the best way for that group of people to do the show at that moment in time. It's now a different time, a different group of people. *Sweeney Todd* is a masterpiece, a classic, and you can approach it all sorts of different ways.[92]

His minimalist version of *Sweeney Todd* was surprisingly powerful.

There is nothing new in this, Doyle said in a 2006 interview published in the *St. Petersburg Times*. "The Greeks were doing it. Shakespeare was doing it. Brecht was doing it. I think what's happened is we've become more rarefied in how we make theater happen. This is just trying to get back to something a little more primal in some senses and, hopefully, honest."[93]

Robert Hurwitt summed it up succinctly in his commentary about *Sweeney Todd*'s touring production for the *San Francisco Examiner*,

> As the vengeful Sweeney slashes his way through his clientele, the imagination more than fills in for the missing props and gory spouts of blood of Prince's

operatic-scale production. It isn't that Doyle and orchestrator Sarah Travis's reimagined *Sweeney* is superior to Prince's long-standard vision. But [this] *Sweeney*... holds its own as an equally thrilling musical melodrama of the first order and contains some exhilarating revelations as well.[94]

The Kids Are All Right

School Edition (2007 and beyond). In the early 1990s Freddie Gershon, the chairman of Music Theatre International (MTI), which manages licensing for numerous musical theater productions, met with Sondheim. He had an idea to expose young people to Broadway shows by creating smaller-scale versions of well-known works.

Sondheim initially proposed *Sweeney Todd*, believing that its guts and gore would appeal to young performers. Gershon was wary. "I need a show that's not offensive to principals or to teachers. I said, 'I want to do *Into the Woods*, because if I only stick with Act I, it's a kids show.'"[95] The quick success of that adaptation with the support and collaboration of Sondheim and James Lapine paved the way for more adaptations, including a "School Edition" of *Sweeney Todd* that was piloted at four high schools in 2007 before it was offered nationwide. Sondheim worked closely with MTI and iTheatrics, MTI's educational arm, to adapt the show for young performers.

School editions sometimes include cuts in songs, lyrics, or the show's book. For *Sweeney Todd School Edition* the wigmaker's sequence and the Judge's self-flagellation number, "Johanna," were eliminated. Adjustments are often made to vocal ranges and keys for less mature voices. The music itself is modestly simplified and accommodations are made in the area of casting.[96]

MTI's rental package for schools can include a CD with synthesized orchestral accompaniment if needed. Other materials include a director's guide, a study guide for the classroom and a technical theater guide providing suggestions for building special props and set pieces, such as Sweeney's barber chair.

Some lyrics were adapted by Sondheim for younger audiences. For instance, the Beggar Woman's promiscuous advances to Sweeney and Anthony on the

London pier in "No Place Like London" have been toned down to "Ow would you like a little kiss, dear?/I'll be your girlfriend."[97]

The Starstruck Performing Arts Center One in Stuart, Florida, a city of 18,000 located north of West Palm Beach, was one of the schools that piloted the *Sweeney Todd School Edition* in a November 2007 production. The role of Pirelli was performed by a teenaged girl. "Inspired by the use of a woman in the role in [John Doyle's] recent Broadway revival [2005], Starstruck opted to take advantage of the abundance of its strong contingent of female talent and do the same."[98]

The Starstruck production in Florida was enthusiastically received by local audiences generally unfamiliar with Sondheim's musicals, including *Sweeney Todd*. Today *Sweeney Todd* has become a popular and frequent choice for high schools with sophisticated theater programs. According to MTI's website,

> This special School Edition has been masterfully adapted, working directly with Mr. Sondheim to retain the dark wit and grand scope of the original work, with a few lyric and key changes to facilitate high school productions. At the show's core is a challenging score of epic proportion with two tasty tour-de-force roles in Sweeney and his comic female accomplice, Mrs. Lovett.[99]

In mid-2024 the MTI website's listed thirty productions of *Sweeney Todd School Edition* for the year—in Arizona, California, Colorado, Florida, Georgia, Indiana, Iowa, Maryland, Massachusetts, Michigan, North Carolina, Oregon, Pennsylvania, Texas, Utah, and Virginia (as well as several in the United Kingdom and one in Mexico). Looking ahead to 2025, another ten were already planned (Figure 5.3).

Figure 5.3 *Mountain Youth Musicals produced* Sweeney Todd School Edition *in Evergreen, Colorado, in 2024. This is the scene for "God, That's Good." Provided by Mountain Youth Musicals, Evergreen Colorado.*

Staunton and Ball Make Audiences Squirm

Chichester Festival Theatre (October 6–November 5, 2011). British director Jonathan Kent staged *Sweeney Todd* in a production called "utterly chilling, thrilling [and] as dark and uncomfortable as any I've ever seen," according to reviewer Mark Shenton. Kent's staging advanced *Sweeney*'s Victorian setting to the 1930s; he cast veteran British screen and stage performers Imelda Staunton as Mrs. Lovett and Michael Ball as Sweeney.

Shenton wrote that Staunton brought "both her wit and grit as she perfectly balances abrasive comedy with the character's desperate need." The handsome, boyish Ball surprised everyone with a "relentlessly unsympathetic" portrait of Sweeney, singing "with a voice from the gods but a heart cast in stone that is full of both power and magnitude."[100]

Kent's staging moved the story forward by a century to London in the 1930s. Commenting on its 2012 transfer to the *Adelphi Theatre* (March 20–September 22, 2012, 207 performances) in London's West End, the *Guardian*'s Michael Billington wrote,

> Jonathan Kent's production, which . . . leaves me grasping for superlatives, has given the piece a fresh look without destroying its essential fabric. . . . We now watch as the 20th-century chorus of the working poor retell the legendary fable of the demon barber. This has the dual advantage of retaining the story's Victorian echoes while reminding us that inequality and injustice remain a permanent scar on city life.[101]

The production received three 2012 Olivier Awards: Best Revival and Best Actor and Actress for Ball and Staunton.

A Rock-n-Roll Sweeney

Landless Theatre Company (August 7–31, 2014), then a twelve-year-old theater in Washington, D.C., undertook an audacious production of *Sweeney Todd*, presented at the Warehouse Theatre. It was a "prog-metal" adaptation of Sondheim's show, thought by one Sondheim expert to be "the most radical rethinking of Sondheim's lush and musically romantic score."[102]

Early in 2014 Sondheim gave his blessing to the adaptation. "Yes, I did indeed give them my O.K." he told the *New York Times*, "on condition that they don't cut anything or change the order of things without my express permission. Since I believe that what keeps theater alive is its openness to reinterpretation from generation to generation, I look forward to seeing (and hearing) what they do."[103]

Melissa Baughman directed the production. "*Sweeney* is a natural fit for prog-metal," she said in a released statement. "Aside from the dark story of murder and revenge, the score is operatic and intricate."[104] The genre of prog-metal was derived from progressive rock bands that blended classically trained and jazz musicians with rock-and-roll groups such as King Crimson and Emerson, Lake & Palmer. Heavy metal was eventually added to the mix. (Emerson, Lake & Palmer's 1971 rendition of Mussorgsky's *Pictures at an Exhibition* exemplifies this evolution.) Landless's production of *Sweeney Todd* marked the first time a preexisting musical was presented as a prog-metal show.[105]

Six arrangers, calling themselves the Fleet Street Collective, collaborated on the production's score: Andrew L. Baughman (Landless's producing artistic director who also played Sweeney), Spence Blevins, Lance LaRue, Ray Shaw, Andrew Siddle, Alex Vallejo, and Charles W. Johnson (the production's music director). Their arrangements were orchestrated for six instruments: piano, synthesizer, two seven-string electric guitars (capable of producing power chords), a five-string bass with an extended range, and double-kick drums. According to Sondheim expert Mark Horowitz, "Aspects of *Sweeney Todd*'s score—particularly the frequent meter changes—are often elements of prog-metal, and this quality was one of the reasons the piece attracted the creators of this staging."[106]

Andrew Baughman was inspired by George Hearn's performance on the 1980 video of *Sweeney*'s original production. "He was a pretty metal Sweeney Todd, growling like a beast, popping the vocals up octaves when the rage overtook him. We knew that we wanted our metal *Sweeney* to speak to a new generation of theatergoers."[107]

Director Melissa Baughman called prog-metal "a passionate form of music that has structural similarities to classical. Both tell emotional stories. By selecting classical-based scores that would not traditionally be thought of as metal and challenging ourselves to adapt them into various styles of metal, it creates a whole new emotional relationship with the script."

The creative team did not change the text, aside from a few cuts approved by Sondheim. He said he would attend rehearsals only if the company invited him. "Nothing is more distracting to a director and cast than having the author within eyesight while they're trying to invent and experiment. It will be an exhilarating learning experience for me whether I like the result or not."[108]

How Small Can We Go?—Pie & Mash Shop

Starting in the early 1990s, numerous small-scale revivals proved that intimate productions of *Sweeney Todd* were just as likely to succeed as those on a larger scale. But in 2014, perhaps the show's most radically constricted staging was produced in *Harrington's Pie & Mash Shop* (October 21–November 29, 2014), London's oldest such enterprise. Produced by the Tooting Arts Club, it used just eight actors and three musicians in an intimate space that could accommodate audiences of just thirty-five people.

Tooting is a south London district of which the club's cofounder, Rachel Edwards, said, "there was nothing in the neighborhood, no real cultural provision at all."[109] Tooting Arts Club had no official venue, regularly identifying local spaces and businesses to collaborate with. As a child Edwards visited Harrington's regularly with her father. As an adult, walking past the shop, which first sold meat pies in 1908, Edwards noticed Anton's barbershop directly across the street. The enterprising producer used a Kickstarter crowdfunding campaign to build a budget and made arrangements with the two businesses to present an immersive production of *Sweeney Todd* that experienced sold-out performances including a three-week extension during October and November 2014.

The barbershop served as the gathering place for preshow and intermission drinks in a backroom with an old-fashioned barber chair. For the performance, audience members were escorted across Selkirk Road to the tiny café. According to the *Sondheim Review*, "Once inside, the shop's blackboards offering jellied eels and liquor cast you directly back to the era of the Penny Dreadful."[110]

The Tooting production was even smaller and more constricted than John Doyle's actor/musician version a decade earlier. Directed by Bill Buckhurst with orchestration and music supervised and arranged by Benjamin Cox, the show featured Australian actor Jeremy Secomb as Sweeney and Irish television and stage performer Siobhán McCarthy as Mrs. Lovett. They were accompanied by three musicians wedged into the eatery's tiny space to play piano, violin, and clarinet. Performers mingled with the audience and sang and danced between and on top of the shop's trestle tables and counter. *Sweeney Todd*'s second act opening number, "God, That's Good!" drew the audience into the performance as the rabble devouring Mrs. Lovett's meat pies—sans human remains, of course.

An intrigued Sondheim attended the final performance of the initial run of the Tooting production in London. He then recommended it enthusiastically to his friend and eminent London producer Sir Cameron Mackintosh, who offered a vacant space, the former Avalon Club, on Shaftesbury Avenue in London's West End. The pie shop was rebuilt there in the spring of 2015 and continued to play to sold-out houses with sixty-nine seats (March 12–May 16, 2015).

Edwards was urged to find another London venue, but she had larger ambitions. "I was like, 'No, the next place it needs to go is New York,'"[111] she said. "We're talking about this being a kind of essentially English gothic tale. But ultimately its home is New York. A lot of support and love of the production has come from [there], so it felt very much like this has to be the next thing we do." London mayor Sadiq Khan agreed that theater art could be universal. "Culture is the glue that binds different cities together and different cultures together. It's international. It translates."[112]

An Off-Broadway venue, the *Barrow Street Theatre* was engaged. A traditional 199-seat facility, its stage featured a set designed by Simon Kenny that recreated a slightly enlarged version of the "truly unremarkable" London pie-and-mash shop with bench and table seating for 130. It began previews on February 14, 2017, and officially opened on March 1, 2017. Attendees were invited to enter the space ninety minutes before each performance to mingle and eat potatoes and pies. (Onetime White House executive pastry chef

William "Bill" Yosses was the official pie maker throughout the New York run, providing a choice of chicken pot pie, vegetarian pot pie, or Beef Wellington.)

Secomb and McCarthy from the London production initially reprised their roles, as well as Duncan Smith (Judge Turpin) and Joseph Taylor (Tobias). They were joined by Broadway veterans Matt Doyle (Anthony) Alex Finke (Johanna), Betsy Morgan (Pirelli and the Beggar Woman), and Brad Oscar (The Beadle).

Writing for the *New Yorker*, Hilton Als praised the production's scenic design as reinforcing "the show's depiction of English class distinctions—the many lives spent in service to the few—by creating a pinched, claustrophobic, dimly lit environment."[113] Describing McCarthy's Mrs. Lovett, Als added, she

> looks like something that died and came back not as a ghost but as ectoplasm with a voice. Wild-haired and hollow-eyed, slightly crouched in a conspiratorial stance, she knows what the world is made of: haves and have-nots, those wot got theirs and those wot haven't. . . . Mrs. Lovett is an incredible comic creation, a dirty Cockney doll, always looking for the main chance.[114]

Ben Brantley gave the imported production a mixed review in the *New York Times*. He observed that Secomb's take on Sweeney was relentlessly intense and jokingly suggested that the production be retitled "Screamy Todd." He concluded his remarks saying, "That high-decibel interpretation is not out of keeping with the production as a whole. This demon barber and his friends are here to rattle you with a sustained, cathartic 'Boo!' that sends you into the night with few nagging worries that Sweeney may still be waiting for you, in your dreams if not in your building lobby."[115]

Once Secomb and McCarthy departed from the New York production, they were replaced by Broadway regulars Carolee Carmello and Norm Lewis on April 11, 2017; Thom Sesma and Sally Ann Triplett succeeded that pair in February 2018 for the balance of the run through August 26. The production recouped its $1.2 million investment in twenty-four weeks, then continued for another year.[116] When it closed, its 558 performances enabled it to lay claim to the longest run of *Sweeney Todd* on record, besting by one Hal Prince's original staging, which had 557.

The Barrow Street Theatre production received the 2017 Lucille Lortel Award for Outstanding Musical, the 2017 Off-Broadway Alliance for Best Musical Revival and the 2017 Theater Fans' Choice Award for Best Off-Broadway Musical. It was named "Best of the Year" for 2017 by *Time*, *Entertainment Weekly*, *The Hollywood Reporter*, *Huffington Post*, *Variety*, *Forbes*, *BuzzFeed*, and *The Daily Beast*.

Back to Epic Basics: Josh Groban

A production of *Sweeney Todd* at Broadway's *Lunt-Fontanne Theatre* (March 26, 2023–May 5, 2024) featured popular singer and occasional Broadway performer Josh Groban. It was directed by Thomas Kail (a Tony Award winner for his staging of Lin-Manuel Miranda's *Hamilton*), and it proved that the epic staging of *Sweeney Todd*'s original production by Hal Prince from forty-three years earlier still had appeal. Built on a capitalization of $14.5 million, the 2023 production featured twenty-five actors and an orchestra with twenty-six musicians. A writer for the *New York Times* wryly observed, "We're used to *Sweeney Todd* deconstructed. Can it be reconstructed?"[117]

Groban had let it be known that he yearned for an opportunity to play the leading role in a major Broadway revival. He had made his Broadway debut in *Natasha, Pierre, & the Great Comet of 1812* in 2016, and he was eager to take on a leading role he had dreamed of since he was in junior high school in Los Angeles. (He saw the 1994 production of *Sweeney Todd* by East West Players in Los Angeles when he was thirteen years old.[118])

Once Kail was persuaded to direct, he enlisted Alex Lacamoire, another *Hamilton* alum, to conduct the full-fledged orchestra. Also recruited was Steven Hoggett, who had served as movement director for *Harry Potter and the Cursed Child* in 2018 and the Tony Award-winning two-part revival of Tony Kushner's monumental, *Angels in America* in 2018.

Even with a creative A-team in place and a performer with Groban's marquee name recognition, there were doubters as to whether the romantic baritone had the necessary gravitas to carry off the role. His voice was certainly suited to Sondheim's lush score, but as a boyish, even genial 42-year-old, could Groban measure up to the terrifying standard established by Len Cariou in 1979?

"That's actually one of the reasons I was attracted to doing it," Groban told the *New York Times*. He believed that "the way to earn a connection with the audience that's frightening on a deeper level than, 'Hey, that's the monster in the room,' is to find whatever humanity there is between that guy and whoever's sitting in the audience."[119]

Early on, Groban spoke with Michael Cerveris, the actor who played Sweeney in John Doyle's 2005 actor/musician production. They exchanged thoughts about the emotionally draining and exhausting role. "Michael and I had a drink before we started previews, and I was lucky enough to kind of sit with him and get some wonderful advice and support.... And he said, 'Just wash it off in the sink, man. Like, when you take the makeup off, take it all off, you know?'"[120]

Director Kail intended to showcase the show's strains of longing, both by Sweeney and the lovelorn Mrs. Lovett. "What we're really keen to explore," he said, "is can you make something thrilling, something entertaining, something hilarious, something scary—and can we also break your heart?"[121] Casting the versatile Broadway regular Annaleigh Ashford (who played Dot in the 2017 Broadway revival of Sondheim's *Sunday in the Park with George* opposite Jake Gyllenhaal) as Mrs. Lovett delivered a major component of the chemistry Kail had in mind (Figure 5.4).

Figure 5.4 *Pop vocalist Josh Groban played Sweeney Todd in a 2023 Broadway revival opposite Annaleigh Ashford as Mrs. Lovett. Both were nominated for Tony Awards. Sara Krulwich/The New York Times/Redux.*

Scenic designer Mimi Lien's stupendous stonework set recreated Victorian London and featured a towering crane. The production was evocatively lit by multiple Tony winner Natasha Katz. Everything about the production was on a grand scale.

Hoggett carefully choreographed the ensemble and kept a laser focus on every aspect of stage movement. He spent time working with the actors who played Sweeney's unfortunate victims. That included a full day of "being slid down the chair into a pit so I could show all the actors how not to bang your chin and where the floor is; we were offering $5 rides."[122]

There was praise for Hoggett's stage pictures: "This *Sweeney Todd* can already put movement ... in its win column for seamlessness. The choreographer creates a vocabulary for the chorus—sometimes in silhouettes enhanced by lighting designer Natasha Katz—that adds to the sense of a world staggered by cruelty and misery. Redemption in *Sweeney*, after all, exists in strictly limited supply."[123]

Sondheim planned to attend the cast's first reading in late November 2021. Unfortunately, he passed away on Thanksgiving night, just two days before the scheduled event. Ashford, known for her flair for physical comedy but also for heartfelt drama, had been eager to work with Sondheim again after her 2017 experience with *Sunday in the Park with George*. Saddened by Sondheim's passing, she focused on his score. "He gives you these little clues. Because it's a puzzle." She imagined conversations with him. "I ask for help getting through the puzzles for the night"—how to unlock a character's motivation, how to land a joke. "Usually we find an answer. Or at least a version of the answer."[124]

Such efforts paid off. Groban and Ashford each received Tony nominations, and she won the Drama Desk Award for Outstanding Lead Performance in a Musical. Another cast member, Ruthie Ann Miles, turned in a Tony-nominated performance as the Beggar Woman.

Miles took in-depth look, deeply researched approach to her role. "I wasn't interested in her being crazy," she told an audience of theater critics in November 2023.[125] "I'd only ever seen this kind of like a comical toggle between crazy sad lady and crazy prostitute. . . . I wanted her to be completely sane." Miles assembled all the lines she spoke and what other characters said about the Beggar Woman. It occurred to her that the broken woman might suffer from dissociative identity disorder [previously called "multiple personality disorder"]. She dug into this with a psychiatrist acquaintance who agreed that it warranted further exploration.

Miles identified an array of different personalities.

> Well, this sounds like a very virtuous person. This sounds like an apocalypse hunter. This sounds like a very sad woman. This sounds like a prostitute. I actually found 13 different [people]. Even though I knew who every single person was, this was too much. . . . I knew who the gatekeeper was. I knew who allowed the alters to come out and then go back in.

She whittled the crowd down to eleven, then nine. Then "finally, I'm at eight." She built her performance around these insights.

> I wanted to show the Beggar Woman from the lens of a real mental health crisis. All she wants is to find home, to find normalcy. She tried to kill herself with poison. Her mind is obviously addled. Obviously she's in pain. She was a virtuous woman who was gang raped. . . . She had never experienced this kind of pain. Her husband was taken away.

That gave Miles a path to the musical's revelation late in the show that she's actually Lucy Barker, Sweeney's wife, not dead but all but erased by trauma. "I wanted to show the many different ways that she tries to come out. She loses herself, but she's slowly finding her way home. . . . She's finally found her love again, but he is not the love she used to know. She allows herself to die because this man she loved so much is no longer there." Miles's fascinating insight added tremendous depth to her performance and resulted in her Tony nomination.

Playing the adolescent Tobias Ragg, Gaten Matarazzo (previously cast as geeky adolescent Dustin Henderson in five seasons of the Netflix sci-fi drama/horror series *Stranger Things*) was repeatedly praised for his performance. Calling the twenty-year-old actor "a revelation as Tobias," a *USA Today* review[126] said "his tender 'Not While I'm Around' is an emotional highlight." Confessing in a *Playbill* interview that playing Toby was "a dream role,"[127] Matarazzo said he worried about "creating a caricature . . . of falling into what had been done before." By focusing on Toby's history as the mountebank barber Pirelli's assistant, he got over that concern.

"Not While I'm Around" was a key moment in which Toby promises to protect Mrs. Lovett as she is seeing that he knows too much. Claiming that he often felt nervous throughout the show, Matarazzo felt he could relax during that song. "That's the one scene where I'm like, 'All right, this is the one.'" He praised Ashford, whom he performed the song with, saying her presence helped him settle in and forget his nerves.

Groban overcame the concerns regarding whether he could carry off the role. Jesse Green's *New York Times* review was titled, "The Many Thrilling Flavors of a Full-Scale *Sweeney Todd*," with a subtitle: "Sondheim's Masterpiece, restored to its proper size and sung to the hilt by Josh Groban, makes a welcome Broadway return."[128] Green described the production as "ravishingly sung, deeply emotional and strangely hilarious. . . . Some of the production's humor comes from [Groban's] growing resemblance to an impassive suburban husband whose job happens to be murder, as Ashford's Mrs. Lovett tries to domesticate him."[129] Green especially admired the full orchestra: "You can't believe the difference three trombones make in creating the sound of doom, especially compared to none. Under Alex Lacamoire's musical supervision, the musicians' performance, like that of the ensemble in the choral numbers, is glorious."[130]

Peter Marks's review in the *Washington Post*, observed,

> It does feel with Groban's more demonstrably emotional Sweeney—whose skin is not so pale, and his eye not so odd—that the character could indeed be sitting there beside you, flipping through his Playbill. The choices the production makes will divide *Sweeney Todd* purists, who have grown accustomed to hollowed out killing machines in the title role. But Groban provides ample evidence here that he can carry a Sondheim musical on his own terms, and certainly one in which he is surrounded with as much first-class talent as Kail assembles on West 46th Street.[131]

The rest of the cast featured Maria Bilbao (Johanna) in her Broadway debut, as well as Jordan Fisher (Anthony Hope), Nicholas Christopher (Pirelli), Jamie Jackson (Judge Turpin), and John Rapson (The Beadle). The extraordinary eighteen-member ensemble was comprised of Galyana Castillo, Jonathan Christopher, Taeler Cyrus, Timothy Hughes, Paul Jordan Jansen, Alicia Kaori, Raymond J. Lee, Patricia Phillips, Samantha Pollino, Lexi Rabadi, Nathan Salstone, Kristie Dale Sanders, Stephen Tewksbury, Daniel Torres,

Felix Torrez-Ponce, and DeLaney Westfall. Several ensemble members were understudies for various characters. Additionally, Nicholas Christopher was the standby for Groban's Sweeney, and Jeanna de Waal was at the ready to replace Ashford's Mrs. Lovett.). The production also had five versatile swings who were prepared to step into multiple roles: Dwayne Cooper, Kyrie Courter, Michael Kuhn, Maria Pinero, and Hennesy Winkler.

Kail's production of *Sweeney Todd* received seven 2023 Tony Award nominations. Groban and Ashford were recognized as leading actor and actress in a musical; Ruthie Ann Miles was nominated for her performance as the Beggar Woman. From the creative team, Steven Hoggett's choreography and Mimi Lien's scenic design were also nominated. Natasha Katz's lighting design of a musical was a winner, as was Nevin Steinberg's sound design of a musical.

Nominated for four 2023 Drama Desk Awards, *Sweeney Todd* won three for Outstanding Lead Performance in a Musical (Annaleigh Ashford), Outstanding Lighting Design of a Musical (Natasha Katz) and Outstanding Direction of a Musical (Thomas Kail). The production was also nominated for Outstanding Revival of a Musical.

This revival of *Sweeney Todd* played at nearly 100 percent capacity during the production's entire run. By the end of 2023 the entire $14.5 capitalization had been recouped. Answering the *New York Times* question, "Can it be reconstructed?"[132] the answer was a resounding "yes."

Groban and Ashford left the production in mid-January 2024. As of February 9, they were replaced by a pair of respected Broadway performers, Aaron Tveit and Sutton Foster. The final performance happened on May 5, 2024. The production's total run was 406 performances (following twenty-seven previews which began on February 26, 2023).

6

Sweeney Settles the Musical Score

After attending a 1973 performance of Christopher Bond's adaptation of a Victorian melodrama about *Sweeney Todd* in London, Stephen Sondheim quickly recognized an opportunity. "It struck me as a piece that sings."[1] His immediate instinct was to turn the story into a serious musical—perhaps unlike any musical ever created up to that time—but a musical nonetheless. It was one of the rare moments in his career when he identified a story he personally wanted to musicalize.

Bond's production employed music, but its tunes were rollicking British music hall ditties that encouraged the audience to sing along. They came between scenes and did not advance the story or offer insights into characters. (The script for Bond's adaptation contains no description or suggestions for accompanying music.) Sondheim initially planned to adapt Bond's script into the book for his musical as well as composing melodies and writing lyrics.

He had not done that kind of writing before. Sondheim routinely collaborated with book writers who shaped the plot: Arthur Laurents for Sondheim's early shows (*West Side Story*, *Gypsy*, and *Anyone Can Whistle*), Burt Shevelove and Larry Gelbart for his first outing as a composer and lyricist (*A Funny Thing Happened on the Way to the Forum*), George Furth (*Company* and *Merrily We Roll Along*), James Goldman (the TV musical *Evening Primrose* and *Follies*), Hugh Wheeler (*A Little Night Music*), John Weidman (*Pacific Overtures*, *Assassins*, and *Bounce/Road Show*), and writer—and director—James Lapine (*Sunday in the Park with George*, *Into the Woods*, and *Passion*).

He abandoned book writing rather quickly. "I did the first twenty minutes and I realized I was only on page five of Bond's script. So at that rate, the show would possibly have been nine hours long. And I realized I didn't know how to cut it."[2] At that point, Wheeler was recruited. By that time Sondheim had immersed himself in Bond's script, characters, and plot. Based on his early perception that the piece would "sing," he had already started to think seriously about the show's sound and score. His familiarity with Bond's adaptation and characters was his springboard to begin to shape the lyrics and music for *Sweeney Todd*. He leaned heavily on Bond's script. The first spoken lines in Bond's adaptation as Anthony and Sweeney arrived in London:[3] "I have sailed the world, beheld its fairest cities, seen the pyramids, the wonders of the east. Yet it is true—there is no place like London." Sweeney responds: "You are young. Life has been kind to you." Compare these lines to Sondheim's opening song, "No Place Like London" and his inspiration is obvious, although he ends this passage ominously: "You will learn."

Sondheim often hewed closely to Bond's text, even before Wheeler began to draft the libretto. In a conversation with public radio interviewer Terry Gross, Sondheim's writing process was broadly explored. She asked, "I know the first thing that comes for you is the story. You only write songs in the context of character and story.... When you're writing music and lyrics yourself, which comes first for you?"[4]

Sondheim explained that those aspects informed one another, so he was often working on them simultaneously. But as his preparation, he typically studied what the book writer was drafting—"Until something's on paper, I have nothing to imitate."[5] His explanation, while not specifically about *Sweeney Todd*, sheds light on how he went about creating the sound for this show: "If looking for a kind of musical atmosphere for the piece, particularly when I'm first beginning to write the piece, I will improvise or think of various melodic ideas and sometimes—often—harmonic ideas, chord sequences and things like that. So I'm collecting a little kind of—the materials for a scrapbook."[6]

The score of *Sweeney Todd* began to take shape as Sondheim worked from Bond's moody, psychological script. But he also fondly recalled haunting movie scores by Hollywood composers, especially Bernard Herrmann. He recognized in Bond's adaptation that it was "material for a musical horror story ... held together by ceaseless underscoring that would keep an audience in suspense and maybe even scare the hell out of them. It would, in fact be my tribute to Bernard Herrmann and *Hangover Square*."[7]

A Recipe Blending Horror and Romance

When Sondheim and director Hal Prince recruited Len Cariou to play Sweeney, they shared an early draft of Wheeler's script. Cariou, who had starred in their 1974 production of the lyrical *A Little Night Music*, wondered if they'd taken leave of their senses. But after further consideration, he observed, "If he writes a really romantic score, this might be interesting. . . . This guy's pretty smart, you know."[8]

Romantic? Really? Slit throats, serial murders, and meat pies filled with human remains? But Sweeney's pursuit of vengeance resulting from the evil Judge Turpin's ruin of Sweeney's loving marriage to Lucy and his appropriation of their daughter Johanna for immoral purposes, provided powerful rationale—if not justification—for his vile acts. The loss of love can surely be a path to madness. In another twisted form of love, Mrs. Lovett's devotion to the Sweeney, whose razors she stored for fifteen years while he was exiled, is the product of her misguided obsession that they are meant for one another. In truth, the juxtaposition of romantic melodies and horrific story events proved to be both "riveting—and extremely disturbing."[9]

Musical Theater or Opera?

Sweeney Todd's romantic, sophisticated score has been the catalyst for an ongoing debate about how to categorize the show. Most fundamentally it was, of course, a Broadway musical, a show created by Broadway royalty—Sondheim, Prince, Wheeler, orchestrator Jonathan Tunick, conductor Paul Gemignani, and Tony Award-winning actors Angela Lansbury and Cariou—for a Broadway audience. It was perhaps more tragic and horrifying than most musicals, but earlier in his career Sondheim had written lyrics for the tragic *West Side Story*, which ended with several deaths. As mentioned elsewhere in this book, Prince and Sondheim disagreed fundamentally about staging *Sweeney*: while Sondheim imagined an intimate, scary production, Prince convinced that an epic staging was the right choice.

That made sense with Sondheim's monumental score, which used numerous musical elements commonly employed by grand operas. In 1984, five years after Prince staged the show's debut on Broadway, he directed productions of *Sweeney Todd* for Houston Grand Opera and New York City Opera. Since then, it has been produced by numerous opera companies and numerous concert stagings featuring operatic voices backed by major symphony orchestras.

Sondheim refused to be pinned down: he subtitled *Sweeney Todd*'s libretto, calling it "A Musical Thriller." In *Finishing the Hat* he offered a possible category, calling it a "dark operetta." But he had second thoughts about that idea. He then offered another possibility, paying homage to movie score composer Bernard Herrmann: "What *Sweeney Todd* really is is a movie for the stage."[10] That was a large part of his willingness to allow film Tim Burton to adapt it cinematically in 2007.

Responding to Prince's operatic productions in 1984, *New York Times* classical music critic Donal Henahan asked, "Why Can't Verdi Voices Handle Sondheim?" He pointed out that "the attempt to actually sing the Sondheim score, which relies heavily on a dramatic *parlando* or speaking style, mainly showed how far from the operatic vocal tradition the work lies. The score, effective enough in its own way, demanded things of the opera singers that opera singers as a class are reluctant to produce."[11]

Henahan distinguished operatic style from Broadway "belting," which he defined as a "pushed tone production . . . used by [musical theater] actors and singers in putting across spoken lines and recitative." (Classic Broadway star Ethel Merman's clarion voice is an example; Patti LuPone and Bette Midler are more recent examples.) This was a style "implicit in the vocal writing of virtually all Broadway composers," Henahan pointed out, but missing in most operatic works. Critic Martin Gottfried made a similar point: "*Sweeney Todd* has its occasional operatic moments," he observed, "but its music overall has the chest tones, the harmonic language, the muscularity, and the edge of Broadway theater."[12]

In a 1989 essay for *Musical Quarterly*, "On the Verge of Opera," George Martin stated that *Sweeney Todd* is "generally acknowledged to be the most conventionally operatic of Sondheim's works."[13] Martin suggested that Sondheim put together the work in a manner similar to that of "any opera composer, by giving the principals distinguishing motifs."[14]

Martin cited the melody used for the first appearance of the Beggar Woman, "Alms! Alms," as being heard again near the finale when Sweeney tragically and finally recognizes her as the sad remains of his beloved wife Lucy. (It's also foreshadowed entirely within the organ Prelude before the Beggar Woman sings it. It's expanded by Sweeney lamenting "And my Lucy lies in ashes" in Epiphany, and then musically reprised upon his tragic realization at the end of Act 2.) Similarly, the romantic melody of Anthony's exclamations about the wonders of London recurs when he rhapsodizes upon seeing Johanna and falling instantly in love.

In 2000 when the New York Philharmonic mounted a concert presentation of *Sweeney Todd*, Sondheim's longtime orchestrator Jonathan Tunick suggested in a *New York Times* interview, "Opera is associated with classical music and its style of singing, where the voice and the notes are more important than the text."[15] He continued, "Opera is generally defined as sung throughout, and it is generally driven by the music. The attitude on casting in opera is you look for someone who can sing."

On the other hand, according to Tunick, in a musical such as *Sweeney Todd* the search is for an actor "who can best play the role and, if the music needs adjusting, that will be done. The cast of an opera is chosen for the voice. The cast of a musical is chosen for acting and voice." Tunick concluded, "By no definition is *Sweeney Todd* an opera. It is not sung throughout. It is driven by the drama, and it is cast by dramatic type. With *Sweeney Todd*, Stephen Sondheim has achieved what many have attempted and failed: a successful American musical drama."[16]

Over time the consensus judgment regarding *Sweeney Todd*'s score has coalesced around the notion it was Sondheim's greatest feat of musical composition. Gottfried called it "the most abundant, most assertive, most passionate music of his life."[17] The score has exactly the power and sweep that evokes the strong emotions typical of many grand operas. It can amuse, horrify, frighten, and overwhelm. *Sweeney Todd*'s finale leaves audiences and performers exhausted, drained by carnage and vengeance, while at the same time startled and saddened by Sweeney's unwitting and tragic murder of his own wife. It resembles the scores of the greatest grand operas—Verdi's *Aida* and *La Traviata*, Puccini's *La Bohème* and *Tosca*, Wagner's *Tristan und Isolde*—driven by overwhelming emotions and typically ending with tragic deaths. That certainly can be said of

Sondheim's spectacular score for *Sweeney Todd*, one of the most compositionally complex scores ever written for the musical theater stage.

In a thoughtful observation in a *New York Magazine* essay in March 1979, Alan Rich pointed out that many critics had applied the term "opera" in their critiques of *Sweeney Todd* "as either praise, damnation, or something indecisive in between." He went beyond that distinction: "I am astounded by the musical solidity of the piece, the use for example, of the recurring 'ballad,' each time more urgent based on wide-ranging variations on the 'Day of Wrath' plainchant."

Rich observed that the second act resolves with a long, cohesive set of musical numbers and minimal dialogue. "If that makes it an opera, so be it, but I don't see why the term has to be used; there is no definition of opera that works for more than one composer at a time. I am more interested that Sondheim, in this dazzling, amazingly varied score, has tried so much, and brought off so much."[18]

A Horror Movie for the Stage

In truth, *Sweeney Todd*'s disconcerting, unnerving and often discordant score owes at least as much to music written for classic film dramas from the 1940s as it does operatic traditions.[19] As a precocious teenager, Sondheim fell in love with the musical textures and melodies he experienced at the movies. "I liked theater," Sondheim wrote in *Finishing the Hat*, his first volume of lyric studies, "but I loved movies, and movies of every kind: dramas, comedies, short subjects, and especially trailers."

Sondheim was especially enamored with the romantic, melodic film scores for dramatic movies that were popular during his teenage years in the 1940s. At the age of fifteen, he saw director John Brahm's 1945 noir thriller *Hangover Square* with his friend Jamie Hammerstein (son of lyricist Oscar Hammerstein II and Sondheim's early mentor). It told the fictional story of George Harvey Bone, a gifted classical music composer and pianist who became a berserk serial killer when he heard certain high-pitched, discordant sounds. He started fires to disguise a series of murders he committed, then suffered from troubling amnesia. The unbalanced Bone's melodramatic story culminated when he performed his avant-garde piano concerto alone in a concert hall that he had set ablaze.

Sondheim was so taken with composer Bernard Herrmann's moody score for *Hangover Square*—especially Bone's piano masterpiece, the strident, discordant "Concerto Macabre"—that he returned to the movie theater for a second viewing the same day. He memorized the first page of music that appeared on the screen for a few seconds before it and Bone were engulfed in flames. At home he played it repeatedly from memory and even wrote a fan letter to Herrmann, the winner of the 1941 Academy Award for his score for *The Devil and Daniel Webster*. Herrmann subsequently created memorable scores for Alfred Hitchcock's *Vertigo* (1958), *North by Northwest* (1959) *Psycho* (1960), and *The Birds* (1963). Years later Sondheim said he could still play the concerto from memory.

In an interview in 1993, Sondheim said,

> Herrmann had a way of making suspense lushly musical, and he had a harmonic line which I thought was just right for *Sweeney*. I didn't consciously copy him, but it was *Hangover Square* that started this kind of thought process in my head. The reason there's so much music in *Sweeney Todd* is that I thought every time the music stops the audience will remember they're in a theatre and that these events are ridiculous. That's what good film scoring does.[20]

Sondheim used music to sustain suspense even when nothing was happening onstage. "Herrmann's harmonic language is always unresolved, so something is always going to happen. There's constant motion, but the harmony is never quite resolved."[21] That became a useful device for the score of *Sweeney Todd*.

Sondheim's score for *Sweeney Todd* never lets up. It sustains constant tension that builds throughout the tale, seldom interrupted by typical musical theater endings (called "buttons" or "stingers"). As with a horror movie score, even as the story unfolds narratively, a steady undercurrent of musical foreboding runs beneath the action. *Sweeney Todd*'s entire harmonic structure, including a funereal organ, electronic sounds, and skittering woodwinds create the menacing, Gothic feeling Sondheim sought for the frightening tale. Without a doubt, the triggering discordant chord that caused the Bone's psychotic breaks in *Hangover Square* was the inspiration for the jarring factory whistle that sounds as Sweeney dispatches his victims.

Sweeney Todd differed considerably from traditional musical theater: almost 80 percent of the show is performed with music, even when characters are speaking rather than singing. After its Broadway opening in March 1979, Harold Clurman, drama critic for *The Nation*, accosted Schuyler Chapin, then general manager of the Metropolitan Opera, to demand, "Why didn't you put this on at the Met?" Chapin replied, "I would have put it on like a shot, if I'd had the opportunity." Interviewed by Sondheim biographer Meryle Secrest, Chapin added, "And I would have. There would have been screams and yells and I wouldn't have given a damn. Because it is an opera. A modern American opera."

Sondheim, however, refused to pigeonhole the show. Over the years, he repeated his belief that the classification of *Sweeney Todd* varied according to where it was produced it and who watched it: "For me, an opera is something that is performed in an opera house in front of an opera audience. The ambience, along with the audience's expectation is what flavors the evening. . . . Opera is defined by the eye and ear of the beholder."[22] And, of course, it follows that a musical is performed on a Broadway stage for an audience of musical theater fans.

Graham Skipper, a horror film fan, called *Sweeney Todd* "Sondheim's Grand Guignol horror masterpiece: presented as larger than life, with a bloody tale of revenge at its center and plenty of bloodletting. This nightmare opera ultimately becomes a searing indictment of the class system and an exploration of love, loss and madness. It is both bloody spectacle and character-driven drama."[23]

Skipper compared it to "the greatest horror films [that] subvert expectations and surprise us with deeper meaning lurking below the surface." He added, "Similarly, Sondheim's work uses the platform of musical theatre to peel back the layers of human darkness, pain and uncertainty."[24] Sondheim's tentative classification of *Sweeney Todd* as a "dark operetta" makes sense in these terms. What's more, by creating a romantic score Sondheim was able to evoke powerful emotions.

Writers in a 2015 feature in *The Sondheim Review* proposed that "Ultimately, *Sweeney Todd*'s reputation as an opera seems less securely tied to its musical continuities than to its original grandiose presentation—more director Hal Prince's doing than Sondheim's—and its timing, coming at the end of a decade that saw Andrew Lloyd Webber develop his own version of the operatic musical."[25] In 2003 theater critic Terry Teachout offered this judgment: "Regardless of whether *Sweeney Todd* is a true opera, it is without doubt one of the 20th century's most powerful and thought-provoking pieces of musical theater."[26] That's a reasonable place to leave this argument.

Sweet Angela Lansbury as Amoral Mrs. Lovett

Sondheim composed Mrs. Lovett's songs with Angela Lansbury in mind. From his mentor Oscar Hammerstein II he learned the advantages of writing for an established star. Sondheim and Arthur Laurents had recruited Lansbury for the role of the "Mayoress" in their ill-fated 1962 show, *Anyone Can Whistle*. It was her first time to sing onstage. Despite that show's embarrassingly short run, it opened the door for future musical theater opportunities. In 1966, Lansbury starred in Jerry Herman's *Mame*, winning her first Tony Award.

Just as Sondheim had written lyrics for *Gypsy*'s Madame Rose with Ethel Merman in mind as well as *Company*'s bitchy Joanne, a perfect fit for Elaine Stritch, he crafted the role of Mrs. Lovett to Lansbury once he and Prince had signed her to play the role of *Sweeney*'s immoral baker. "It's not so much that you tailor the material, but you hear the voice in your head whether you want to or not."[27]

Sondheim preferred to work on filling out a show's score after the major roles were cast. As he wrote the score for *Sweeney Todd*, he gave each main character a basic musical theme (in operas these are called "leitmotifs") "to serve as a starting point for their songs. Each of their songs would depend on the previous one, until the end, when they would all collide."[28]

Lansbury met Sondheim at his home where he shared some of the music he was creating with her in mind. She recalled,

> The first song he wrote was "By the Sea," and he said, "Angie, I've written a song in which you have no time to breathe whatsoever." Steve always took some kind of delight in doing that and presenting one with that kind of challenge and then saying, "Well, yes, but you can catch a breath here and you can catch a breath there. And, of course, most of us who have performed his work find that, indeed, there are places to breathe."[29]

So squarely did he set Mrs. Lovett's songs on Lansbury and her voice, working with her British roots and her affinity for a Victorian music hall style performance, that subsequent performers are almost always compared to the jaunty, amoral character she established—right down to her hairstyle of jaunty topknots and soiled costumes. Sondheim actually enjoyed fitting the role to the actor, but he confessed, "The hardest thing of all was how to take these two really disgusting people and write them in such a way that the audience can rather love them. And I think people did love Mrs. Lovett—yet she doesn't have a single redeeming feature."[30]

Lansbury enthusiastically took on the role, which began with "The Worst Pies in London," with "her Cockney eyes as large as saucers, her topknots dancing on her head, wiping her greasy fingers and slapping roaches off the table with inimitable flair and panache."[31] She provided rhythmic comic relief and counterpoint to Len Cariou's darkly portrayed Sweeney.

Can Anyone Whistle?

Although not exactly a piece of music, *Sweeney Todd*'s most memorable sonic moment is most often a shrieking factory whistle sounded early on and recurring jarringly at various moments, especially when Sweeney slashes a throat. Sondheim's initial idea was not for a blasting whistle, but rather an abrupt, jarring organ chord. The show opens with a gloomy organist onstage playing a prelude.

> At various points in the story he would pound away with all the stops open—something I used to do to scare people at military school and college also, where there was a chapel, and you could make it dark and scare people. Then Hal Prince had the idea of the steam whistle—which turned out, I think to be a much better idea. The grating sound of the whistle is much more unnerving and upsetting than just big, loud, sting chords. So the organ idea eventually was scratched as a presence onstage.[32]

Paul Gemignani, *Sweeney Todd*'s original conductor, in conversation with public radio's Terry Gross, recalled,

> We finally found this actual factory whistle, and we hooked it up to a CO_2 canister, and . . . I operated it, actually, from a switch in the pit. I think we almost all passed out from the sound. But it did what it was supposed to do. It was so intense that they had to keep moving it further away, so the audience wouldn't, you know, like leap out of their seats.[33]

Sondheim's score indicated the blast just once in his musical notation, in the "Prologue" when a pair of gravediggers are seen as the audience enters. A curtain displaying George Cruikshank's caricatured illustration of a honeycombed beehive[34] represented the stratified nineteenth-century British society. It was torn down, accompanied by the deafening factory whistle.

A singular musical notation is the only way the whistle sound is represented in most of the show's score, appearing first at the end of the organ Prelude. It was clearly an editor's addition to the published score rather than something Sondheim inserted. After its early sounding, the whistle's subsequent appearances are cued by stage directions at key horrific moments, as conceived by Prince in the show's original production rather than Sondheim's musical notations.

The repeated jump-scares of the harsh whistle are memorable vestiges of the original production. Ashley Marion Pribyl in her 2019 doctoral dissertation observed,

> Prince used the whistle to begin the show after the organ prelude, to signal the beginnings and endings of scenes, and to amplify moments of heightened tension, such as Todd's murder of Pirelli. The shriek of the whistle served a multiplicity of purposes: first, it startled the audience, creating a sense of unease; second, its similarity to a human scream set the sonic stage for the horror show that Sondheim wanted; and third, the factory whistle became an auditory representation of class oppression, moving Prince's [political] conception of the show into the soundscape of the musical.[35]

According to academic director and essayist Joanne Gordon,

> The combination of eerie organ chords and the screaming blast of the whistle is significant. The organ suggests an ominous "Gothic" atmosphere. Its sonorous chords evoke the period's ponderous system of government, suffocating religiosity, and false gentility. The hard shrill of the factory whistle suggests unambiguously the unremitting oppression of economic power. The earsplitting sound will be used repeatedly to arrest the audience. It conveys a sense of sinister presentiment and is employed with horrifying effect to underscore each murder. The synthesis of eerie organ sounds, and the blaring abrasive factory whistle is used to disturb and unsettle the audience.[36]

Allen Wallach of *Newsday* wrote, "While Sweeney Todd is taking men's lives with his razor, the industrial age is polluting their city and maiming their souls. The scream of horror we hear repeatedly is a factory whistle."[37] Wallach connected the murders with the violence of the Industrial Revolution and vividly described how the sound of pain and the sound of capitalist oppression are elided by the whistle. "Todd may be killing bodies, but corrupt, unfettered capitalism is killing souls."[38]

Critic Howard Kissell suggested, "Apart from its metaphoric aptness, the whistle is a shrewd theatrical device, a way of jolting and chilling the audience. The organ and the whistle say much about Prince's overpowering conception of *Sweeney Todd*."[39] Kissell suggested that the whistle and Prince's overall vision instilled the show with a more modern sensibility. The organ might have been enough to scare naïve nineteenth-century audiences but, according to Kissel, Prince understood that modern audiences needed to be both terrorized and intellectually challenged. The blaring, abrasive whistle fulfilled both needs.

An aural artifact from Prince's original production soundscape is perhaps contextually tied to a more modern world of New York City in 1979, an evolution of an effect that Sondheim envisioned for his score. The factory whistle is, in fact, not required. Those favoring Sondheim's preference for a melodramatic thriller (such as Doyle's scaled-down 2005 actor/musician production) have eschewed it for more intimate horror sounds, such as door slams and footsteps.

Enhancing the Score

Jonathan Tunick was Sondheim's preferred orchestrator for the vast majority of his shows. In fact, Sondheim called him the "best orchestrator in the history of the theater" during a 2011 video interview with Sony Masterworks.[40] Sondheim typically created a piano score for each show as he composed songs and accompaniments. Tunick translated Sondheim's melodies for *Sweeney Todd* into a full-fledged score for an orchestra of twenty-six musicians. He saw his task as providing subtext and color, especially important for *Sweeney Todd*, for which he "conjured a hellacious soundscape for the macabre: agitated strings, blazing horns and frantic xylophones that evoke the scurrying of rats."[41] Tunick also provided new orchestrations for Tim Burton's 2007 cinematic rendition of Sondheim's show, which used an ensemble with seventy-eight musicians.

Once Sondheim had completed his piano score for a stage show, he and Tunick and Sondheim would come together. He would play and sing all the material to give the orchestrator his sense of the style and color of the score. Tunick's job was to give a show like *Sweeney Todd* its full orchestral sound: various strings, brass, reeds, and so on, blended and counterpointed to create powerful effects.

Sweeney Todd's original conductor, Paul Gemignani, marveled at Tunick's contribution to the score for a theater as immense as the Uris (today's Gershwin).

Such a large theater required a masterful orchestration to fill the space without overpowering the delicate moments of the score. Jonathan Tunick, in a feat almost unimaginable, took the score and orchestrated it perfectly in 24 days. That speed is unheard of, and when the orchestra met to play through the orchestrations for the first time, not a single note was incorrect. What Tunick had created in those 24 days is the licensed orchestration today.[42]

Leitmotifs in Sweeney Todd

Sweeney Todd is clearly a masterwork of American musical theater, but despite his disdain for most operas, Sondheim never objected to its being produced by opera companies. "I'm flattered beyond belief that people take this stuff seriously," he said. "Opera, for all my objections to it as an art form, takes music seriously, and Broadway doesn't. Very few of the journalistic critics on Broadway know anything whatsoever about music. Whereas people connected with an opera company know what music is supposed to do and what it can do."[43]

Sondheim composed an intense musical structure for *Sweeney Todd*'s score using many of the devices employed by operatic and film score composers. The density and complexity of *Sweeney Todd*'s score was not initially understood or appreciated by many critics or first-time audiences. It's complexity wove a subtly eerie and menacing undercurrent that resulted in an overwhelmingly unsettling tone for the entire story. In fact, the show's score is a labyrinth of musical sculptures and devices, especially its employment of leitmotifs, a common operatic device.

A leitmotif is a repeated melodic phrase that represents a character, an emotion, or a theme. This short musical phrase is generally tied to a specific person, place, or idea. When a leitmotif is sounded, the audience, consciously or unconsciously, recognizes and likely senses what it means or what is about to happen. Opera composer Richard Wagner used leitmotifs extensively in his *Ring Cycle* operas (1857–64), but the device can be found in less serious works. For instance, "The Imperial March" from the *Star Wars* movies represents the fear and danger personified by the villainous Darth Vader. Another famous leitmotif is the "shark theme" from the movie *Jaws*, composed by John Williams, simply two alternating, accelerating notes in the bass register to signify the menacing approach of the fearsome shark.

Sweeney's Theme Song: "Dies Irae"

In addition to the leitmotifs Sondheim created, his most prevalent leitmotif is the "Dies Irae" theme within passages of music about a man obsessed with vengeance and death. Sondheim borrowed the notes from the Roman Catholic Church's Mass for the Dead, a thirteenth-century Gregorian plainchant melody. "I always found the 'Dies Irae' moving and scary at the same time," Sondheim told chronicler Craig Zadan. He also employed an unsettling and scary minor-major seventh chord, using it repeatedly, he said, as "sort of a personal joke, because it's a chord that occurred in every Bernard Herrmann score."[44]

The "Dies Irae" melody derives from the notes behind the Latin words that begin the Mass for the Dead. The passage foretells the second coming of Christ to oversee Judgment Day. Evoking the sound of bells, it heralds the "Day of Wrath," a moment of reckoning for humankind. The text describes how a trumpet will summon earthly souls before the throne of God. There the saved are delivered up to heaven while the damned are cast down into the eternal, tormenting flames of hell. It's an apt musical underpinning for the vengeance Sweeney intends for those who stole his wife and child, for anyone in a position of power, and eventually for all mankind—"They all deserve to die,"—and, indeed, the "Dies Irae" sounds in the accompaniment.

The "Dies Irae" motif was employed by composers long before Sondheim to evoke death and vengeance. When he was developing the score for *Sweeney Todd*, a tale set in the nineteenth century with a melodramatic flourish, it made sense to deploy this symbol of doom as used by many past composers, including Mozart, Berlioz, Liszt, Saint-Saëns, Mahler, and Rachmaninoff.[45] As with his predecessors, Sondheim appreciated how the oscillating pitches of "Dies Irae" suggested the nightmarish swinging of bells on Judgment Day.[46]

He used the melodic phrase in "My Friends," when Sweeney is reunited with his razors. Although the song is about Sweeney's joy at holding his sharp instruments again, the undercurrent is something more sinister. "It was the inversion of the opening of the 'Dies Irae,'" Sondheim explained. "And although it was never actually quoted in the show, the first release of 'The Ballad of Sweeney Todd,' was a sequence of the 'Dies Irae,' up a third, which changed the harmonic relationship of the melodic notes to each other."[47] Without digging deeply into the complexities of music theory, it's apparent that Sondheim's repeated use of this musical phrase throughout the score of *Sweeney Todd* achieved the desired effect.[48]

His repeated employment of "Dies Irae" becomes a fearsome signpost during many moments in the show. The phrase "Swing your razor wide, Sweeney" is set on these notes, powerfully voiced by the chorus of downtrodden Londoners singing "The Ballad of Sweeney Todd" as the Demon Barber makes his first appearance, rising from the grave. They recur throughout the score. The company invokes the theme again and again when it repeats "The Ballad" during scene transitions: "Lift your razor high, Sweeney!" and "Swing your razor wide." It crashes through at the end of Sweeney's "Epiphany" and enters again frighteningly just after the liberated Johanna slips free—only to barely escape being murdered by Sweeney. As the story's finale unspools, the chorus again calls out, "Swing your razor high, Sweeney!" a final invocation of the melody.

Other leitmotifs and recurring themes are woven into *Sweeney Todd*. For details, refer to Appendix 2, "Song-by-Song Commentary."

A Chorus of Individuals

An unusual feature of *Sweeney Todd* is Sondheim's use of the chorus of downtrodden London citizens, employed in a manner similar to choruses in ancient Greek tragedies that comment on the action. Sondheim generally avoided choral writing, based on his observation that it seemed unnatural for a lot of people to be completely united in song. But it made sense for *Sweeney Todd*.

The singers in the show's company are onstage from its first moments, often performing individual lines of the fearsome "Ballad of Sweeney Todd" and returning frequently between scenes of action to remind audiences of Sweeney's demonic nature and course of destruction. They also enliven the crowd for Sweeney's barbering contest with Pirelli and later the voracious customers demanding more and more of Mrs. Lovett's pies in the Act II opener, "God, That's Good." But much of their performing in those scenes are as individuals within a unified crowd. The two scenes are linked with the same melody used by Tobias to promote Pirelli's "Miracle Elixir" and Mrs. Lovett's meat pies.

Music Director Paul Gemignani was singularly challenged to inject variety into the company's choral singing.

> I literally memorized the color of everybody's voice and then when I came up to another section of the "Ballad of Sweeney Todd," I'd completely turn it upside down, and we never used the same person twice for solo lines. So over the course of the evening, the same tune sounded just a little different each time you heard it.[49]

"Epiphany": A Play in a Single Song

The frightening monologue number "Epiphany" demonstrates Sondheim's ability to assemble a fully developed play within a single song. He portrayed a series of mood swings when the vengeful barber's mind cracks and increasingly detaches from reality. As pointed out by Signature Theatre's Anika Chapin in an informative video, "Key plot elements using music communicate on a deeper emotional level, while the lyrics communicate on a language level. Every human understands that music speaks to us on an emotional, visceral level."[50] In "Epiphany," Chapin explained, Sweeney goes from

> a man who is rightfully angry about a great harm done to him and who wants revenge against the person who did that harm to a man who has decided that he will kill innocent people. He has a breakdown and comes back together as a new version of himself with a new purpose, and this all takes place within the song . . . in less than four minutes. The music and lyrics give us a full portrait of exactly what is going on in Sweeney's head and heart during this pivotal moment, the ingredients of his change from a sane man to an insane one.[51]

Musically the song repeatedly shifts keys and meter. "There's a lot going on," according to video blogger Kevin Lynch. "This is the cathartic moment, and you can hear it in the music—it alternates between [Sweeney] going out of his mind and yearning for Lucy and Johanna, what he's lost. It's probably one of the hardest songs in the show."[52] The audience needs to see and hear how Sweeney's mind is shattering and witness his dawning attraction to mass murder. Chapin points out that the music behind the first lyrics "is tense, and these booming angry notes are loud and low enough that you can literally feel them in your body. You can physically feel his rage, and it is terrifying."[53]

Anthony Hope's excited and unexpected entrance into Sweeney's shop interrupts the barber's first opportunity to execute Judge Turpin. In his fury, "Epiphany" reflects the turning point of his madness as his grievances expand to all of humanity. It took Sondheim a month to craft this complex number. Once Sweeney's mind is shattered and reformed, the stage directions have him directly and fiercely addressing the audience. He is menacing and ice cold: "Welcome to the grave," he intones. "I will have vengeance. . . . Sweeney's waiting!"

His final declaration claiming to be alive at last, when Sweeney sings, "And I'm full of joy!" with harshly discordant notes beneath the word joy is surely one of the most chilling moments in any musical or a play. That's the exact point when Sweeney becomes a new, horrifying, assuredly insane version of himself. He has a new purpose, well beyond mere revenge against a single man.

Now he's eager to murder indiscriminately and punish everyone. Sondheim's music brilliantly carries us to this moment.

Fresh Air interviewer Terry Gross asked Sondheim about the song's concluding chords which "are so dark there. There is no joy." Sondheim replied, "Well, that's the idea." He explained that he put a big, consonant chord on the end because Hal Prince wanted to evoke applause for Len Cariou's performance. Sondheim chose to unnerve audiences by using a dissonant chord immediately after the consonant chord. It got nervous applause.

Cooking Up Some Comic Relief

To follow the stupefying blow delivered by "Epiphany," Sondheim crafted "A Little Priest," surely the show's most gruesome (and memorable) number. The distance from Pirelli's murder to meat-pie cannibalism is traveled in short and wickedly entertaining order. The dark but jolly eight-minute number reveals Mrs. Lovett's seductively opportunistic suggestion to work with Sweeney in an abhorrent partnership that's professionally productive and subconsciously sexual.

The catchy waltz-time number is weird and quirky, a pragmatic extension of Mrs. Lovett's coquettish, Cockney nature first introduced in "The Worst Pies in London." "A Little Priest" comically takes the form of a "list song." Sondheim admired such numbers by songwriter Cole Porter featuring funny, clever rhymes, and images, often spicing them with sexual innuendo and double-entendre toward a big, satisfying ending.[54] As Sondheim worked on the lyrics for this song, he generated an astonishing array of possibilities—40 pages of notes and lyric sketches, considering more than 100 professions for Mrs. Lovett to propose to Sweeney as potential contents for her pies (Figure 6.1).[55]

The mad waltz of "A Little Priest" cements the devious, not to mention repellent, partnership between Mrs. Lovett and Sweeney. Not only are they disposing of the bodies of Sweeney's victims by feeding them to unwitting, ravenous customers, at a metaphorical level they are demonstrating the cannibalism imposed by the English class system—"It's man devouring man, my dear." There's a kind of manic justice: "How gratifying for once to know—that those above will serve those down below!"[56] Of course, this fiendish notion

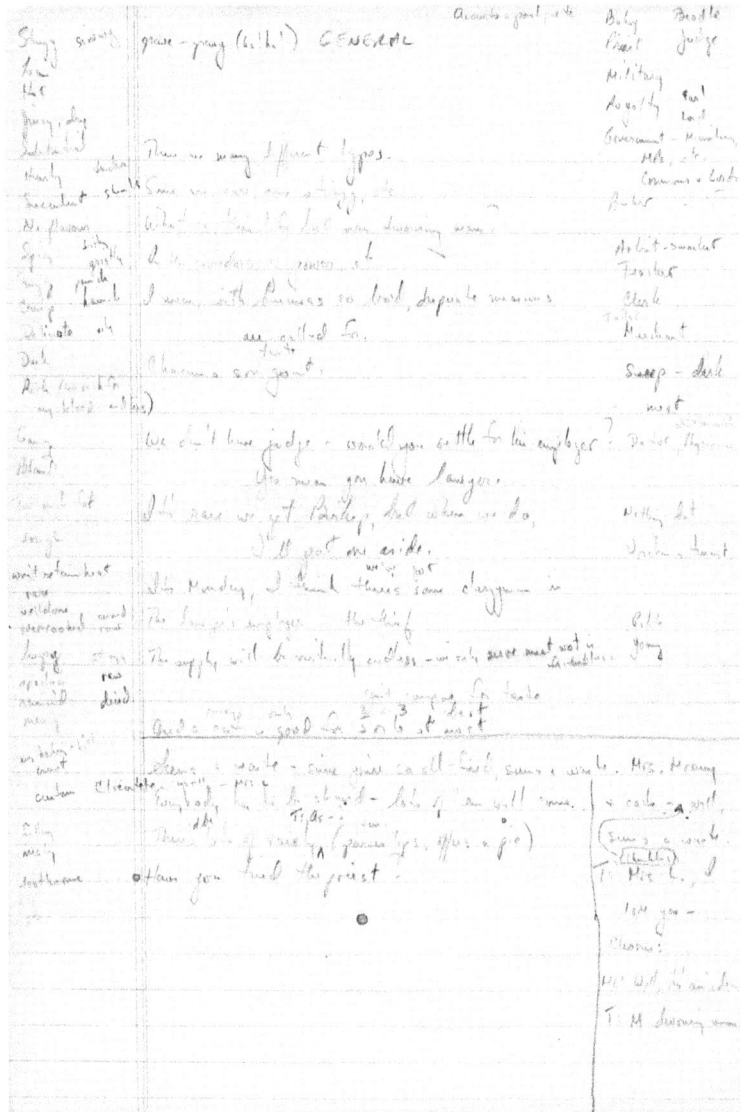

Figure 6.1 *A page from Sondheim's lyric sketch for "A Little Priest" includes his brainstorming various professions to become pie fillings.*
© *The Sondheim Estate.*

of recycling puts a perfect final touch on *Sweeney Todd*'s first act, bringing the audience down from Sweeney's madness to a riotously funny conclusion.

The song also shows Mrs. Lovett advancing her matrimonial scheme to ensnare Sweeney. He is momentarily engaged, but not for long since he is singularly focused on revenge while she is being merely opportunistic. Their contest of double-entendres, appraising potential "customers" as pie fillings, resolves as their mindsets "harmonize" in a delirious ideology as they set each other up.

One more sign of Sondheim's genius: as the second act winds down to the show's tragic denouement, the grieving Sweeney finally realizes that Mrs. Lovett has deceived him: Lucy did not die, she became the Beggar Woman, whom he has just murdered. Totally mad, Sweeney waltzes with Mrs. Lovett once more to the mad melody of "A Little Priest"—and flings her into her own oven.

The Frightening Epilogue

For the *finale ultimo*, individual players—Tobias, Johanna, and Anthony, the Beggar Woman, Judge Turpin, Pirelli, the Beadle—reassemble onstage, eventually joined by ghastly Sweeney and Mrs. Lovett. They sing a fierce rendition of "The Ballad of Sweeney Todd" that eventually involves the entire company pouring out shrieking warnings to the audience. They imply that Sweeney—or at least his attraction to righteous vengeance—remains in our midst: "No one can help, nothing can hide you—/ Isn't that Sweeney there beside you."[57] Of course, the "Dies Irae" motif worms its way through their powerful choral delivery. The "Day of Wrath" has indeed arrived.

The script's final, baleful stage direction brings the show to a stunning close featuring shrieking, skittering violins: *The company exits. TODD and MRS. LOVETT are the last to leave. They look at each other, then exit in opposite directions, MRS. LOVETT into the wings, TODD upstage. He glares at us malevolently for a moment, then slams the iron door in our faces. Blackout.*[58]

The orchestra continues to crank away powerfully as the living and the dead return to the stage for a reprise of the "Ballad of Sweeney Todd." The music flows across final bows until Sweeney slams the iron furnace door, and there is shocked silence—followed by rousing applause—the final piece of evidence of how Sondheim's magnificent score makes *Sweeney Todd* a true masterpiece.

7

Take Sweeney Home to Listen Recordings

The enthusiastic reception by critics and audiences for the original Broadway production of *Sweeney Todd* was undoubtedly reinforced and expanded by the release of the show's original cast recording in May 1979, just weeks after the March 1 opening. Using realistic audio recreation of numerous aspects of Prince's production, it was conceived as a "radio play" that told the story with the addition of dialogue and sound effects. The twenty-six-piece orchestra that performed in the pit at the Uris Theatre was expanded to forty musicians for the recording. Featuring the memorable (and Tony Award-winning) performances of Len Cariou and Angela Lansbury Lovett, the two-disk recording continues to be the definitive rendition of Prince's 1979 production.

Several subsequent and variously staged productions have also resulted in additional recordings that demonstrate Sondheim's musical mastery as well as the show's versatility. Prince's stagings for the Houston Grand Opera and New York City Opera paved the way for performances featuring opera singers, including a series of concert stagings in the late 1990s, culminating in a 2000 event featuring the New York Philharmonic and resulting in an impressive recording that encompassed virtually the entire score.

A recording of British stage director John Doyle's intimate, actor/musician production on Broadway in 2006 offers a very different take on the show and its score. Featuring Michael Cerveris in the title role and veteran Patti LuPone as Mrs. Lovett, this Broadway cast recording demonstrated the performers' talent and versatility as musicians as well as actors. It also represented a convincing demonstration that Sondheim's score can work just as well in a small production. Sondheim's original desire for *Sweeney Todd* to be a small, scary show was demonstrated effectively. Doyle won the 2006 Tony Award for Best Direction of a Musical, and the production's double-compact disc cast recording provided permanent evidence of the show's unusual mastery of words and music.

Tim Burton's 2007 cinematic adaptation took *Sweeney Todd* off the stage and into the dark, brooding corners of Victorian London. With Sondheim's approval and enthusiastic engagement, the film, minus the chorus and the bloodcurdling "Ballad of Sweeney Todd," resulted in a soundtrack recording that leans heavily on the largely untrained singing voices of Johnny Depp as Sweeney and Helena Bonham Carter as Mrs. Lovett. They were both successful actors, but their vocal performances separated from the film on this recording are less than satisfying. Nevertheless, it has its pluses—especially with a much-expanded orchestra and memorable performances by several supporting actors.

The continued popularity of twenty-first-century *Sweeney Todd* stage productions culminated in a 2023 Broadway revival featuring pop star Josh Groban in the title role. His resonant baritone was a fine instrument for Sweeney's songs. He was paired with past Tony Award winner Annaleigh Ashford, who turned in an amorous, libidinous take on Mrs. Lovett. Staged by director Tommy Kail and musical director Alex Lacamoire, Groban's and Ashford's performances received 2023 Tony nominations among eight for the production, including Best Revival of a Musical. The production's excellent twenty-six-piece orchestra can be appreciated via the 2023 original cast recording, which was nominated for a Grammy in the category Best Musical Theater Album.

NOTE: Six of the most memorable sound recordings of Sweeney Todd are the focus of this chapter. Commentaries regarding video recordings of some of these performances can be found in previous chapters (in addition to the chapter devoted to Tim Burton's film).

Original Cast Recording with Len Cariou and Angela Lansbury: Sweeney Todd, The Demon Barber of Fleet Street (RCA RED SEAL, CBL 2-3379, 1979). In early

1979 there was considerable advance interest in *Sweeney Todd*'s imminent arrival on Broadway on March 1, including a potential cast recording to be overseen for RCA by veteran producer Thomas Z. Shepard. He had previously won a Grammy for his original cast recording of Sondheim's *Company* (1970). In 1976, he produced the original cast recordings of *Pacific Overtures* (1976) and London productions of the composer's *A Little Night Music* (a Grammy winner) and *Side by Side by Sondheim*. Shepard, himself a composer, conductor, music arranger, and pianist as well as a respected producer, had a well-established working relationship with Sondheim and director Hal Prince.

Early in 1979, Sondheim performed his *Sweeney Todd* score for Shepard and his wife Irene at the home of Mary Lea Johnson, heiress to the Johnson & Johnson pharmaceutical company. She and her husband Martin Richards were backers of the show. A few weeks later, Prince invited the Shepards and fifty or so others to his Manhattan townhouse for a preview of most of the score with Sondheim singing and playing the piano. By then Mathilde Pincus, Sondheim's copyist, was providing Shepard with the piano/vocal scores of the show's songs. A working copy of Hugh Wheeler's libretto had been shared with Shepard so he could begin to map out the recording's production. "Unlike any prior musical I had ever encountered," Shepard has written, "*Sweeney Todd* thrived on breaking the rules, on expanding the boundaries of American musical theater."[1]

RCA president Bob Summer expressed an early concern that the commitment to record *Sweeney Todd* might have been a mistake based on rumors about the gruesome tale. Shepard pushed back:

> I took the plunge and assured him that we had a masterpiece on our hands, and that RCA's unofficial commitment to record whatever Sondheim wrote would continue to enhance our catalogue, no matter what. Bob agreed. This unspoken commitment to Sondheim and to his publisher, Tommy Valando, had held RCA and Sondheim together for most of his productions in the 1970s.[2]

Working with Sondheim, Prince, Wheeler, conductor Paul Gemignani, orchestrator Jonathan Tunick, and others, Shepard established a plan for a recording "constructed like a radio play that would guide the listener through

Figure 7.1 *Thomas Z. Shepard (left) produced* Sweeney Todd's *original cast recording, working closely with Sondheim and director Hal Prince.Photofest.*

the story with the judicious use of dialog, sound effects, and using our technological resources, our stereo tools, in order to achieve aural perspective and motion." (Figure 7.1).

Several changes from the musical as performed onstage were made for the recording. Some tempi were faster to make up for the absence of stage movement. Two sections cut from the stage performance in previews were restored: parts of "The Contest," between Sweeney and Pirelli to see who can quickly pull a tooth, and Judge Turpin's self-flagellation during his *mea culpa* performance of "Johanna."³ To give the recording a fully symphonic sound, the twenty-six-piece orchestra that played the show in the Uris Theatre pit was augmented with fourteen additional players—doubling the number of strings, adding a French horn, and an additional percussion player.

Shepard effectively included the startling shriek of the piercing factory whistle that sounded onstage whenever there was danger or death. (At the Uris, this was triggered live from the orchestra pit by conductor Paul Gemignani.) Shepard and his sound engineers recorded several iterations of this jolting effect and added it during postproduction, along with the sounds of coins, the barbershop entry bell, and customers' footsteps.

When Sweeney's victims were dispatched down a chute from his barber chair to the basement, Shepard had to come up with a way to replicate that sound on a stereo recording that's limited to motion left and right, not up and down. He described the contribution of his associate producer Jay David Saks.

In 1979 he was young, healthy, and particularly athletic. So Jay became Sweeney's sonic victims. With microphones hovering above him, he didn't seem to mind shoving himself around the floor many times over, until we got the thuds and swishes that seemed to work best. He was also very willing to throw himself to the ground to replicate what it might sound like when a fresh corpse lands.

An hour's worth of recording generated the necessary effects. "For the final mix," Shepard explained,

> we positioned the sound of the chair hard right. We then took the sliding on the floor as we electronically travelled it from hard right to hard left at a speed as if it were free-falling vertically. As the "corpse" got to the left side, we added the loud, dull thud as the body of the victim (Jay's) lands hard in the left loudspeaker. We nicknamed the entire venture "The Horizontal Laundry Chute."[4]

Shepard's recording schedule was accomplished using six three-hour sessions on March 12 and 13, 1979, resulting in twenty-nine separate sections, "each one tailored or adapted from the way the material was performed in the theater"[5] about ninety total minutes of material in total.

The recording was released in May 1979 in double-LP and double-cassette formats.[6] It received an enthusiastic review by John Rockwell in the *New York Times*.

> The cast for the Uris run of *Sweeney Todd* boasts not only Mr. Cariou and Miss Lansbury, whose superb theatricality and serviceable voices come through strongly on disk; but a fine, healthy-voiced subsidiary cast. The orchestra has been beefed up slightly for recording purposes, and the production of Thomas Z. Shepard (who has considerable classical-music recording experience) incorporates enough of the sound effects of the show to lend a chilling sense of verisimilitude. The album comes with plenty of pictures of the stage production and a booklet that includes an essay by Robert Kimball and the complete libretto. All told, it's a terrific show, whether you call it musical or opera, and it makes for a terrific listening experience on records.[7]

Other reviews offered similar praise. In *The Theatermania Guide to Musical Theater* (2004), Robert Sandla wrote:

Even if there were dozens of recordings out there, the original Broadway album would be definitive. Len Cariou as the alternately brooding and enraged barber, Angela Lansbury as the warm-hearted yet cold-blooded Mrs. Lovett, Victor Garber and Sarah Rice as the young lovers, Edmund Lyndeck as the creepy, unjust Judge Turpin—they all leap off the disk and grab you by the throat.[8]

Sandla awarded the *Sweeney Todd* original cast recording a five-star "Superlative, outstanding" rating.

Alan Rich in an August 1979 *High Fidelity* review of the recording wrote, "Whatever the eventual fate of *Sweeney Todd* in the theater, on records the status of Sondheim's accomplishment has been preserved with exceptional intelligence.... A masterly original piece of musical theater has, for once, been given its due."[9] Paul Wittke, writing another review for *High Fidelity* in April 1980 called the recording "exceptional" and praised the cast and the chorus as "superb." He summed up his commentary this way: "The recording was made with intelligence and fidelity. Technically, it is one of the finest show recordings ever produced."[10]

In 1980, Shepard's *Sweeney Todd* original cast recording won a pair of Grammys, one for the recording and one for Shepard personally. In 2014, it was one of twenty-five recordings added permanently to the National Recording Registry of the Library of Congress, a list of materials chosen for preservation "as cultural, artistic and/or historical treasures, representing the richness and diversity of the American soundscape."[11]

For most critics, fans, and scholars, this is the definitive recording of Sondheim's musical theater masterpiece. In a web-based overview of *Sweeney Todd* recordings in 2023, Matt Koplik stated, "There will always be room for differences of opinion as to what score represents the very best of Sondheim, but when it comes to *Sweeney Todd*, only one recording is truly essential: this one."[12]

Booklet: The 2005 reissue of the original cast recording in compact-disc format included a sixteen-page booklet featuring five pages of appreciative liner notes by Broadway producer and director Richard Jay-Alexander:

The newly remastered version simply cannot be improved upon. It vividly brings into sharper details some of the salient moments in the show and boasts an incredibly skilled cast that knows exactly what it is doing, under the musical direction of the legendary Paul Gemignani, a frequent Sondheim collaborator. Hearing it again, one is constantly mesmerized by the way it so thoroughly conveys the story from beginning to end and still "chills," in Jonathan Tunick's most impassioned and visceral orchestrations.

Two 2-page spreads offer 16 black-and-white photos by Martha Swope and Van Williams of original cast members and scenes from Prince's original production. BONUS TRACKS: The album's second disk includes a pair of performances recorded live during *Sondheim: A Celebration at Carnegie Hall* on June 10, 1992, with the American Theatre Orchestra conducted by Paul Gemignani: "Symphonic Sondheim: *Sweeney Todd*" (orchestrated by Don Sebesky and featuring Jerry Hadley, Eugene Perry, and Herbert Perry) and "Green Finch and Linnet Bird" performed by operatic soprano Harolyn Blackwell.

2001 Concert Recording with George Hearn and Patti LuPone: Sweeney Todd: Live in Concert (New York Philharmonic Special Editions, NYP 2001/2002). Director Lonny Price's three-evening concert production of *Sweeney Todd* with the New York Philharmonic (May 4–6, 2000) at Lincoln Center's Avery Fisher Hall featured opera and musical theater performers.[13] Patti LuPone was Mrs. Lovett, and George Hearn reprised the role he played twenty years earlier when he succeeded Len Cariou on Broadway and toured with Angela Lansbury. (This touring production with Lansbury was preserved on video that year.)[14] Hearn was a last-minute replacement for Welsh opera start bass-baritone Bryn Terfel, originally contracted to play Sweeney. He withdrew because of back pain that eventually required surgery. Hearn's performance was widely praised.

The concert cast also featured Davis Gaines as Anthony, Neil Patrick Harris as Toby, and Audra McDonald as the Beggar Woman. Operatically trained singers in the cast were soprano Heidi Grant Murphy as Johanna, bass Paul Plishka as a menacing Judge Turpin, and tenors John Aler as the Beadle and Stanford Olsen as Pirelli. The forty singers of the New York Choral Artists played the chorus of bedraggled Londoners. The concert's final performance received a fifteen-minute standing ovation.

Plans fell through for a video recording which would have aired on PBS's "Great Performances." Deutsche Grammophon decided against producing a cast recording. At that point, the Philharmonic decided to make its own live recording, which was released in 2001.[15] Veteran recording producer Tommy Krasker oversaw the project, working with co-producer Lawrence L. Rock.

In his assessment for the *Theatermania Guide to Musical Theater Recordings*, Robert Sandla praised the orchestra. "With all due respect to those dedicated souls who toil in Broadway pits, hearing Stephen Sondheim's most ambitious score played by instrumentalists of this caliber—and by an orchestra of this size—is thrilling. Conductor Andrew Litton reveals himself to be a Broadway baby at heart, and the New York Philharmonic soars through the *Sweeney Todd* score with grandeur and drive."[16] Sandla's entry in the guide awarded the two-CD recording three stars, defined as "Recommended."

In addition to all the music Sondheim composed, the Philharmonic's live recording includes much of show's dialogue, which means that *Sweeney Todd*'s narrative is clearly told and with high energy. (The accompanying 130-page booklet provides the complete libretto and photos of the concert production, as well as essays by Sondheim, Price, and several performers.) Audience reaction ranging from extended applause to knowing laughter is an effective component of the recording,[17] enhancing the ambience of live performance. The thirty-seven separate tracks across two disks (Act 1, Act 2) generally flow from one scene to the next, often with bridging dialogue. This is undoubtedly the most complete commercial recording of *Sweeney Todd* available —125 minutes of concert performances.[18]

Steven Suskin praised the clarity of the recording.

> One of Sondheim's many strengths—one often overlooked—is his brilliant multi-part writing. Other shows have vocal arrangements; Sondheim weaves tapestries of melody which miraculously complement each other, often with character-specific lyrics. "Kiss Me," for example, or the quartet version of "Johanna"; or the phenomenal second act opening "God, That's Good," with Sweeney, Lovett and Tobias going their separate ways against the full chorus.

These—and several other numbers—are infinitely more effective here, simply because you can distinctly hear the notes and comprehend the words.[19]

In 2001, Scott Ross wrote in *The Sondheim Review*,

Among the joys of this resplendent CD is the opportunity to hear this score anew—to embrace again its brooding sonorities, its coruscating highs, its many hair-raising dramatic climaxes, it's chilling undertones of passion and madness, it's cunning variations on the "Dies Irae," all tied together and immeasurably enhanced by Jonathan Tunick's extraordinarily rich orchestrations, perhaps the finest ever written for an American musical.[20]

Booklet: A 128-page booklet accompanying the two-CD set offers an essay by Sondheim, another by the New York Philharmonic's Music Director Kurt Masur, and a third by James Keller, the orchestra's program annotator. Director Lonny Price wrote an informative piece about "Staging Sweeney," which is followed by more than a dozen interviews with the artists, including conductor Andrew Litton and stars George Hearn and Patti LuPone. Brief biographies of each featured artist are also included. The entire booklet is illustrated with numerous color photos and includes a fifty-page libretto of *Sweeney Todd* as it was performed in 2000 at Avery Fisher Hall.

2005 Broadway Revival Actor/Musician Cast Recording with Michael Cerveris and Patti LuPone: Sweeney Todd (Nonesuch 79946, 2006). John Doyle's reconceptualized 2005 actor/musician revival of *Sweeney Todd* earned 2006 Tony Awards for him for Best Direction of a Musical and for Sarah Travis for Best Orchestrations. It also made for a remarkably different original cast recording. The pared-down "orchestra" consisted of the ten actors who performed the show as inmates in an insane asylum. They also played Travis's reorchestrated score, which comes through in the cast recording in a new and different way: "though the score loses its grandeur, the show becomes chillingly personal . . . with each of them switching back and forth from actor to musician seamlessly."[21]

Doyle's staging had been refined by a series of presentations across England, making considerable demands on his British actors who had to memorize lines, movement and, especially, the full score, which was performed without sheet music. The cast of ten remained onstage for the entire performance. Eleven days after the Broadway production opened at the Eugene O'Neill Theatre, Doyle's New York cast went to Avatar Studios for two days of recording (Monday and Tuesday, November 14–15, 2005), overseen by Executive Producer Robert Hurwitz; recording engineers were Tom Lazarus, Peter Doris, and Chad Lupo. The resulting double-compact disk has eighty-eight minutes of material.

A review of the recording in the *Houston Chronicle* pointed out:

> Nonesuch's two-disc set of the . . . revival is a knockout—a strikingly different rendition, but just as powerful in its own right. If it loses a little in sheer grandeur and scope, it gains in intimacy, immediacy and intensity. It's not just having smaller forces at play. Astute editing deletes bridging passages (no longer needed) and, for most songs, drops the "button"[22] The streamlined result is more tightly focused, relentlessly advancing the bloodthirsty plot, while making the consistent daring and genius of Sondheim's soaring music and incisive lyrics more apparent than ever. . . . Sarah Travis' new orchestrations are resourceful, the unexpected combinations of instruments displaying the score's melodic beauty, rich harmonic underpinnings and dark colorations. In graduating from epic to chamber music, *Sweeney Todd* has grown edgier and more percussive.[23]

The cast recording did not add musicians, as had been the practice for several of Sondheim's previous cast recordings. "While the intricacy of the instrumentation is, in the theatre, a marvel, it's bound to be less impressive on disc," wrote Ken Mandelbaum. "Which is not to say that Sarah Travis's new orchestrations aren't admirable, especially when one considers the requirements of the staging. They're satisfying even to one familiar with the original, grandiose Jonathan Tunick orchestrations. Indeed, Travis's work serves to demonstrate how well Sondheim's score can come across even in a reduced instrumentation."[24]

Classical music critic Donald Rosenberg offered some insightful observations in *The Sondheim Review*.

> Nonesuch's recording of the new production . . . can't reproduce much of the vibrant virtuosity that Doyle and company conjure onstage, but

it is a jolting and thrilling experience on its own energizing terms. The performance is so different from the two previous recorded incarnations . . . that it immediately takes a distinctive place in the life of this most resilient of musical theatre works.[25]

This recording was nominated for the 2006 Grammy Award for Best Musical Show Album.

Booklet: The eighty+ page booklet packaged with the recording features an essay by renowned British stage director Jeremy Sams, "Where Do We Put *Sweeney*?"; and others by John Doyle, the production's director, "Staging *Sweeney Todd*"; Tony Award-winning orchestrator Sarah Travis, "A Musical Jigsaw"; and a detailed synopsis by music and theater producer Sean Patrick Flahaven. Color photos from the stage production on the inside front and back covers are by Paul Kolnik; black-and-white images from the recording session are by Bruce Glikas.

Motion Picture Soundtrack with Johnny Depp and Helena Bonham Carter: Sweeney Todd, The Demon Barber of Fleet Street (Nonesuch 368572–2, 2007). Don't go listening for the chorus of foreboding citizens of London singing "The Tale of Sweeney Todd" on the soundtrack of Tim Burton's cinematic adaptation of *Sweeney Todd*. The film kept a tight focus on the faces and reactions of leading characters, so Burton chose to excise all the chorus singing. (The easily recognized melody of "The Tale of Sweeney Todd" became pulse-pounding underscoring for the film's opening credits.) The crowd scenes for the barbering contest and the ravenous crowd demanding Mrs. Lovett's meat pies were no longer opportunities for choral singing.

Burton and veteran recording producer Robert Hurwitz were the soundtrack's executive producers, with Mike Higham serving as the album producer.[26] A huge seventy-eight-musician orchestra conducted by Paul Gemignani was recorded prior to the commencement of filming by Jake Jackson and Geoff Foster at London's Air Lyndhurst Studios. With fifty-two more players than supported the 1979 Broadway production at his disposal, Jonathan Tunick expanded his brilliant orchestrations. Advance recordings of the actors singing their songs were used during shooting so they could match their performances to the pre-recorded music.

Depp and Bonham Carter's vivid cinematic characters did not translate effectively to the soundtrack. Both have serviceable voices, but their ranges were limited, and Depp's gentle tenor—while occasionally pushed into anger and fury—seldom sounds as threatening as any of the baritone stage performers who played the Demon Barber, especially during the devastating number "Epiphany."[27] Minus the film's visuals to show the presence and character of Mrs. Lovett, Bonham Carter all but whispers her way through a breathy rendition of "The Worst Pies in London," and her narrow range rendered her less convincing as the mordant villainess of the piece. She did shine on "By the Sea," a lighter number, and she conveyed the irony of "Nothing's Gonna Harm You" sung with sweet young Ed Sanders as Tobias Ragg.

As the Beadle, Timothy Spall is unctuously oily; Alan Rickman's evil Judge Turpin doesn't get much time on the recording, although he certainly had the deeply menacing, bass voice required for this especially creepy role. Anthony (Jamie Campbell Bower) and Johanna (Jayne Wisener) come across as truly eager, nervous adolescents; she does an acceptable job warbling through "Green Finch and Linnet Bird." Laura Michelle Kelly's presence as the Beggar Woman was narrowed, so the recording affords only few vocal clues about her secret as Sweeney's damaged wife Lucy. Several minor players turn in fine moments: Comedian Sacha Baron Cohen milks the role of the scheming barber Adolfo Pirelli for all it was worth, and ten-year-old Sanders is the first true child to convincingly portray earnest, innocent Tobias.

Burton's film was recognized with Academy Award and Golden Globe nominations. However, the seventy-two-minute soundtrack recording's most noteworthy element is the orchestral accompaniment, featuring Tunick's magnificent orchestrations.

Booklet: The seventy-eight-page booklet is almost entirely filled with the film's lyrics but without connecting narrative. It is illustrated with numerous production photos that often depict the washed-out cinematic color palette that Burton used throughout. He provided a brief note for the booklet's opening page, declaring that "Of all musicals, *Sweeney Todd* is my favorite." He added: "What makes these recording so unique is that they are performed by actors who for the most part had no formal musical training. I believe this gives the songs a different dimension than any previous version."

2012 London Revival with Michael Ball and Imelda Staunton: Sweeney Todd (First Night Record CASTCD 113, 2012). This production, staged by British director Jonathan Kent, originated in September 2011 at England's Chichester Festival Theatre. On the strength of award-winning performances by the leading veteran actors—Michael Ball as Sweeney and Imelda Staunton as Mrs. Lovett—it quickly transferred to London's West End at the Adelphi Theatre in March 2012. (It closed in September 2012 after 207 performances.)

The cast recording was released in April 2012 (First Night Records), the first British commercial recording of this very British show. However, purchasers quickly recognized it as a selection of highlights (although not so designated on the packaging). They were dismayed about the absence of "Poor Thing," "Green Finch and Linnet Bird," "Ah, Miss," "Pirelli's Miracle Elixir," and "The Contest." These were likely omitted to keep the recording to a single seventy-four-minute disk. But these absences mean that the roles of Johanna and Pirelli are barely present. Jonathan Tunick reduced his standard orchestration (typically twenty-six musicians) to just fifteen but claimed "that there are no significant changes other than a generally lighter texture and more open voicing necessitated by the smaller compliment."[28]

Kent's production shifted the story to 1930s London and the city's working poor of that era who were suffering from the worldwide Depression. The director also focused on the show's violent shifts of tone, making them all the more unsettling—such as the jarring transition from the frightening "Epiphany" to the dismayingly jaunty "A Little Priest." Ball began initially playing Sweeney as a man with a legitimate grievance who slowly becomes a demonic serial killer. Critic Michael Billington praised Staunton's performance as Mrs. Lovett "as a pinafored loner whose residual moral sense is quickly overcome by her love of profit and lust for Sweeney."[29]

Writing for *Variety*, David Benedict observed that "with the dynamite pairing of Michael Ball and Imelda Staunton . . . this staging is anything but cautious. But instead of immensity, this incarnation has scalding intensity."[30] Another writer said, "They quite simply provide a masterclass in musical theatre."[31] Nevertheless, this truncated representation of *Sweeney Todd* is the least favored of the show's several cast recordings.

2023 Broadway Revival Cast Recording with Josh Groban and Annaleigh Ashford: Sweeney Todd: The Demon Barber of Fleet Street (Warner Records Inc., 2023). Josh Groban fans love this beautifully sung recording of *Sweeney Todd*. When the production opened in March 2023, some critics claimed the star, who personally pursued this production, lacked the requisite gravitas to play the Demon Barber. Despite such claims, he was nominated for a Tony as Leading Actor in Musical. Over the run of the show, he grew into the acting demands of the role and, by the revival's performances late in 2023, negative judgments were no longer being voiced. The cast recording was made just a week after the production opened, with Groban and fellow performers already in fine voice, especially Annaleigh Ashford as Mrs. Lovett and Ruthie Ann Miles as the Beggar Woman (both also Tony nominated). The result is a fine recording of Sondheim's masterpiece.

That being said, this ninety-three-minute offering will be most often compared to the 1979 original cast recording. Len Cariou's Sweeney will probably never be matched; on that recording his acting and his singing truly define the role. Groban was a worthy successor, although his stage performance on the revival recording lacks Cariou's fiendish texture. Nevertheless, his rendition of Sweeney's mind-snapping "Epiphany" is chilling, especially on its dissonant final note.

In 1979, Angela Lansbury gave the comedic role of the amoral Mrs. Lovett its most iconic performance. Ashford spun it differently with a strong dose of physical humor and some slapstick which occasionally surfaces, although she seldom evinces the cold ruthlessness of Lansbury or LuPone. Instead, her unstinting lust for Sweeney is omnipresent.

Ruthie Ann Miles's portrayal of the Beggar Woman was built on a framework of multiple personalities, and she rotated through these in fascinating ways that are admirably captured on this recording. She's a central figure in the chaotic, rapidly performed "City on Fire."

In a brief appraisal of this recording the *New York Times*' Jesse Green observed that "the glorious score is largely unchanged. The orchestrations are only slightly tweaked," although the startling factory whistle was not used in this production, instead relying on discordant orchestral "stings." Green asks, "What's the added value of this nth recording of the Sondheim masterwork? As you might expect from a cast headed by Josh Groban as the vengeful barber, the answer is the beautiful singing." The actor's early shortcomings in acting in the huge stage production "are utterly absent on the album, turning numbers like Sweeney's 'Epiphany' into murderous arias as big as any in opera. Under Alex Lacamoire's musical supervision, the performances—not just Groban's but the ensemble's—go for the throat, over and over."[32]

Booklet: The thirty-two-page booklet enclosed with the double-compact disc is mostly a transcription of *Sweeney Todd*'s lyrics as performed in this revival. A two-page essay "He Trod A Path That Few Have Trod," by Peter Marks of the *Washington Post* and eight color images from the production are also featured. On its final page, the booklet dedicates the album to "Stephen Sondheim and Hal Prince, two masters of their craft who continue to teach us."

8

"Isn't that Sweeney there beside you?"
Cultural Impact

When *Sweeney Todd* debuted on Broadway in 1979, it was largely unprecedented. Few shows had ever featured such a through-composed and complex score as the one Sondheim created. Possible artistic forerunners might have been George Gershwin's *Porgy and Bess* (1935), a show Sondheim deeply admired, or Leonard Bernstein's *West Side Story* (1957), with lyrics by 26-year-old Sondheim. But Sondheim's own musical inspiration, especially from Bernard Herrmann's chilling movie scores, made *Sweeney Todd* a show the likes of which had never been produced on Broadway.

At Sondheim and Hal Prince's behest, playwright and novelist Hugh Wheeler transformed Christopher Bond's adapted melodrama script into a literate and coherent libretto that was paired with Sondheim's astonishing score. Wheeler drew on the psychological motivation Bond had conceived with Sweeney seeking vengeance for his wrongful and corrupt treatment by Judge Turpin. He also refined some of Bond's plotting to make the whole story even more devastating.[1]

Sondheim's ability to write insightful lyrics gave more depth and texture to *Sweeney Todd*'s characters. Songs such as "My Friends" and "Epiphany" provided vivid insights into Sweeney's tragically twisted mind as he sinks to increasingly violent emotional depths. Mrs. Lovett's "Worst Pies in London," a jaunty but repellent comic number, quickly established her zeal and willingness to expand her business by any means and to win Sweeney's attention in the bargain. Her Act II duet with Toby, a simpleminded boy, "Nothing's Gonna Harm You," revealed frightening irony as he earnestly pledges to protect her from harm while she recognizes he must be eliminated.

Prince's immense original Broadway production set a powerful precedent for large-scale, epic productions. The ragtag Londoners opened the show with "The Ballad of Sweeney Todd" as he emerged from a grave. Sweeney and Mrs. Lovett's hilarious scheming about menus for "A Little Priest" concluded with her raising a rolling pin and Sweeney his glistening razor, a madly victorious image that became the show's most iconic. The horrific finale, as Sweeney discovers he has murdered his wife, evokes gasps from most theatergoers, as does his horrifying waltz of Mrs. Lovett into the fiery oven.

Sweeney's baleful glance over his shoulder at the show's conclusion implies that he knows others are capable of similar obsession. As evidenced by numerous productions of the show worldwide since 1979 (including a major motion picture), *Sweeney Todd*'s impact lives on. For more than a half-century, it has been lurking around theatrical corners as frightening as ever. In fact, *Sweeney Todd*'s influence has expanded beyond theatrical productions to broader culture and consciousness.

Writing a Horror Movie

Before Sondheim and Prince delivered *Sweeney Todd* to Broadway in 1979, the bogeyman murderer's fearsome reputation was pretty much a British phenomenon. From the mid-nineteenth to the mid-twentieth century, his name and reputation were invoked in England to chasten misbehaving children: "Behave yourself or Sweeney Todd will catch you and turn you into a meat pie." Very few people in the United States knew about the Victorian serial killer.

That included British actor Angela Lansbury, whom Sondheim and Prince cast as Mrs. Lovett. She was at home in Ireland when she received a telegram from them inviting her to their new project. "I didn't know the original play at that time, but one grows up knowing the name Sweeney Todd and one is immediately frightened."[2] Even though she wasn't a candidate for the title role, Lansbury understood the show's potential and welcomed the opportunity.

Sondheim's love of macabre and gory tales fueled his desire to create something new and different in the world of musical theater: "What I wanted to write was a horror movie."[3] When he shared his enthusiasm for the project with Prince, the director needed to be convinced. "Hal is not the fan of melodrama and farce that I am," Sondheim said, "I think they are my favorite forms of theater."[4] When Prince tuned in to the story as one of revenge with a possibility for social commentary, he came on board. He overlaid Sweeney's horrific story in the crushing grip of the Industrial Revolution in Victorian London. Sondheim was convinced that it could be a scary story about obsession, but he understood how it could succeed—artistically and successfully—with Prince's epic concept.

Previous musicals had told serious stories—Gershwin's *Porgy and Bess*, Rodgers and Hammerstein's *Carousel*, or even *West Side Story* by Bernstein, Laurents, and Sondheim—but a tale about a serial killer with a gigantic dollop of cannibalism felt like a step too far for many theater fans. In general, the majority of musicals were seen as entertainment, not a means to frighten audiences. The general notion was to leave such tales to those who liked being scared and encourage them to go to creepy movies. But when Sondheim's towering, bloody "musical thriller" debuted, tastes began to evolve.

In Michael Kantor and Laurence Maslon's *Broadway: The American Musical*, they point out that

> Although it was not the object of the exercise, Sondheim and Prince showed that there was nothing you couldn't put into a musical if you did it artfully and with integrity. You could gain the audience's sympathy for a serial killer; you could even get a couple of really boffo laughs out of his deranged accomplice. Sondheim and Prince were only the most daring of the Broadway practitioners who sought, throughout the last hundred years, to push the envelope. With *Sweeney Todd*, they slashed it wide open.[5]

Paving the Way

In 1979, *Sweeney Todd*'s unique blend of musical styles and genres, as well as its deep dive into the darker depths of storytelling, was a mixture of high and low entertainment that was new to Broadway.[6] Several productions in the 1980s and 1990s followed a similar path by adapting classic stories into musicals—Victor Hugo's nineteenth-century novel became the megahit *Les Misérables* (1987) and Puccini's tragic opera *La Bohéme* was modernized as *Rent* (1996). Other stories were musicalized: *Little Shop of Horrors* (1982) was originally a low-budget 1960 horror comedy about a carnivorous plant; the roots of *Carrie* (1988) were in Stephen King's blood-soaked 1974 horror tale about a persecuted teenage girl.

Sweeney Todd showed the opportunities for more serious storytelling, especially stories that avoided traditional happy endings that had been typical of "Golden Age" Broadway musicals from the 1940s and 1950s. Jason Robert Brown's *Parade* (1999) retold the true story of a 1915 lynching in Georgia. *Spring Awakening* (2006) was about teenage sexuality, angst, and suicide in nineteenth-century Germany. And *next to normal* (2009) was the story of a modern woman with bipolar disorder grappling with depression and some uniquely distorted reality. *Fun Home* (2015) used dark humor to dig into personal identity, homosexuality, and suicide.

The phenomenally popular and award-winning *Hamilton* (2015) by Lin-Manuel Miranda told the story, both tragic and joyous, of a significant figure from American history. W. Anthony Sheppard pointed out that *Hamilton*'s "prologue was modeled on the opening of *Sweeney Todd*, with each character singing about the title character before the title character speaks."[7] Tony Award winners such as *Hadestown* (2019), which dug back into mythology for a fanciful story about poverty and lost love, and *A Strange Loop* (2022), about a queer man struggling to write a musical, proved that shows with engaging scores could address just about any subject.

Sweeney Todd marked an inflection point in musical theater that invited greater experimentation in subject matter told with seriously composed music—stepping beyond happy tunes and flashy choreography—that added considerable power and depth to storytelling. Sondheim's masterpiece paved the way for serious, character-driven scores to find success on Broadway and beyond.

Sondheim himself personally exercised this newfound freedom to explore stories never previously imagined for Broadway. Especially *Assassins* (1990), his own show about people who sought fame by shooting American presidents, and *Passion* (1994), telling an almost unbelievable love affair between a handsome soldier and a sickly, unattractive woman, are difficult stories about off-kilter characters. Treated seriously in musicals, Sondheim learned through *Sweeney Todd* that audiences could be reached with an astute blending of score, characters, and story.[8]

Sweeney Todd is one of the very few works of musical theater that has led a double life, spending time in the world of opera, starting almost immediately after its Broadway debut. In 1984, Prince staged it for opera companies in Houston and New York City; Lyric Opera of Chicago produced it in 2002 with renowned baritone Bryn Terfel in the title role. It was produced at England's Opera North (in Leeds, 2002) and London's Royal Opera House (2003). While it's not quite standard opera repertory in the twenty-first century, when contemporary opera companies decide to present a new work ("new" at least by opera standards, where classic productions date from the nineteenth century) with strong audience appeal, *Sweeney Todd* is often the first choice.

Sweeney Todd's adaptability—enhanced by Sondheim's willingness to permit and work with directors who took new approaches to stage the tale—also helped broaden its impact. Prince initially doubted the financial wisdom of Sondheim's wishes to make the show intimate and scary, and his epic approach held sway for a decade or so. (The grand scale of the original on Broadway was surely a part of what got the attention of opera companies.)

But Sondheim's instinct for smaller staging has proved equally durable, adaptable, and impactful—from early productions teasingly called "Teeny Todd" to unusual theatrical approaches such as Doyle's actor/musician production early in the twenty-first century. Burton's 2007 cinematic adaptation, which stripped away the tale's storytelling frame and focused on fierce human emotions and gallons of spurting blood, proved that the tale could reach even broader audiences, especially with screen star Johnny Depp as the spooky, sexy, murderous barber.

No one can help, nothing can hide you — Isn't that Sweeney there beside you?

Today, the "Tale of Sweeney Todd" is so familiar that it can be referenced and adapted into popular entertainment. The public now has at least a passing acquaintance with the story of the malevolent Demon Barber. That's one more sign of how Sondheim's masterpiece has had a far-reaching impact on contemporary culture, well beyond that of most Broadway musicals. Here are a few examples of the tale's appearance in modern media.

In 2003, a satirical show by Joanne Bogart and Eric Rockwell, *The Musical of Musicals (The Musical)*, used a classical melodrama plot ("I can't pay the rent") to parody the works and styles of several renowned creators of musical theater: Rodgers & Hammerstein; Jerry Herman; Andrew Lloyd Webber; Kander & Ebb; and, of course, Sondheim.[9] The Sondheim parody, amusingly titled "A Little Complex," is set in a New York apartment complex inhabited by a bevy of neurotics: the crazed landlord Jitter (as unbalanced as Sweeney) is an unappreciated artist who plots to murder his tenants. They include a young woman, Jeune, obsessed with birds (think Johanna twittering her way through "Green Finch and Linnet Bird"); Billy, a deep-thinking composer (like Sondheim himself); and Abby, a pessimistic alcoholic (like Elaine Stritch as *Company*'s acid-tongued Joanne: "Everybody dies!" or Mary Flynn, *Merrily We Roll Along*'s often drunk and sardonic novelist). The Sondheim parody is full of tortured lyrics and dissonant melodies, and things don't end well for most of the characters.

In October 2009, the long-running animated television series *The Simpsons*, in its twentieth annual Halloween installment of "Treehouse of Horror," very loosely parodied *Sweeney Todd* in "There's No Business Like Moe Business." The episode's third and final seven-minute segment told a story of Homer Simpson's death that leads to a blood-infused microbrew served at Moe's Tavern. The episode ranged well beyond Sondheim's show, including a few pokes at Andrew Lloyd Webber's *Phantom of the Opera*.

The Office, a mockumentary TV sitcom about employees at a mundane branch office of a paper company in Scranton, Pennsylvania, used *Sweeney Todd* as a key element in "Andy's Play," the third episode of the series' seventh season in 2010. Andy (B. J. Novak) is an ineffective salesman inclined to sing at inappropriate moments. In a community theater production of *Sweeney Todd*, he is cast as the romantic Anthony Hope. To promote the production at the Loose Screw Playhouse, Andy and his castmates invade the office, flash mob style, to perform "The Ballad of Sweeney Todd." Most of the *Office* drudges are mystified, and no one knows anything about *Sweeney Todd* except Michael (Steve Carell), the manager, who auditioned for the title role but was not cast. No one is eager to attend Andy's performance, but several of them do—and the production has some comic interruptions, including Andy's cell phone ringing in the middle of a scene and Michael booing the actor chosen to play Sweeney. Surprisingly, the musical numbers from the show used in the episode—"The Ballad of Sweeney Todd"; "Johanna," sung by Andy; and "By the Sea"—are capably performed . . . much to everyone's surprise.

Schmigadoon, the 2021–3 musical comedy series on Apple TV+ satirized and paid homage to classic musicals. Its second season was set in a gritty city ("Schmicago") and had its way with Broadway shows from the 1960s and 1970s. Stars performed in an array of mash-ups of well-known titles: Kristin Chenoweth and Alan Cumming led a tuneful parody of *Sweeney Todd* with a set of high-spirited orphans, in the style of *Annie*. Chenoweth played Miss Codwell, stitching together Mrs. Lovett and *Annie*'s cruel, child-hating Miss Hannigan; Cumming was Dooley Blight, a vengeance-seeking butcher whose failing business required an injection of fresh meat. In this twist on *Sweeney Todd*, it's Miss Codwell who plans to use the rambunctious orphans for pie fillings in Blight's shop. They perform "Good Enough to Eat," a clever parody of "A Little Priest" with an amusing slice of *Annie*'s "It's a Hard-Knock Life." The episode includes two other amusing *Sweeney* song parodies. Chenoweth sings "The Worst Brats in Town," inspired by Mrs. Lovett's "The Worst Pies in London," and Cumming marches through "There Was a Butcher," inspired by *Sweeney Todd*'s "Poor Thing."[10]

In the twenty-first century, *Sweeney Todd* has become a legendary masterpiece, adored by Broadway performers. A particularly striking piece of evidence was part of the 2017 edition of the Easter Bonnet Competition, a benefit for Broadway Cares/Equity Fights AIDS. This annual New York City event celebrates six weeks of fundraising by actors who perform on Broadway, Off-Broadway, and in national touring productions. It features performers who sing, dance, and wear elaborate, specially designed Easter bonnets. In 2017, the cast of Lin-Manuel Miranda's Tony Award-winning *Hamilton* performed a spot-on parody of *Sweeney Todd*. Miranda played "Demon Barber Sweeney Todd," a title that perfectly matched the rhythm of "Alexander Hamilton," that character's introductory line in Miranda's hit production. The entire *Hamilton* company, employing some signature moves by choreographer Andy Blankenbuehler choreography, offered a condensed parody of *Sweeney Todd*. It culminated with Jonathan Groff, who played *Hamilton*'s petulant King George III, coming forward wearing an immense meat pie bonnet in place of his costume crown.[11]

Putting It Together

Just how important and influential is *Sweeney Todd*? In 2024, it was ranked by the Broadway website *Theatermania* as one of the most indispensable American musicals. Journalist Zachary Stewart wrote,

> Walk into any bar in Hell's Kitchen, and you'll be inundated with opinions about what stories can and cannot be turned into musicals. Stephen Sondheim spent his entire career pushing against such narrow-minded opinions, most forcefully with *Sweeney Todd*, the best deployment of horror in a Broadway musical. Sondheim and book writer Hugh Wheeler tell the story of a Fleet Street barber driven mad by revenge—and by the pie shop proprietress who sees him as the key to her happily-ever-after. The menacing wind and string triplets in the opening number perfectly set the skin-crawling tone. But in typically Sondheim fashion, humor grows in the darkest of places, like the brilliant first act closer "A Little Priest," which is itself an indictment of dog-eat-dog capitalism. No other musical is simultaneously so satisfying and sickening.[12]

There is plenty of consensus about the cultural impact of *Sweeney Todd*. Academic Joanne Gordon summed it up concisely: "In its operatic boldness, its schizophrenic synthesis of elemental comedy and tragedy, it approaches the greatness of total theater. It elicits both intellectual excitement and shattering emotional intensity. By crossing all the accepted boundaries of musical theater, Sondheim has redefined, regenerated, and dignified the genre."[13] One might even call it "bloody good"!

Appendix 1
Sweeney Todd Productions Worldwide

Stephen Sondheim's *Sweeney Todd* has been staged around the world, particularly but not exclusively at opera houses, throughout the late twentieth and early twenty-first centuries. After its poorly received London debut in 1980, it became a popular staple produced by theater and opera companies across Great Britain. But its appeal spread well beyond England. It gained acceptance with numerous international opera companies around the world, especially in Australia, thanks to early productions in the 1980s. Perhaps directors sought to redeem the Commonwealth nation's reputation as the desperate place of painful exile to which Benjamin Barker was wrongly exiled by the lecherous Judge Turpin.

A quick search indicates that since 1987, there have been at least fifty-five professional and amateur Australian productions of *Sweeney Todd*. Since the original production's Broadway debut in 1979, Sondheim's masterpiece has become a worldwide phenomenon, sometimes in English and occasionally in remarkable translations.

Australia

The first "down under" staging of *Sweeney Todd* was in April 1983, an amateur production by the Cheltenham Light Opera Company (CLOC) at Monash University's Clayton Alexander Theatre in Melbourne. It was directed by

David Wilson, with Ken Taylor serving as musical director. Donald Cant won an award for his performance as Sweeney Todd; June Lownds played Mrs. Lovett.

Gale Edwards directed Australia's first professional production of *Sweeney Todd* in Adelaide for The State Opera of South Australia (September 1987). The much-praised cast included Lyndon Terracini as Todd, Nancye Hayes as Mrs. Lovett, and Peter Cousens as Anthony. In September 1987, the Melbourne Theatre Company presented *Sweeney Todd* directed by Roger Hodgman. With a pit orchestra of ten musicians, it was performed at the Melbourne Playhouse. In 1988, Hodgman's production toured to Her Majesty's Theatre in Sydney and Riverstage in Brisbane. Peter Carroll played Sweeney; Geraldine Turner, the renowned Australian musical theater performer, was Mrs. Lovett. She was recognized as the Female Musical Theatre Performer of the Year in 1988 by the Australian Entertainment Mo Awards, one of many awards she received during her long career.

In 2015, Victorian Opera and New Zealand Opera co-produced *Sweeney Todd* with performances at Australia's Melbourne Arts Center (July 16–25) and in New Zealand at Auckland Civic Theatre (September 17–24), in Wellington's St. James Theatre (September 9–October 5), and finally in Christchurch's Isaac Theatre Royal (October 12–15). Directed by Stuart Maunder, with Phoebe Briggs as musical director, the production featured international opera star, baritone Teddy Tahu Rhodes, a native of Christchurch, as the Demon Barber. Antoinette Halloran was Mrs. Lovett. Rhodes made Sweeney an uncompromising villain. According to one reviewer, "It is surely the ultimate accolade that you can hardly wait for the next appearance of a character who is so utterly unlovable."[1] Another commentator said Halloran as Mrs. Lovett "cooks up a brilliant incarnation of the villainess of the piece, more potent for remaining human at every point."[2]

In June 2019, for *Sweeney Todd*'s fortieth anniversary, a limited run was presented by Life Like Company at Her Majesty's Theatre in Melbourne and Darling Harbour Theatre in Sydney. It starred Anthony Warlog as Sweeney, Gina Riley as Mrs. Lovett, Debra Byrne as the Beggar Woman, Michael Falzon as Adolfo Pirelli, Jonathan Hickey as Tobias Ragg, and Daniel Sumegi as Judge Turpin.

The fiftieth anniversary season of the Sydney Opera House included a production of *Sweeney Todd* (July 26–August 27, 2023), again shared with New

Zealand Opera. Ben Mingay played the murderous barber. His performance persuaded the audience to invest in Sweeney's humanity and recognize the effects of the deep hurt caused by his experiences, even when he was at his most horrifying. Antoinette Halloran reprised her 2015 performance as Mrs. Lovett, matching Mingay with her superb comic timing and precise vocals. The director was again Stuart Maunder. Scenic design using dark wood was by Roger Kirk (also costumes); Phillip Lethelean and Jason Morphett designed the lighting. Sound reproduction, thanks to Jim Atkins's fastidious design, was admirable. Conductor Simon Holt led a nine-piece musical ensemble. The cast included Margaret Trubiano (Beggar Woman), Jeremi Campese (Tobias). Ashleigh Rubenach (Johanna) and Harry Targett (Anthony) were the lovers, Dean Vice (Judge Turpin) and Kanen Breen (Beadle). Benjamin Rasheed played Pirelli as well as Jonas Fogg.

Japan

Tokyo's Imperial Theater, the longtime flagship of the Toho, Inc., entertainment company, was Japan's first Western-style theater, built in 1911. It presented a very early *Sweeney Todd* production in 1981: Matsumoto Koshiro played Sweeney, and Otori Ran was Mrs. Lovett. Other performers included Nakamura Tako (Judge Turpin), Yamaya Hatsuo (Beadle), Sawada Ayako (Johanna). Avant-garde theater director Suzuki Tadashi staged the show with a precise, tense, and exciting flavor using a Japanese translation by Kurahashi Ken and Kai Marie.

Amon Miyamoto, the founding artistic director of the Kanagawa Art Theatre and one of the foremost Japanese interpreters of Sondheim's works, staged and choreographed *Sweeney Todd* in 2007 at Tokyo's Nissey Theatre. His production was subsequently presented in 2011 (Aoyama Theatre, Tokyo), in 2013 (Aichi Arts Center, Nagoya; Aoyama Theatre, Tokyo; Theater BRAVA!/Osaka; and Kanagawa Arts Theatre); and in 2016 (Tokyo Metropolitan Theatre; Theater BRAVA! In Osaka, and the Nagoya's Aichi Arts Center). In 2024 it was revived by the Japan-British Society at Tokyo's Tatemono Brillia Hall (March 9–30). That production starred Masachika Ichimura as Sweeney and Shinobu Otake as Mrs. Lovett.

Israel

The first performance of *Sweeney Todd* in Israel was by the **Israeli National Opera** in 1982 using a Hebrew translation by lyricist, translator, poet, and broadcast personality Ehud Manor. In 1991, the **New Israeli Opera** mounted a full production, directed by David Alden and sung in English. Veteran star Timothy Nolen was Sweeney, and future Broadway star Roger Bart, age twenty-nine, was Tobias. Israeli opera singer and teacher Robin Weisel-Capsouto played Mrs. Lovett. In September–October 2020, it was back on a stage in Israel with a new translation by director Roi Dolev; musical direction by Yuval Goldstein.

Spain

On April 5, 1995, in Barcelona, *Sweeney Todd* had its Spanish premiere in a translation into the Catalan dialect by Roser Batalla and Roger Peña. The production of the Drama Centre of the Government of Catalonia opened at the Theater Poliorama and subsequently moved to the Apollo. It was staged by the renowned Spanish director Mario Gas. The cast was led by Constantino Romero as Sweeney and Vicky Peña as Mrs. Lovett. Maria Josep Peris was Johanna, Muntsa Rius played Tobias, Pep Molina was Anthony. Xavier Ribera-Vall portrayed Judge Turpin and Teresa Vallicrosa as the Beggar Woman. The production's critical acclaim and warm audience reactions drew Sondheim to Barcelona; he expressed delight with the production. It subsequently moved to Madrid. The production received more than fifteen awards.

Finland

The Finnish National Opera performed *Sweeney Todd* in Helsinki in rep from September 9, 1997, to October 10, 1998. Sweeney was played by Sauli Tiilikainen; Ritva Auvinen was Mrs. Lovett. Staffan Aspergren directed the production.

Iceland

The Icelandic Opera performed *Sweeney Todd*, translated into the Icelandic language by Gísli Rúnar Jónsson, in the fall of November 2004, the first time the show was produced in that North Atlantic island nation. It was directed by Magnús Geir Þórðarson. The production's scenic design resulted in the most complex, multilayered set ever constructed by the opera company; its designers were Freyr Hilmarsson and Stigur Steinbórsson. A traditional barber chair was redesigned so Sweeney's victims could be dropped to Mrs. Lovett's bakehouse basement. Ágúst Ólafsson played Sweeney.

Philippines

Repertory Philippines produced *Sweeney Todd* (November 13–December 13, 2009), the same company that staged its Philippine premiere in 1982. Menchu Lauchengco-Yulo played Johanna in that original production. In 2009, she was Mrs. Lovett. She was joined by Audie Gemora as Sweeney. "For all the varied productions and roles they have been through, they both agree on one thing as far as *Sweeney Todd* is concerned: It is a dream come true."[3] The 2009 production also featured Liesl Batucan (Beggar Woman), Robbie Guevara (Beadle), Robbie Zialcita (Pirelli), Franco Laurel (Anthony), Lena McKenzie (Johanna), Marvin Ong (Tobias), and Roger Chua (Judge Turpin).

Bobby Garcia's production of *Sweeney Todd* happened a decade later in 2019, with Broadway star Lea Salonga as Mrs. Lovett. It was presented at the Theatre at Solaire in Manila by the Atlantis Theatrical Entertainment Group. Garcia staged the production; musical direction was by Salonga's brother Gerard, leading the FILharmoniKA Orchestra. Philippine rock star Jett Pangan played Sweeney. Other cast members were Gerald Santos (Anthony), Nyoy Volante (Pirelli), Mikkie Bradshaw-Volante (Johanna), Ima Castro (Beggar Woman), Andrew Fernando (Judge Turpin), Luigi Quesada (Tobias), and Arman Ferrer (Beadle).

A review in the *Philippine Daily Inquirer* observed that director Garcia

> set his sights on finding that elusive sliver of sanity amid the deafening madness. His *Sweeney* is no primal scream, but a prolonged, muffled psychotic breakdown unraveling on the derelict, multi-story car depot designed by David Gallo, a renowned Broadway designer, and lit with masterly exactitude by Aaron Porter. This scene of industrial decay serves as a magnified stand-in for the state of mind of its leading characters.[4]

France

In 2010, Lee Blakeley successfully staged Sondheim's *A Little Night Music* at Théâtre du Châtelet, a nineteenth-century theater and opera house with 2,500 seats. A year later (April 22–May 21, 2011), Blakeley returned to stage a brilliant new production of *Sweeney Todd*, the second time for the Châtelet to stage a work by Sondheim. It recreated nineteenth-century Industrial Revolution London down to the smallest detail and was sung in English.

A forty-six-piece orchestra (twenty-seven strings) was enthusiastically led by American conductor David Charles Abell, bringing out the score's color. The set was designed by Tanya McCallin, and lighting was overseen by Rick Fisher. Rod Gilfry played Sweeney, and Caroline O'Connor was Mrs. Lovett, a performance praised by Sondheim, who personally attended. Other cast members were Rebecca de Pont Davies (Beggar Woman), Rebecca Bottone (Johanna), and Jonathan Best (Judge Turpin). Pascal Charbonneau took on the role of Tobias, and his sweet tenor made "Not While I'm Around" a high point.

France's second oldest opera company, Opéra de Toulon, which opened in 1862, broadened its repertoire in the twenty-first century with occasional musical theater productions, including Sondheim's *Follies* in 2015. That production's success led to another well-received Sondheim show the following year: *Sweeney Todd* (November 11–13, 2016), performed in English and directed by Daniel Glet. Olivier Bénézech conducted the Opéra de Toulon's orchestra and choir. Jérôme Pradon starred as Sweeney with Alyssa Stillburn playing Mrs. Lovett. Other performers included Sarah Tullamore (Beggar Woman), Maxime de Toledo (Judge Turpin), Thomas Morris (Pirelli/Fogg), Sinan Bertrand (Beadle), Sarah Manesse (Johanna), Ashley Stillburn (Anthony), and Julien Salvia (Tobias).

Poland

Sweeney Todd's Polish premiere took place at Teatre Rozrywki, Chorzow, Poland, on May 1, 2012. The production continued in repertory through May 1, 2014. Jacenty Jędrusik played Sweeney; Maria Meyer was honored with the 2013 Golden Mask award for her performance as Mrs. Lovett.

Canada

Toronto's Canada Stage Company produced *Sweeney Todd* (March 27–April 19, 2003) at the Bluma Appel Theatre. Sheila McCarthy, a regular at Ontario's Stratford Festival, played Mrs. Lovett. George Masswohl was Sweeney. Morris Panych was the director and choreographer; Bruce Kellett was the musical director. Scenic design was by Ken McDonald, costumes by Nancy Bryant.

Quebec City-based Théâtre Décibel produced the French-speaking world premiere of the show. Translated by Joëlle Bond, the production was presented from October 28 to November 8, 2014, at the century-old Théâtre Capitol de Québec at Place d'Youville. The cast included Renaud Paradis as Sweeney and Katee Julien as Mrs. Lovett, Jean Petitclerc as Judge Turpin, Sabrina Ferland as the Beggar Woman, Pierre-Olivier Grondin as Anthony Hope, Andréane Bouladier as Johanna, and David Noël as Tobias. Louis Morin was the stage director; Guillaume Saint-Laurent was the musical director.

Scotland and Wales

In 2010, Scotland's leading theater for musicals, Dundee Rep, produced a modern dress take on Sondheim's masterpiece, set in an environment of shipping containers and a gantry crane. Staged by James Brining and designed by Colin Richmond, the *Guardian*, calling the production "rich, vivid and rewarding," described it, saying, "for all its throat-slashing gore, *Sweeney Todd* owes as much to the arc of Greek and Shakespearean tragedy as it does to Victorian melodrama. Like Macbeth, the murderous Todd is defeated by the same compulsion that brought him greatness in the first place."[5] Brining's production featured David Birrell's Sweeney as "cool and enigmatic, self-contained, focused on revenge." Ann Louise Ross was Mrs. Lovett.

In the autumn of 2015, Brining's *Sweeney Todd* was revived by the Wales National Opera for its "Madness" season. It was a co-production with the West Yorkshire Playhouse and the Royal Exchange Manchester. With David Arnsperger as Sweeney and Janis Kelly as Mrs. Lovett, it was performed in Cardiff before touring to Southampton, Bristol, Llandudno, Oxford, Liverpool, and Birmingham. The production was based on Brining's 2010 smaller production at Scotland's Dundee Rep.

South Africa

South African theater manager Pieter Toerien produced *Sweeney Todd* at his Montecasino Theatre in Johannesburg (October 10 to December 13, 2015). From there, it transferred to Cape Town's Theatre on the Bay (February 19 to April 9, 2016). Directed by Steven Stead and designed by Greg King, the production featured an all-star South African cast led by Jonathan Roxmouth as Sweeney and Charon Williams-Ros as Mrs. Lovett.

South Korea

The first Korean production of *Sweeney Todd* was in Seoul in 2007, translated into the Korean language. It was named the year's Best Foreign Musical for its artistic and quality presentation.[6] But it was not a bestseller with Korean audiences, who at the time preferred more bright, lyrical music theater. *Sweeney Todd*'s dissonant music and strong language telling the story of bloody revenge failed to capture sufficient public interest. However, tastes evolved, and by 2016, it was staged by the OD Company, and its serious drama and storytelling were more deeply appreciated. When that production was repeated in 2019, it was a hit.[7]

In 2022, produced by Shin Chun-soo at Seoul's Charlotte Theater (December 1, 2022–March 5, 2023), it featured three women rotating in the role of Mrs. Lovett. All three—Jeon Mi-do, Kim Ji-hyun, and Lina—were returning to the role, having appeared in one of the 2016 or 2019 productions. The women agreed that the role was demanding. "I really had a hard and stressful time playing Mrs. Lovett in 2019, which was my first time. But this time around, I was able to have more fun because I was already familiar with the lines, staging and the music."[8] Three actors—Lee Kyoo-hyung, Shin Sing-rok, and Kang Pil-suk—also rotated in the role of Sweeney. Kang Pil-suk said, "This is a show with incredible energy both in its music and the plot. It is very exciting as an actor to be able to absorb all that energy and relay it to the audience."[9]

The Korea Herald described the 2023 production of *Sweeney Todd* as one that was "warming up the cold winter season."[10]

Mexico

The first Mexican production of *Sweeney Todd* (July 7–September 30, 2018) happened at Cia de Teatro Musical Salle in Mexico City. It was directed by Ricardo Diaz and produced by David Cuevas of the Coyoacanense Cultural Forum. Beto Torres (Sweeney) and Lupita Sandoval (Mrs. Lovett) led a cast of Mexican performers that included José Andrés Mojica, Mario Beller, Eduardo Ibarra, Alejandra Desiderio, Sonia Monroy, Daniel Paéz, and Adrian Mejia.

It was again presented in Mexico City at the 260-seat Milan Theater (October to December 2023) where it was presented by Vatru Entertainment and Ícaro Comapñía Teatral. After winning numerous Metro Theatre Awards (the Tony Awards of Mexico City for best musical, director, costume design, scenic design, lighting, makeup, actress, supporting actress, supporting actor), it was extended to March 3, 2024, with its final performances being completely sold out.

Director Miguel Septién translated the show into Spanish, (*El Barbero Asesino de la Calle Fleet*). His version is now the Spanish translation licensed by Music Theatre International. His work was praised by critic Mariana Mijares, who stated that Septién was in charge "not only of direction but also of stage movement" and that the show "demonstrates his maturation . . . even down to the way he shows the Sweeney murders, inviting the viewer to join his game, without needing to see a single drop of blood in the process."[11]

Dano Coutiño was the production's musical director, leading five musicians on piano, flute, trombone, violin, and contrabass; together, they created the sound of organ prelude. The cast included Quecho Munõz (Sweeney), Flor Benítez (Lovett), Eduardo Siqueiros (Turpin), Jimena Parés (Beggar Woman), Luisa Cortés (Johanna), Ervey Ortegón (Anthony), Andres Elvira (Pirelli), José Grillet (Beadle), and Diego Enríquez (Toby). Here's a link to the trailer for this riveting production: https://tinyurl.com/SweeneyMexico2023

Switzerland

An English-language production of *Sweeney Todd* was presented from December 9, 2018, to January 11, 2019, at Opernhaus Zurich. International opera star Bryn Terfel was recruited to play Sweeney, and Angelika Kirschlager was Mrs. Lovett

Denmark

Sweeney Todd was produced by the Royal Danish Opera (November 23, 2019, to February 22, 2020) at the Copenhagen Opera House, a venue often compared acoustically to the Sydney Opera House. It was performed in English with Danish surtitles. James Brining, who staged modern dress productions previously throughout Great Britain (see "Scotland and Wales" above), and Caroline Chaney were the stage directors; the conductor was Ian Ryan. Paul Knudsen and David Kempster alternated in the role of Sweeney; Susanne Resmark and Alyssa Anderson played Mrs. Lovett in various performances.

Sweden

As early as March 1989, Swedish opera fans saw a production of *Sweeney Todd*, presented by Wermland Opera, featuring Björn Eduard as Sweeney and Anne Bolstad as Mrs. Lovett. It was conducted by Ole Wiggo Bang. The show's popularity continued in Sweden, including a four-week production in May and June 2008 by the Göteborg Opera with Michael McCarthy as Sweeney and Rosemary Ashe as Mrs. Lovett.

Swedish interest in Sondheim's masterpiece perhaps culminated in 2022. The Stockholm newspaper *Dagens Nyheter* proclaimed, "If you're going to play a musical on the national stage, you should start with *Sweeney Todd*." Michael Cavanagh staged it in an English-language production with Swedish surtitles for the Royal Swedish Opera (December 13, 2022–February 10, 2023). Ola Eliasson portrayed Sweeney (*Svenska Dagbladet* declared, "what a thunderous voice he has!"[12]) and Karolina Blixt was Mrs. Lovett (her "burlesque [performance was] the most vivid character of the show."[13]) The Royal Swedish Orchestra and the Royal Swedish Opera Chorus were conducted by David Björkman.

Appendix 2
Song-by-Song Commentary

Sondheim constructed the score of *Sweeney Todd* almost as if it were a puzzle with interlocking pieces and mystery clues. As mentioned in Chapter 6, he used the "Dies Irae" motif (derived from the opening notes of the medieval Roman Catholic "Mass of the Dead") as a thread to bind together the music and the Demon Barber's storytelling. In Joanne Gordon's *Art Isn't Easy*, she wrote, "with its widely recognized message of doom and its vision of horrors, guilts, and irreversible decisions of the Day of Judgment, [the motif] provides a key to the morbid complexity of Sweeney's character."[1]

In this appendix, *Sweeney Todd*'s musical numbers are discussed in order and in greater detail to demonstrate how they fit together, relate to one another, use musical motifs as clues to identify character and situation, and inject greater meaning into Sweeney's tragic tale. Listening to the incomparable original cast recording from 1979 (or to the New York Philharmonic's very complete live recording from 2001, which includes much of the show's spoken dialogue) while reading these notes is highly recommended.

Prelude and "The Ballad of Sweeney Todd"

The first music heard in most productions of *Sweeney Todd* is a Prelude full of the sinister chords of funereal organ music. Sondheim based these on the invocation "Kyrie eleison" ["Lord, have mercy"] from Roman Catholic church liturgies.[2] In *Sweeney Todd* they are often played furiously by a cadaverous organist with his back to the audience, a mysterious, frightening figure. This polytonal organ Prelude is full of foreshadowing: Lucy's "lament" theme "Alms, Alms" and Johanna's "Green Finch" theme, as well as the four notes of the Dies Irae melody.

It suggests that we are about to witness a scary silent movie with musical organ accompaniment. Sondheim envisioned *Sweeney Todd* as a "horror musical," and these opening notes are how he launched the tone for eerie, frightening storytelling.

"The Ballad of Sweeney Todd" is the show's theme song, repeatedly sung at key moments by the chorus (sometimes using solo lines or subsets of those performers; at one point it's harmonized by a trio; at another moment, a quintet handles it). This powerful and spooky number puts the "tale" in motion and establishes a pace for the show's momentum.

Sondheim began composing his musical score with this ballad. "Once I decided that there was going to be some kind of storytelling thing, then I went right for it. And then the rest of the score was pretty well composed in sequence . . . it started with 'The Ballad of Sweeney Todd.' Absolutely. The very first thing I wrote."[3]

As the curtain rises, a pair of working-class laborers are digging a grave. They stop to tear down a large drop bearing Cruikshank's cartoonish image of a beehive depicting the stratified, oppressive Victorian society. The organ music is startlingly drowned out by the shriek of a factory steam whistle.

The workers are joined by a dozen or so men and women, the downtrodden citizens of nineteenth-century London, looking like ghostly characters in a gaslit melodrama. As a chorus and individually, they menacingly sing "The Ballad of Sweeney Todd" straight to the audience. It sounds like a fearsome folk ballad. A single voice proclaims, "Attend the tale of Sweeney Todd," and another follows.

As the Ballad winds down, we hear "Swing your razor wide, Sweeney!" The Ballad climaxes with "a vocal scream—the sopranos on a brutally high C-sharp—that rivals the factory whistle."[4]

The balance of the song provides a chilling overview of what's to come as Sweeney rises from the grave with haunting words that the singers shrilly repeat. The lyrics use sententious, stilted Victorian rhetoric, especially the slightly antique word "attend." It has a double meaning—urging us to follow Sweeney's story but also as a reminder to pay heed to its moral lesson. (The ballad finishes with the tried-and-true storytelling trope of not giving away the ending.)

Reviewing *Sweeney Todd*'s original cast recording, Paul Wittke described "a scurrying low accompanying figure [that] reflects the sinister, disturbed tortured mind of Todd." He added, "The solemn funereal beat in the orchestral accompaniment gives the score its relentless, tragic processional movements. . . . As the plot thickens and twists, so does the musical element falling into place with hammer stroke accuracy."[5]

The ballad is sounded repeatedly throughout the show as a reminder of Sweeney's ghastly agenda. Writing about the score, scholar Larry Avis Brown said,

> To create a sense of gloom, Sondheim begins the piece in a very low register and adds a scurrying, low accompanying figure that periodically crescendos slightly as if something were about to happen and then does not. In this show, song is almost inseparable from dialogue; there are no comment songs, no inner monologues and no narrators as in previous shows. Nevertheless, the ballad establishes an overall presentational quality to the drama.[6]

The ballad echoes across the entirety of *Sweeney Todd*, from the opening to the finale. In between are a half dozen reminders from the chorus of the Demon Barber's bloody swath.[7] Although the ballad was one of the most iconic aspects of Sondheim and Prince's original production and many subsequent revivals, director Tim Burton's cinematic version removed all of itsiterations, relying instead on the hurtling momentum of the central characters' stories. (Practically speaking, it was also how Burton was able to trim the three-hour musical down to a riveting two-hour film.)

"No Place Like London"

As the weary and vengeful Benjamin Barker—now going by the name Sweeney Todd—and the earnest young sailor Anthony Hope arrive in London after their long sea voyage from Australia, their differing perspectives are evident. Anthony gushes buoyantly as he sings the song's ebullient title, while Sweeney glowers, responding in a minor key—an ironic, negative twist on the same words.

They are approached by the Beggar Woman, who slips back and forth between pitiful begging and graphic sexual solicitation (using language Sondheim largely invented).[8] It's the composer at his cleverest, tantalizing audiences with musical clues regarding her true identity. Her brief bawdy tune recurs at several crucial moments: it's the melody played elegantly by a string quartet in a scene recollecting the rape of Lucy Barker at Judge Turpin's party, the first step in her descent into the Beggar Woman. It makes its final appearance when the orchestra performs it as a dirge when Sweeney realizes that he has unwittingly murdered his wife.

"The Barber and His Wife"

As Sweeney finishes his diatribe about the injustices of London and beyond, he sings yearningly of a "foolish" barber who had a lovely wife, Lucy, and a baby daughter, Johanna. His recollection is full of tenderness, and it's obvious that he is describing his own story. It turns quickly to pain and loss as he explains how the corrupt Judge Turpin convicted the barber unjustly of a crime and transported him to Australia so he could have his way with Barker's innocent wife.

"The Worst Pies in London"

Sweeney wanders into Mrs. Lovett's pie shop, who's had almost no customers for weeks. She recognizes him immediately but doesn't let on as she runs through the challenges faced by her struggling business. Her pies are the "worst," she tells him, as she flicks flies off her dough, drops it on the floor, dusts it off, and continues rhythmically pounding and shaping the pie crust. She is certain a competitor is filling pies with the remains of stray cats.

With a driving beat, accented by her pounding the dough and swatting insects, Mrs. Lovett sings of her plight as "a woman alone," switching back and forth between two different moods—frantic and practical in 4/4 time and wistful and passionate in 3/4 time. Sondheim's skill at blending music and action gives a capable performer plenty of complex physical business.[9]

Mrs. Lovett is eager for Sweeney to become more than a customer. She treats him to an all-but-inedible pie that he spits on the floor. He asks about her upstairs room, and she explains that it belonged to a barber who was unjustly transported to Australia. Of course, she's seeking to confirm that this odd man is, in fact, Benjamin Barker, whom she lusted after fifteen years earlier.

"Poor Thing"

The melody of "The Barber and His Wife" returns shortly, as Mrs. Lovett restates her version of the barber's "foolishness." But in her version, it's the barber who was "beautiful" rather than his wife—and her own romantic feelings are evident. She's eager to be certain that the man before her is indeed Benjamin Barker, who has returned to London.

Mrs. Lovett relates the story of Lucy being assaulted by Judge Turpin, assisted by the Beadle at a lascivious private party that is reenacted in a dumb show performed upstage. The dance music,[10] played by a string quartet, is the same melody as the Beggar Woman's tune from the opening scene, another early clue to her true identity. Lucy is described as the victim of a horrible transgression.

Sweeney becomes increasingly agitated as Mrs. Lovett sings "Poor Thing," retelling the story of Lucy's violation. His agonized outburst identifies who he is. He insists he is no longer Benjamin Barker. He has become Sweeney Todd, a man obsessed with vengeance. She tells him Lucy "swallowed poison" and that Judge Turpin took in Johanna as his ward, facts that deepen Sweeney's towering rage.

"My Friends"

Mrs. Lovett retrieves the pair of chased-silver, straight-edge razors that Benjamin Barker left behind when he was banished to Australia. She has saved them for fifteen years, convinced he would return. They are valuable, but she never sold them to supplement her meager income. She gives him the tools he needs to return to barbering. But due to his maniacal obsession, he immediately sees them as the means to avenge the wrongs done to him and his family.

His response to receiving the razors, "My Friends," is *Sweeney Todd*'s most passionate, almost operatic music, a tender love song to shaving implements with bloody potential. Caressing them tremulously, he addresses them in intimate, personal phrases, calling them his "faithful friends." Michael Cerveris, who played Sweeney in John Doyle's 2005 actor/musician production, said, "Musically, it's sort of opening a door into a part of Sweeney that you haven't seen yet. You know, there is this loving person in him, and there's a tenderness that you see in that song, in relation to these cold pieces of steel."[11]

Music in a minor key only occasionally appears in Broadway musicals, but it's an essential element of "My Friends." "Although use of the minor key does not always indicate mysterious and sinister moods," scholar Larry Avis Brown pointed out, "here it combines with haunting lyrics as a foreboding sign that Sweeney's sanity might be in question. Establishing a spiritual bond with one's razors is not exactly the occupation of a sound mind."[12]

Teaching this number to music students in a master class, Sondheim told a young singer that the song was written with "a trance-like quality. The reason that I wrote this rhythmically so squarely is because he's falling into a state of almost semi self-hypnosis. So it must have that feeling. . . . This is a ritual."[13] Sondheim also explained that the opening lines have many sibilant "S" sounds to give them a whispered quality.

The number employs the "Dies Irae" motif—although it's masked by an inversion, with a note from the chord that's not the root now in the bass position—another foreboding clue to Sweeney's murderous intentions. Brown puts it in the context of the sinister melody coming in the next number: "In 'Epiphany' the motif appears subtly in the low brass accompaniment starting just before the lines, 'They all deserve to die! Tell you why, Mrs. Lovett, tell you why.' On this day of wrath, Sweeney's razor becomes the Grim Reaper's sickle as he executes justice on the human race for its sins."[14]

Conductor Paul Gemignani, asked by public radio host Terry Gross to choose a number that sticks with him, cited this song. "What's so wonderful about this moment?" she asked. Gemignani said, "Well, the beauty of the music and the irony of the idea, it gives you something to perform. It's not 32 bars in 4/4 time. It's a beautiful melody . . . [an] intense, dramatic moment that's taking the story from one place to another. That is the theater to me, musical or otherwise."[15]

It's truly a melodramatic horror movie scene as Sweeney brandishes a glistening razor and declares that his arm is complete again—as a tool of bloody destruction.[16] While this is happening, Mrs. Lovett makes futile, musically counterpointed attempts to draw attention to herself as Sweeney's devoted friend. But he remains oblivious.

"Green Finch and Linnet Bird"

After the foreboding ending of "My Friends," the story shifts to a simpler character, Johanna Barker, Sweeney's sweetly innocent daughter. She is essentially a prisoner as the ward of the lascivious Judge Turpin, who intends to marry her and keep her away from the world. She identifies with the caged singing birds that can be purchased from a street vendor passing by. "Green Finch and Linnet Bird" is a beautiful, heartrending soprano aria with a chirping, almost birdlike accompaniment. It's in the style of an "art song," which is how Sondheim described it.

But its winsome melody belies how Johanna, rather simpleminded and flighty, nevertheless recognizes that she is indeed a captive. Since she cannot fly, she yearns for the birds to teach her how to sing. Her song does not end on the first scale degree ("Do") as many melodies resolve. Rather, perhaps conveying a lack of fulfillment, it lands on the unresolved fifth scale degree ("Sol").

Peering out her upstairs window, she spies Anthony Hope wandering by, and they feel an instantaneous—indeed melodramatically coincidental—connection.

"Ah, Miss"

The romantic song Anthony breathlessly sings, having exchanged a fleeting glance with Johanna and instantly fallen in love, begins with a few bars of the same melody he sang in the show's opening when he professed his wonder at the beauties of London. As he is about to depart, the Beggar Woman appears—unknown to Johanna, she is in fact the girl's mother, Lucy Barker, permanently damaged and unrecognizable. Anthony asks her about the young lady. She tells him Johanna is harshly protected by the unscrupulous judge. She propositions Anthony again, then runs off. He buys a singing bird for Johanna, and she comes down to the street to accept his gift.

"Johanna" (Anthony)

Anthony sings an ardent aria, as masculine for him as "Green Finch" was feminine for Johanna. It's an outright love song, imbued with aching tenderness. "Sondheim has been criticized throughout his career for writing cold, unemotional music," wrote Steven Suskin, "but this is a fallacy; 'Johanna' is sheer beauty in music."[17] It has almost no dissonant harmonies.

Sadly, the bird Anthony intends for Johanna has its existence cut short when Turpin appears and orders the Beadle to send Anthony packing. To underscore the seriousness of the Judge's bidding, the Beadle wrings the bird's neck, a not-so-subtle message that Johanna's circumstances could be dire, and the implications for Anthony are no better. Left alone on the street, the young sailor continues to voice his passion and concludes that he must steal her away.

"Pirelli's Miracle Elixir"

Following Anthony's violent treatment by the Beadle, "Pirelli's Miracle Elixir" is a long jaunty scene of comic relief. It demonstrates Sondheim's ability to combine music, lyrics, and dialogue as an entertaining, performable sequence. With church bells ringing, a street urchin, Tobias Ragg, wearing an ample wig, exuberantly delivers a rhythmic, thumping, rapid-fire sales pitch to a crowd assembled at St. Dunstan's Marketplace. (The bells are a sort of counterpart to the "Dies Irae" theme.)

The elixir, in truth just foul-smelling snake oil, is guaranteed to "Banish Baldness." It's obviously a quack product from "Signor Adolfo Pirelli—Haircutter, Barber, Toothpuller to His Royal Majesty the King of Naples." His thinly veiled pose as a world-traveling cultured gentleman suggests he is "Eyetalian," according to Mrs. Lovett, who adds, "All the rage, he is."

Simpleminded Toby's job is to attract a crowd with his infectious, heavily rhymed song accompanied by a tin drum.[18] It's a gleeful showcase that encompasses several rhythmic styles, starting with a sort of march and then jumping to a double-time polka. The assembled throng does not sing as a chorus: instead, individuals voice endorsements and skepticism. This range of reaction is more natural than a unified choral response.

Mrs. Lovett and Sweeney observe the crowd from the sidelines. He passes judgment—announcing the elixir to be nothing more than a mixture of piss and ink. Toby struggles desperately to obscure this revelation, while the barber and Mrs. Lovett respond to the rhyming sales pitch with their own sly rhymed remarks.

"The Contest"

Flamboyant Pirelli bursts from behind the curtain of his caravan with a dramatic flourish, wearing an elegant suit. He seeks to charm the crowd and sell his elixir with grand pronouncements and promises. Sweeney interrupts and challenges him to a barbering contest; he asks the Beadle to judge. The contest is obviously part of Sweeney's plan to win support for his shop, but it's clear his underlying intention is for the Beadle to recommend his services to Judge Turpin. After the contest, the Beadle nearly recognizes Sweeney ("it seems your face is known to me"), but Mrs. Lovett distracts him with an explanation that he's her cousin from Birmingham.

Toby's gleeful pitch and Pirelli's ostentatious song as he shaves a man from the crowd are diegetic numbers.[19] Pirelli hams it up from start to finish and concludes by hitting an unnaturally high note. He has examined Sweeney's razors and recognized an opportunity to expose Sweeney as an escaped criminal, a fatal mistake on Pirelli's part.

Sondheim and Wheeler's conception of the scene originally also included a tooth-pulling competition. It remains in the libretto, but it was cut from the original Broadway production to reduce the show's running time.

The scene concludes with another iteration of the ballad sung by members of the company, a reminder that Sweeney is carrying out his nefarious plan to lure Judge Turpin to his shop.

"Johanna" (Judge Turpin)

Perhaps the most audacious number that Sondheim and Hugh Wheeler created for *Sweeney Todd* is a scene during which Judge Turpin spies through a keyhole on his innocent young ward Johanna while whipping himself with a scourge and achieving an orgasm. It was trimmed from the original production to reduce the show's length. But the song was recorded and can be heard on the original cast album, performed by actor Edmund Lyndeck.

The judge's self-inflicted beatings are built into the music for this rendition of "Johanna." Critic Stephen Citron called the scene "a daring foray into prevalent Victorian hypocrisy, for the judge's voyeurism coupled with his religious exhortations for deliverance from his filthy thoughts lead him to spontaneous orgasm."[20]

Reviewer Paul Wittke observed,

> The words are lecherous; the music mounts with smoldering passion, rising and falling in exhaustion.... His vacillating emotions become more turbulent until the surge of pleasure and pain... ending with the final outcry. ... The orchestra underscores a writhing Ravelian waltz, tempestuous and decadent.... One can literally hear the sting of whips on the flesh in this masochistic scene.[21]

In fact, Judge Turpin's salacious actions show him to be nearly as obsessed as Sweeney. In productions when the number is retained, it is generally rewarded with tepid applause. Shortly after this moment, the judge enters Johanna's chamber and announces his shocking intention to marry her.

In *Finishing the Hat*, Sondheim wrote, "Just as I had hoped with 'Gee, Officer Krupke' [in *West Side Story*] to be the first songwriter in Broadway history to use 'Fuck you' in a lyric, so I had hoped here to be the first to have a character reach an orgasm in the middle of a song."[22] Although it was cut from *Sweeney Todd*'s original production, the number remains in the libretto and is occasionally performed.

"Wait"

In Mrs. Lovett's upstairs room, Sweeney waits impatiently for the Beadle to arrive, the first step in luring Judge Turpin to his execution. She tries to calm him and steer him past his obsession. The song is offered as a soothing lullaby about how she plans to brighten the room with flowers to relieve the gloom.

Sweeney's first guest is Pirelli, who reveals himself to be Daniel O'Higgins, a onetime apprentice to Benjamin Barker. He completely drops his Pirelli persona and threatens to turn Sweeney over to the Beadle. The Demon Barber makes short work of dispatching Pirelli and pushes his nearly dead body into a trunk.

Three tenors from the chorus sing another iteration of "The Ballad of Sweeney Todd" with an echo of the "Dies Irae" motif.

"Kiss Me"

In Johanna's room she is hysterically panicked about the Judge's marital intentions. Anthony is with her, heedless of the Judge's threats about calling on her. They address one another formally as "Miss" and "Sir," echoing lines from their first encounter. He tries to distract her with insistent kissing. It's a rapid musical exchange between them, with him seeking kisses from her; she excitedly reaches higher and higher in her vocal register, but before long, she calms slightly and orders him to kiss her. They urge one another in a dangerous direction—he moves from kissing her to proposing marriage on Monday, as they plan to run away together.

"Ladies in Their Sensitivities"

The scene changes again to Beadle Bamford strolling with Judge Turpin. He expresses his concern that Johanna seems reluctant to accept his marriage proposal. The sycophantic Beadle suggests that it's because the Judge needs a shave, and ladies are easily offended by an unkempt appearance. It's evident that the seed Sweeney planted during the shaving contest has taken root. The Beadle is steering the Judge to Sweeney's shop.

He croons this fawning number (written for a high tenor) with an off-kilter 5/8 meter that underscores his unnerving mood. It excites the Judge, who is convinced he can win over Johanna's reservations with a bit of tonsorial cleanup and a dash of cologne. Their conspiring is overtly repellant. The following scene weaves between this song and the lovers, who continue to nervously plan their escape.

"Pretty Women"

Judge Turpin arrives at Sweeney's parlor seeking a shave, and the barber promises "the closest I ever gave" with his tongue firmly (and dangerously) in his cheek. They launch into a musical conversation about the beauties of women, "a madrigal-like air set with Victorian lyrics."[23] It's a beautiful counterpoint, accompanied by a moody French horn and a bassoon. Turpin hums and Sweeney whistles the merry tune as he sharpens his razors. The two men perform an odd duet sung by a lascivious masochist and a homicidal maniac. But their song is alluring and curiously appealing.

"I try to use song in unexpected ways," Sondheim said in a 1988 interview. "I like surprise, because I think that's the essence of theater. Over a period of years, I've tried to learn how not to write the expected. . . . *Sweeney*'s full of them, [especially] 'Pretty Women': You're expecting a murder, and you get a love song instead."[24]

The melody of "My Friends" is sounded again as Sweeney is on the brink of slashing the Judge's throat. But before he can, Anthony bursts in, exclaiming to the barber about his plan to free Johanna. Judge Turpin hears enough to depart furiously before Sweeney can swing his razor. Anthony is brusquely expelled for disrupting this opportunity to execute the judge.

"Epiphany"

The noisy commotion in the shop brings Mrs. Lovett upstairs to discover what has happened. Sweeney is furious, and she is unable to calm him. In this song, Sondheim mixed many of the motifs from earlier in the show, including horrifying dissonances and echoes of the "Dies Irae" melody. "The music is jarring, frenetic, leaping back and forth between phrases as Sweeney's mind begins to crack. The judge's escape has pushed him beyond the point of no return. Now his price is all mankind."[25]

In a completely bloodthirsty rage, Sweeney turns directly to the audience and threatens to extinguish all mankind. "It took Sondheim a full month to write this key number on which all further action and believability in the play depends. Instead of vowing vengeance on one guilty man, he pledges to murder humanity, shouting, 'They all deserve to die.'"[26]

"I had to motivate Todd from wanting to kill one man to wanting to kill all men, the moment at which we felt Bond's play was weakest," Sondheim told an interviewer. "To demonstrate musically that his mind is cracking I switched between violent and lyrical passages, and had rapid rhythmic shifts, from quick to slow. His murderous vengeance announced to a chugging engine-like theme [the *Dies Irae* motif disguised] alternates with a keening threnody for his wife and his daughter."[27] It's the same tune as "Alms, Alms," the first half of the Beggar Woman's theme. The number's percussive chords reflect his increasing loss of control, characterized as "the sound of a mind unhinged yet working out a logic all its own."[28] The vacillation of tempi is a more horrifying version of the switches heard earlier in "The Worst Pies in London."

Sweeney's mad "epiphany" concludes the number. He bellows, "The work waits, I'm alive at last, And I'm full of joy!"[29] The word "joy" lands on a chilling, unexpected chord. "What's going on in Sweeney's head is dissonant," he told radio interviewer Terry Gross.

> In fact, I originally didn't bring the number to a hand [evoking applause], but had it end on a dissonant chord with kind of violent harmonics, meaning very, very high, shrill sounds. And Hal Prince said, "You know, Len Cariou has worked so hard while he sings that song. You've got to give him a hand." So I put a big chord on the end, and that big chord still strikes me as wrong. And so even in the printed copy—that is, the piano vocal score that's published—I put two endings in—those who want to give it a big, nice consonant chord at the end to get a hand from the audience and those who want to do what I wanted to do, which was to let the thing dribble out into the next scene.[30]

Is Sweeney a monster or a victim of horrific circumstances? Martin Gottfried described "Epiphany" as "a nervous breakdown in song."[31] He suggested that it "concludes with the perverted 'And I'm full of joy!' Todd is elated by the commitment to kill, and yet the outburst endows him with a measure of sympathy and even heroism. He will not seem monstrous to the audience; instead, he will appear a victim, abused and agonized." That judgment ultimately will be made according to the actor and the audience watching him.

"A Little Priest"

Coming down from the crazed pitch of the concluding notes of "Epiphany," Mrs. Lovett matter-of-factly says, "That's all very well." She presses on with how they might dispose of Pirelli's body. Quickly a "bright idea" pops into her head, sounded with a familiar light bulb chime. It takes Sweeney several more words of encouragement before he gets her drift. By that time, the audience has fully grasped where Mrs. Lovett is steering the plan. In a sense, we are fully and willingly brought along for the gory ride.

"A Little Priest" offers eight minutes of dark comic relief following the heart-stopping "Epiphany." According to Brown,

> This pair of songs at the end of Act I is the most significant musical addition which Sondheim made to Bond's version. In the play Sweeney's mental collapse and the subsequent "meat pie connection" take place in less than half a page of dialogue, much too quickly for the full psychological impact. Sondheim carefully reveals the developing ideas in Sweeney and Mrs. Lovett's demented minds.[32]

In her 2019 doctoral dissertation, Ashley Marian Pribyl wrote that Sondheim said his cue for "A Little Priest" came from a stage direction concluding Act I of Christopher Bond's melodrama: "They both start to giggle, then fall into one another's arms laughing helplessly as—the CURTAIN falls."[33]

As Mrs. Lovett describes her ghoulish solution to the shortage of fillings for her meat pies, the waltzing music hall melody of "The Worst Pies in London" returns, reinforcing the connection to her conniving ways. Of course, this time it's considerably more wicked than flicking flies and catching feral cats. Once Sweeney tunes in to her suggestion, "A Little Priest" switches back and forth "between two dueling waltz idioms. Todd's swirling aristocratic Viennese strains, which always begin with a reference to the world at large, alternate with Mrs. Lovett's rag-tag clog waltz, which she always initiates in order to introduce the next flavor of the moment."[34]

While Sweeney's goal is vengeance, Mrs. Lovett's is selfishly derived. "There's a survivor element to Lovett," actor Josh Groban told an NPR interviewer. "And they're both looking for a means to achieve what they need. These duets are crafted so brilliantly—to be able to show both of those plans happening simultaneously."[35]

As the pair runs through an extended array of gruesome pie fillings, the song's lyrics are, as Paul Wittke observed in his review of the original cast recording, "a masterpiece of gallows humor. They, like the show, may not be to everyone's taste, but there is no denying their linguistic and musical intelligence."[36]

Based on a careful study of the composer's lyric sketches for "A Little Priest," Mark Eden Horowitz discovered that Sondheim considered more than 150 professions and personality types for possible fillings for Mrs. Lovett's pies.[37] See Figure 6.1, p. 167. Their ghastly propositions are interspersed with witty repartee. "Sondheim has said that he likes the combination of the spoken and the sung and, indeed, it does add to the variety of colors and textures in this long number. These spoken breaks are also very much in the vaudeville and British music hall traditions that inform the number's style."[38]

Sweeney's obsession with revenge interrupts Mrs. Lovett's jolly pursuit of their collaboration with "Have you any Beadle?" She puts him off with a suggestion to wait until next week. But he pushes through the distraction. In the final verse, he's at it again, forcefully shouting, "I'll come again when you have judge on the menu." At that moment, the descending scale also uses D flat and G flat to give the scale the Dorian feel of the "Dies Irae." Mrs. Lovett then hands him a meat cleaver, telling him, "We have something even better: Executioner."[39]

The song and Act I conclude with Sweeney and Mrs. Lovett triumphantly embracing and raising their arms; she is brandishing a rolling pin and he the cleaver, in a frightening celebration.

Act II

"God, That's Good!"

Mrs. Lovett's tasty new pies have developed such a following that she has expanded her shop to offer *al fresco* dining. Act II of *Sweeney Todd* opens with a remarkable, multiple perspective scene. She is now simultaneously the baker, the waitress, the cashier, and the major-domo of a frantic scene with customers extolling the virtues of her pies—now filled with Sweeney's murderous carnage—and demanding more and more, shouting, "God, that's good" and "More hot pies."

Tobias has become Mrs. Lovett's promoter, and the melody he used for "Pirelli's Miracle Elixir" to recruit customers for the charlatan barber and his sham hair-growing tonic is now extolling Mrs. Lovett's baked products. Writer Stephen Citron said, "With overlapping vocal lines over a full chorus generally screaming 'God, that's good!' as they swill pies and ale, it is as complicated and many-faceted as Verdi's second scene of *Aida* and certainly as intense."[40]

Sweeney Todd's second act builds upon the psychologically motivated first act, and the score becomes a concerted march to the finale, launched by this rollicking number. There's more going on than simply a voracious crowd. Sweeney anxiously awaits the delivery of his new trick chair that will deliver victims to the bakeshop's basement where they can be ground into pie filling. Once it arrives, he needs to test the mechanism. He sends a bundle of books down the chute, using the same pounding meter of "God, That's Good!" He tells Mrs. Lovett that he'll "Knock three times" to signal his next delivery.

The parallel storylines weave together as Sweeney extols his chair as "fit for a king," while Lovett's pies are praised with the same phrase by her rabid customers.

"Johanna"

More interweaving begins with four characters involved in the reprise of "Johanna"—Anthony, Sweeney, the Beggar Woman, and Johanna herself. First, Anthony sings his lilting ballad of passion for the young woman. Sweeney, in his barbershop, sings about her yellow hair, but it's obvious he's recalling Lucy, her mother. He mourns his loss of both of them but recalls their beauty. The Beggar Woman (the sad, damaged person who was once Lucy Barker) begins to sound Cassandra-like warnings of "Mischief" and "City on fire!" There is a glimpse of Johanna imprisoned at Fogg's Asylum and pining for Anthony. Sweeney is murdering almost everyone who enters his shop, sending them down to the grinder. He spares one man accompanied by his wife and child, perhaps a momentary recognition of his former, foolish self.

"By the Sea"

Mrs. Lovett tries to calm Sweeney by playing her harmonium and daydreaming about a vacation and the idyllic life she fervently hopes will soon be hers. "By the Sea," complete with seagull calls, is a bouncy, fast-paced number.[41] But Mrs. Lovett is half-crazed herself, and Sweeney pays almost no attention to her overtures. He remains obsessed with getting his razor on Judge Turpin's throat. Their present reality intrudes when she suggests that at the seaside he can bring along his "chopper." Apparently, in her mind, their gruesome undertaking has a bright future.

Wigmaker Sequence

Not a song per se, but a scene that's key to the development of *Sweeney Todd*'s final moments. Sweeney rhapsodizes to Anthony about the colors and textures of human hair using the same unnerving 5/8 meter from "Ladies in their Sensitivities" and "Pretty Women." Armed with this information, the plan is for the young sailor to pose as a wigmaker and rescue Johanna from Fogg's Asylum, where Judge Turpin and Beadle Bamford have imprisoned her.

A quintet of chorus members sings another brief iteration of "The Ballad of Sweeney Todd," this time describing the barber's fixation on not missing a second opportunity to execute the Judge.

"The Letter"

Sweeney drafts a brief missive to Judge Turpin, the lines of which are sung as he writes by individual members of the quintet. He reports that Anthony has abducted Johanna, but she is now in Sweeney's custody, housed in his shop for the evening. He invites the judge to come and find his ward repentant and ready for marriage. He delivers the letter to Turpin's home.

"Not While I'm Around"

The next scene finds Tobias and Mrs. Lovett in her deserted outdoor dining area. She has knitted a muffler for the ragamuffin boy, and he is grateful for her motherly attention. He tells her he would do anything for her. He fears that "demons are prowling" and suggests he's concerned about "a man wot was bad." She warily questions him to discover what he suspects.

He sings the show's most touching number, "Not While I'm Around," pledging his unwavering devotion to her, accompanied by harp, cello, French horn, and oboe. As she attempts to distract him with an errand, she takes out the purse she took from Pirelli's body when she and Sweeney disposed of him. Tobias recognizes it immediately and questions how she came to have it. She says Sweeney gave it to her. To discourage his further questions, she sings the same words he just sang to her. But now, accompanied by a flute and off pitch violins, they have frighteningly different double meanings.

The tune is sweetly simple as sung by the innocent boy, but Mrs. Lovett's version darkens the number with an ironic undertow. It's clear that Toby knows too much and must be eliminated. She takes him to the bakehouse basement and shows him how to prepare the meat for pie filling, putting it through the grinder three times—recalling Sweeney's "Knock three times" rhythmic signal for a body being delivered.

"Parlor Songs"

Beadle Bamford drops in unexpectedly, responding to complaints about foul-smelling smoke from the bakehouse chimney. Mrs. Lovett discovers him playing her harmonium and singing "Sweet Polly Plunkett."[42] She tells him Sweeney is not home with the key to the bakehouse. He stalls by playing a second number about the bells in "The Tower of Bray," with a dozen call-and-response verses. He begins vocalizing, and Toby downstairs starts to sing a "Ding dong!" refrain.

Sweeney's return breaks this off, and Mrs. Lovett encourages the Beadle to accept a complimentary shave—with fatal consequences. Meanwhile, Toby's fears are realized when he discovers a hair and a fingernail in the ground meat, and then the Beadle's body slides down the chute. The boy raises a ruckus, and Mrs. Lovett tells Sweeney he has sorted out what's happening and needs to be silenced permanently.

"City on Fire" and "Searching"

The chorus sings another piece of the ballad, and then the women become the inmates in Fogg's Asylum. Anthony arrives and locates Johanna; Fogg realizes Anthony is not a wigmaker, and he is posing as one as a ruse. Anthony draws the pistol Sweeney gave him but loses his nerve and drops it. Johanna picks it up and shoots Fogg. The lunatics spill out into the street and vocal pandemonium—"City on Fire"—ensues. As part of the commotion, the Beggar Woman has recognized the evil afoot, but no one listens to her alarms. Sweeney and Mrs. Lovett continue to search in the bakehouse for Tobias.

Anthony takes Johanna to Sweeney's shop for safekeeping while he goes for a coach for their escape. The music from "Ah, Miss" and "Kiss Me" is woven into the action, as is "No Place Like London." After Anthony leaves, Johanna sees the Beggar Woman coming upstairs and hides in the trunk. A snatch of "A Barber and His Wife" is sounded as the demented woman enters. She has been searching for the Beadle, but her mind drifts back to former times: she's cradling a doll while the melody of "Poor Thing" recurs, the tune that played the night she was raped by Judge Turpin. She is singing to "My Jo," another reminder of Johanna's family connection.

Sweeney bursts in and sees her as an obstruction to his plan to murder the judge. She recognizes him momentarily: "Hey, don't I know you, mister?" He fails to realize that she is Lucy. He sees the judge approaching, tragically dispatches her, and sends her body down the chute.

"The Judge's Return"

With the Judge back in his clutches, Sweeney tempts him with a few hints that Johanna is eager to see him and persuades him for a quick shave. The melody of "Pretty Women" returns, and the men seem to share their appreciation of feminine traits. Sweeney brashly reveals his true identity, hears the factory whistle, and slashes the judge's throat and sends the body sliding down the chute. Sweeney sings a version of "My Friends," a gentle, unbalanced farewell to his razors. Johanna emerges from the trunk and almost becomes a victim herself, but Mrs. Lovett's screams from downstairs distract Sweeney, and the young woman escapes.

The chorus sings the ballad again briefly, leading with the "Dies irae" motif: "Lift your razor high, Sweeney!"

Final Sequence

The judge, not quite dead, has clutched the hem of Mrs. Lovett's dress. Sweeney enters as she drags his body toward the oven. He sees the Beggar Woman and suddenly recognizes that she is Lucy—and painfully realizes that Mrs. Lovett has deceived him from the moment of his arrival. Backed by the melody of "Poor Thing," she says she lied because she loved him.

The mad melody of "A Little Priest" materializes as the pair sing at cross purposes. She tries to convince him to marry her, while he furiously waltzes her toward then into the bakehouse oven. During this fatal duet, they sing to changing time signatures. Her music shifts from 6/8 to 5/8 to 3/8, while his expands with longer notes, from 6/4 to 9/4. Their final waltz is a manic 3/8. When he finally realizes with horror what he has done, Sweeney keens pathetically over Lucy's body in a nearly identical reprise of "A Barber and His Wife." The only difference is a full octave interval on the final word, "naïve."

Toby appears, his hair turned white from shock, singing a haunting nursery rhyme, "Pat-a-Cake." Sweeney pushes him away, but Toby picks up the razor and cuts Sweeney's throat. A crowd enters, including Anthony and Johanna, who are shocked by the ghastly scene.

"The Ballad of Sweeney Todd"

Toby sings the first line of the final reprise of "The Tale of Sweeney Todd." Others follow suit, including the Beggar Woman, Judge Turpin, Beadle

Bamford, and Adolfo Pirelli. Sweeney and Mrs. Lovett rise from the grave. The chorus members join in a shattering crescendo then exit the stage. Sweeney and Mrs. Lovett remain, stare at each other, then head in opposite directions. Sweeney opens the oven, "glares at us malevolently for a moment, then slams the iron door in our faces."[43]

Notes

Chapter 1

1. Craig Zadan, *Sondheim & Company* (New York: Da Capo Press, 1994), 114.
2. Meryle Secrest, *Stephen Sondheim: A Life* (New York: Random House, 1998), 187.
3. Robert Berkvist, "Stephen Sondheim Takes a Stab at Grand Guignol," *New York Times*, February 25, 1979.
4. Stephen Sondheim, "Larger than Life: Reflections on Melodrama and Sweeney Todd," interviewed by Daniel Gerould on September 5, 1979, *Melodrama*, Vol. 7 (New York: New York Literary Forum, 1980), 4.
5. Secrest, *Stephen Sondheim*, 290.
6. Christopher Bond, "Introduction," *Sweeney Todd, The Demon Barber of Fleet Street* by Stephen Sondheim and Hugh Wheeler (New York: Applause Theatre Book Publishers, 1991), 2–3.
7. Zadan, *Sondheim & Company*, 245.
8. Zadan, *Sondheim & Company*, 246.
9. Sondheim, "Larger than Life," 3–4.
10. Sondheim, "Larger than Life," 4.
11. Sondheim, "Larger than Life," 6.
12. Sondheim, "Larger than Life," 3.
13. Sondheim, "Larger than Life," 6.
14. Zadan, *Sondheim & Company*, 246–47.
15. Zadan, *Sondheim & Company*, 245.
16. Zadan, *Sondheim & Company*, 245.
17. Graham Skipper, "Stephen Sondheim: Horror's Musical Maestro," https://fangoria.com, November 30, 2021.

Chapter 2

1. Robert L. Mack, *The Wonderful and Surprising History of Sweeney Todd* (London: Continuum, 2007), 163–64.
2. Peter Haining, *Sweeney Todd: The Real Story of the Demon Barber of Fleet Street* (New York: Barnes & Noble, 1997), 34–35; Mack, *Wonderful and Surprising*, 339.
3. Mack, *Wonderful and Surprising*, 172.
4. Mack, *Wonderful and Surprising*, 173.

5 Mack, *Wonderful and Surprising*, 149. For a more in-depth discussion of such stories, see Chapter 5: "I Shall Have to Polish Him Off: Proto-Myths and Precedents," Mack, *Wonderful and Surprising*, 135–194.
6 Dick Collins, "Introduction to the Revised Edition," *Sweeney Todd: The String of Pearls* by James Malcolm Rymer (Wordsworth Editions, 2005, 2010), x.
7 Collins, "Introduction," xiii–xvi.
8 "Sweeny" is an adjective describing the atrophy of shoulder muscles in a horse, according to the *Shorter Oxford English Dictionary*. "The barber himself was a long, low-jointed, ill-put-together sort of fellow, with an immense mouth, and such huge hands and feet, that he was, in his way, quite a natural curiosity ..." Collins," Introduction," xx.
9 Collins, "Introduction," xxi.
10 Montagu Slater in a 1928 edition of George Dibdin Pitt's script. It's likely that it was this script that Christopher Bond adapted.
11 Haley Moore, "George Dibdin Pitt." *Dictionary of Literary Biography*, Vol. 344: *Nineteenth-Century British Dramatists*. Detroit: Gale, 2008, 295–99.
12 Christopher Bond, "Introduction," Sondheim, Stephen, and Wheeler, Hugh. *Sweeney Todd: The Demon Barber of Fleet Street* (New York: Applause Theatre Book Publishers, 1991), 3. Subsequently referred to as "Libretto."
13 Bond, "Introduction" to Libretto, 4.
14 C. G. Bond, *Sweeney Todd, The Demon Barber of Fleet Street: A Melodrama* (London: Samuel French, 1974).
15 Stephen Sondheim, "Larger than Life: Reflections on Melodrama and Sweeney Todd," interviewed by Daniel Gerould on September 5, 1979, *Melodrama*, Vol. 7 (New York: New York Literary Forum, 1980), 4.
16 Sondheim, "Larger than Life," 8.
17 Stephen Sondheim, *Finishing the Hat* (New York: Alfred A. Knopf, 2010), xx.
18 Meryle Secrest, *Stephen Sondheim: A Life* (New York: Alfred A. Knopf, 1998), 290.
19 Sondheim, *Finishing the Hat*, 332.
20 Craig Zadan, *Sondheim & Company* (New York: Da Capo Press, 1994), 243.
21 Bond, "Introduction," 5.
22 Bond, "Introduction," 5.

Chapter 3

1 Meryle Secrest, *Stephen Sondheim: A Life* (New York: Alfred A. Knopf), 291.
2 Mel Gussow, "Broadway," *New York Times*, August 27, 1976.
3 Craig Zadan, *Sondheim & Company* (New York: DaCapo Press, 1994), 245.
4 Secrest, *Sondheim: A Life*, 295–296.
5 Zadan, *Sondheim & Company*, 246.
6 Zadan, *Sondheim & Company*, 246.
7 Zadan, *Sondheim & Company*, 246.
8 Frank Shanbacker, "Taking a Risk on Broadway: What Convinced Investors to Buy a Piece of *Sweeney Todd*'s Pie?" *Playbill*, July 2, 2015.

9 Zadan, *Sondheim & Company*, 252.
10 Harold Prince, *A Sense of Occasion* (New York: Applause Theatre & Cinema Books, 2017), 226.
11 Zadan, *Sondheim & Company*, 260.
12 Stephen Sondheim, *Finishing the Hat* (New York: Alfred A. Knopf, 2010), 332.
13 Mel Gussow, "*Sweeney Todd*: A little nightmare music," *New York Times*, February 1, 1979.
14 Secrest, *Sondheim: A Life*, 292.
15 Zadan, *Sondheim & Company*, 246.
16 Ashley Marian Pribyl, "Sociocultural and Collaborative Antagonism in the Harold Prince–Stephen Sondheim Musicals (1970–1979)" (PhD diss. Washington University, 2019), 28-29.
17 Roger Pines, "Composer's Note," interview with Stephen Sondheim published in the 2002 Chicago Lyric Opera program, 26–27.
18 Prince, *Sense of Occasion*, 224.
19 Prince, *Sense of Occasion*, 224.
20 Jack Kroll, "Review: *Sweeney Todd*," *Newsweek*, March 12, 1979.
21 Kroll, "Review."
22 Prince, *Sense of Occasion*, 224.
23 Kroll, "Review"
24 Secrest, *Sondheim: A Life*, 299.
25 Margaret Hall, *Gemignani: Life and Lessons from Broadway and Beyond* (New York: Applause Theatre & Cinema Books, 2022), 74.
26 Michael Portantiere, "Brilliant Stuff: Interview with Len Cariou the original Sweeney Todd," *Everything Sondheim*, January 2017, 26.
27 Portantiere, "Brilliant Stuff," 26.
28 Prince, *Sense of Occasion*, 225.
29 Prince, *Sense of Occasion*, 225.
30 Neil Genzlinger, "Franne Lee, Tony Winner Who Also Costumed Coneheads, Dies at 81," *New York Times*, September 1, 2023.
31 Zadan, *Sondheim & Company*, 255.
32 Pines, "Composer's Note," 26.
33 Hall, *Gemignani*, 73.
34 Zadan, *Sondheim & Company*, 256.
35 Zadan, *Sondheim & Company*, 252–253.
36 Hall, *Gemignani*, 69.
37 Zadan, *Sondheim & Company*, 253.
38 Hall, *Gemignani*, 74.
39 Gussow, "Broadway," *New York Times*, February 1, 1979.
40 Portantiere, "Brilliant Stuff," 25–26.
41 Secrest, *Sondheim: A Life*, 299.
42 Eddie Shapiro, *Nothing Like a Dame: Conversations with the Great Women of Musical Theater* (New York: Oxford University Press, 2014), 44.
43 Portantiere, "Brilliant Stuff," 25.
44 Shapiro, *Nothing Like a Dame*, 44.

45 Shapiro, *Nothing Like a Dame*, 44.
46 Zadan, *Sondheim & Company*, 249.
47 Portantiere, "Brilliant Stuff," 26.
48 Shapiro, *Nothing Like a Dame*, 44.
49 Zadan, *Sondheim & Company*, 249.
50 Shapiro, *Nothing Like a Dame*, 44.
51 Shapiro, *Nothing Like a Dame*, 45.
52 Bruce Janiga, "Side by Side with Ken Jennings," interview in early 1998, https://Sondheim.com/features/ken_jennings.html]
53 Richard Eder, "Stage: Introducing *Sweeney Todd*," *New York Times*, March 2, 1979.
54 Shapiro, *Nothing Like a Dame*, 45.
55 Harry Haun, "Len Cariou On a Six Decade Career That's Included Shakespeare, Sondheim, and Selleck," *The Observer*, April 18, 2024.
56 Shapiro, *Nothing Like a Dame*, 45.
57 Shapiro, *Nothing Like a Dame*, 82.
58 Secrest, *Sondheim: A Life*, 248.
59 Angela Lansbury, *Studs Terkel Radio Arkive* (Feb. 19, 1981).
60 Terkel/Lansbury.
61 Terkel/Lansbury.
62 Shapiro, *Nothing Like a Dame*, 87.
63 Terkel/Lansbury.
64 Ethan Mordden, *On Sondheim: An Opinionated Guide* (New York: Oxford University Press, 2016), 108.
65 Stephen Sondheim and Harold Prince, "On Collaboration Between Authors and Directors," moderated by Gretchen Cryer, *Dramatists Guild Quarterly* (16, Summer 1979), 29.
66 Richard Eder, "Introducing *Sweeney Todd*."
67 Hall, *Gemignani*, 76.
68 Michael Portantiere, "Victor Garber: Anthony Hope Springs Eternal," *Everything Sondheim*, April–May 2017, 26.
69 Janiga, Ken Jennings.
70 Janiga, Ken Jennings.
71 Janiga, Ken Jennings.
72 Janiga, Ken Jennings.
73 Janiga, Ken Jennings.
74 Janiga, Ken Jennings.
75 Portantiere, "Victor Garber," 26.
76 Portantiere, "Victor Garber," 26
77 Portantiere, "Victor Garber," 27
78 Portantiere, "Sarah Rice: I Feel You, Johanna," *Everything Sondheim*, June-August 2017, 25–26.
79 Portantiere, "Sarah Rice," 26.
80 Portantiere, "Sarah Rice," 26.
81 Ryan Keating, YouTube interview with Merle Louise (1984), https://tinyurl.com/MerleLouise

82 Keating/Merle Louise interview.
83 Keating/Merle Louise interview.
84 Prince, *Sense of Occasion*, 225.
85 Personal email correspondence with Frank Verlizzo, November 4, 2024.
86 Verlizzo email.
87 Verlizzo email.
88 Michael White, "Monster at the Opera," Sunday Telegraph (London), November 30, 2003.
89 Eder, "Introducing *Sweeney Todd*."
90 Eder, "Introducing *Sweeney Todd*."
91 Walter Kerr, "Is *Sweeney* on Target?" *New York Times*, March 11, 1979.
92 Edwin Wilson, "Sondheim Writes a Musical to Talk About," *Wall Street Journal*, March 16, 1979.
93 Clive Barnes, "Sondheim's *Sweeney Todd*," *New York Post*, March 5, 1979.
94 Kroll, "Review."
95 T. E. Kalem, "Theater: Razor's Edge," Time Magazine, March 12, 1979 https://content.time.com/time/subscriber/article/0,33009,948445,00.html
96 Peter Marks, "Home-Grown Musical Master," *New York Times*, January 25, 1998.
97 Frank Rich, "Review: *Sweeney Todd*," *New York Times*. September 15, 1989.
98 Eder, "Introducing *Sweeney Todd*."
99 Martin Gottfried, Sondheim (New York: Harry N. Abrams, 1993), 146.
100 Zadan, *Sondheim & Company*, 261.
101 Zadan, *Sondheim & Company*, 256.
102 Secrest, *Sondheim: A Life*, 302.
103 Sondheim, *Finishing the Hat*, 376.
104 Hall, *Gemignani*, 77.
105 Alan Rich, "Sweeney Agonistes," *California*, October 1981, 149–150.
106 Rich, "Sweeney Agonistes," 150.
107 Rich, "Sweeney Agonistes," 150.
108 Rich, "Sweeney Agonistes," 150.
109 Rich, Sweeney Agonistes," 150.

Chapter 4

1 Joe Blevins, "Stephen Sondheim was not impressed with the film version of *West Side Story*," April 7, 2016, https://avclub.com
2 Pauline Kael, "The Current Cinema: Shivers," *The New Yorker*, March 20, 1978, 129.
3 Stephen Sondheim, *Finishing the Hat* (New York: Alfred A. Knopf, 2010), 331.
4 Adam Baer, "Wrestling demons," *Los Angeles Times*, December 18, 2007.
5 Baer, "Wrestling demons."
6 Brian Scott Lipton, "Transforming Todd: Screenwriter John Logan talks about the challenge of taking *Sweeney Todd* from stage to screen," theatermania.com, December 10, 2007.

7. Karl Rozemeyer, "Tim Burton Redux: Exclusive Interview," premiere.com, January 15, 2008.
8. Baer, "Wrestling demons."
9. Rozemeyer, "Tim Burton Redux."
10. Mark Salisbury, *Sweeney Todd: The Demon Barber of Fleet Street* (London: Titan Books, 2007), 87.
11. Salisbury, *Sweeney Todd*, 87–88.
12. Salisbury, *Sweeney Todd*, 94.
13. Salisbury, *Sweeney Todd*, 88.
14. Salisbury, *Sweeney Todd*, 93.
15. A. O. Scott, "Murder Most Musical," *New York Times*, December 21, 2007.
16. Terry Teachout, "The Hollywood Musical Done Right," *Commentary*, February 2008.
17. Salisbury, *Sweeney Todd*, 58.
18. Ruben V. Nepales, "Only in Hollywood: From Borat to Pirelli, Sacha Baron Cohen is quite ballsy," *Philippine Daily Inquirer*, December 21, 2007.
19. Salisbury, *Sweeney Todd*, 38.
20. Salisbury, *Sweeney Todd*, 95–96.
21. Salisbury, *Sweeney Todd*, 96.
22. Terry Armour, "Johnny Depp, Tim Burton pour it on in *Sweeney Todd*," *Chicago Tribune*, January 1, 2008.
23. John Jurgensen, "Just Asking: Tim Burton," *The Wall Street Journal*, December 29, 2007.
24. Salisbury, *Sweeney Todd*, 96.
25. Salisbury, *Sweeney Todd*, 96.
26. Salisbury, *Sweeney Todd*, 97.
27. Lipton, "Transforming Todd."
28. Jesse Green, "No Remorse," *New York Times*, December 16, 2007.
29. Green, "No Remorse."
30. Paul Fischer, "A rare audience with Stephen Sondheim," FilmMonthly.com, December 2, 2007.
31. Jesse Green, "Sondheim Dismembers 'Sweeney,'" *New York Times*, December 16, 2007.
32. Lipton, "Transforming Todd."
33. Teachout, "Hollywood Musical."
34. Paul Fischer, "Exclusive Interview: Stephen Sondheim," Moviehole.net, December 28, 2007.
35. Emmanuel Levy, "It's not a stage thing – it's a movie," *Financial Times*, December 22, 2007.
36. Salisbury, *Sweeney Todd*, 73.
37. Salisbury, *Sweeney Todd*, 73.
38. Salisbury, *Sweeney Todd*, 83.
39. Silviane Gold, "Demon Barber, Meat Pies and All, Sings on Screen," *New York Times*, November 4, 2007.
40. Salisbury, *Sweeney Todd*, 74.
41. Anthony Tommasini, "An Actor Whose Approach to Singing Lets the Words Take Center Stage," *New York Times*, January 12, 2008.

42 Tommasini, "An Actor Whose Approach."
43 Sean Patrick Flahaven, "The sounds of Sweeney: Adapting the music from stage to film was an exciting challenge," *The Sondheim Review*, Summer 2008, 16.
44 Salisbury, *Sweeney Todd*, 85.
45 Salisbury, *Sweeney Todd*, 97.
46 Lipton, "Transforming Todd."
47 Steve Daly, "Johnny Depp: Cutting Loose in 'Sweeney Todd,'" EW.com, November 3, 2007.
48 Levy, "It's not a stage thing."
49 Levy, "It's not a stage thing."
50 Armour, "Johnny Depp."
51 Salisbury, *Sweeney Todd*, 30.
52 Salisbury, *Sweeney Todd*, 30, 31, 35.
53 Salisbury, *Sweeney Todd*, 83.
54 Tommasini, "An Actor's Whose Approach."
55 Peter Travers, "Sweeney Todd," *Rolling Stone*, December 13, 2007.
56 Paul Byrne, "Helena makes the cut," *The Independent* (London), January 9, 2008
57 Thomas Floyd, "An oral history of Mrs. Lovett, one of theater's greatest, bloodiest roles," *Washington Post*, April 6, 2024.
58 Salisbury, *Sweeney Todd*, 49.
59 Jesse Green, "The Ballad of Johnny Depp," *New York Times*, December 16, 2007.
60 Salisbury, *Sweeney Todd*, 79.
61 Mark Salisbury, "Helena Bonham Carter's pie-in-the-sky dream," *Los Angeles Times*, December 28, 2007.
62 Salisbury, *Sweeney Todd*, 80-81.
63 Salisbury, *Sweeney Todd*, 50.
64 Floyd, "An oral history."
65 Tommasini, "An actor whose approach."
66 Hank Sartin, "The villain voice: Alan Rickman takes on another bad-Englishman role – this time crooning," *Time Out Chicago*, December 13, 2007.
67 Nick Hutson, "Alan Rickman," BroadwayWorld.com, December 11, 2007.
68 Salisbury, *Sweeney Todd*, 72.
69 Salisbury, *Sweeney Todd*, 62, 65.
70 Nepales, "Only in Hollywood."
71 Salisbury, *Sweeney Todd*, 65.
72 Salisbury, *Sweeney Todd*, 65.
73 Salisbury, *Sweeney Todd*, 83.
74 Salisbury, *Sweeney Todd*, 83.
75 Jonathan Stayton, "Child star of *Sweeney Todd* barber film takes short cut to fame," *The Argus*, January 24, 2008.
76 Michael Portantiere, "Sondheim on film and video," *The Sondheim Review* (Spring 2011), 35.
77 Roger Ebert, "Shave and a haircut, two bits: slight wait for meat pies," *Chicago Sun-Times*, December 20, 2007.
78 Scott, "Murder Most Musical."

79 Peter Marks, "*Sweeney Todd*: A Savory Pie, Any Way You Slice It," *Washington Post*, December 21, 2007.
80 Bob Mondello, "In 'Sweeney Todd,' Blood Will Most Certainly Flow," National Public Radio, December 20, 2007.
81 David Thomson, "Attending the Tale of Sweeney Todd: The Stage Musical and Tim Burton's Film Version," *The Oxford Handbook of Sondheim Studies*, Robert Gordon, ed. (New York: Oxford University Press, 2014), 302.
82 Thomson, "Attending the Tale," 305.
83 Thomas Peyser, "The Sound of Murder," *Style Weekly* (Richmond, Virginia), January 2, 2008.
84 Levy, "It's not a stage thing."
85 Jonathan Zipper, "Sondheim Traces Sweeney's Bloody Trail on Stage and Screen," *Hollywood Today*, December 21, 2007.
86 Norman Lebrecht, "When a movie outshines the outstanding original," *La Scena Musicale*, January 9, 2008.
87 Rozemeyer, "Tim Burton Redux."
88 Marks, "*Sweeney Todd*."
89 Teachout, "Hollywood Musical."

Chapter 5

1 Charles Isherwood, "Cutting 'Sweeney Todd' to the Bone," *New York Times*, October 30, 2005.
2 Ken Mandelbaum, "Preview '05-'06: Attend the Tale," broadway.com, August 1, 2005.
3 Sheridan Morley, "'Sweeney Todd' on a Small Scale," *International Herald Tribune*, June 9, 1993.
4 Stephen Sondheim in a telephone interview in January 2002 with Roger Pines, editorial dramaturg for Lyric Opera of Chicago. Published in the operatic performance program for the 2002–2003 season, 27.
5 Isherwood, "Cutting 'Sweeney Todd.'"
6 Morley, "Small Scale."
7 Meryle Secrest, *Stephen Sondheim: A Life* (New York: Alfred A. Knopf, 1998), 367.
8 Rodney Milnes, "Opera in Britain – *Sweeney Todd*, Royal Opera at Covent Garden, December 15," Opera (March 204), 349–52.
9 Stephen Sondheim, *Finishing the Hat* (New York: Alfred A. Knopf, 2010), 376.
10 Donal Henahan, "City Opera: Sondheim's 'Sweeney,'" *New York Times*, October 13, 1984.
11 Henahan, "Sondheim's Sweeney."
12 Michael Portantiere, "Sweeney Todd," TheaterMania (www.theatermania.com), March 12, 2004.
13 Bernard Holland, "City Opera Review: Supertitles and Meat Pies as Hors d'Oeuvres," *New York Times*, March 11, 2004.
14 Sean Patrick Flahaven, "NYCO Sweeney falls short," *Sondheim Review* (Summer 2004, Vol. XI, No. 1), 23.

15 Stephen Holden, "*Sweeney Todd* Revival on an Intimate Scale," *New York Times*, April 8, 1989.
16 Holden, "Intimate Scale."
17 Frank Rich, "Critic's Notebook: On Stage, the Feminist Message Takes on a Sly and Subtle Tone," *New York Times*, April 19, 1989.
18 Rich, "Feminist Message."
19 Rich, "Feminist Message."
20 Rich, "Feminist Message."
21 Lloyd Rose, "Signature's *Sweeney Todd* Cuts To the Quick," *Washington Post*, September 15, 1999.
22 Nelson Pressley, "*Sweeney Todd* revived at the Signature," *Sondheim Review* (Fall 1999, Vol. VI, No. 2), 8.
23 Peter Marks, "This version of *Sweeney Todd* commits a cardinal sin: It's bloodless," *Washington Post*, May 25, 2023.
24 Morley, "Small Scale."
25 Terry Morgan, "Sweeney Todd – The Demon Barber of Fleet Street," *Variety*, February 13, 2006.
26 Alvin Klein, "For Goodspeed, a Noble Departure," *New York Times*, May 26, 1966.
27 Klein, "For Goodspeed."
28 Paul Taylor, "Theatre: *Sweeney Todd* Leicester Haymarket," *The Independent* (London), November 22, 1996.
29 Taylor, "Sweeney Todd."
30 Taylor, "Sweeney Todd."
31 Mark Shenton, "In London, Cariou returns as Sweeney," *Sondheim Review* (Spring 2000, Vol. VI, No. 4), 7.
32 Matt Wolf, "Sweeney Todd," *Variety*, February 27, 2000.
33 Shenton, "In London, Cariou returns."
34 Shenton, "In London, Cariou returns."
35 Alfred Hickling, "Sweeney Todd," *The Guardian*, April 27, 2002.
36 Richard S. Ginnell, "Hollywood Bowl Orchestra," *Variety*, Sept. 9, 1998.
37 Ginnell, "Hollywood Bowl Orchestra."
38 Stewart, Patrick, *Making It So*, New York: Gallery Books, 2023, 46.
39 March 4, 2017, https://theatreboard.co.uk/thread/2478/patrick-stewarts-idea-sweeney-revival
40 Terri Roberts, "Grammer attends the tale of *Sweeney Todd*," *Sondheim Review* (Spring 1999, Vol. V, No. 4), 8.
41 Sean Patrick Flahaven, "A glorious *Sweeney* in a New York concert," *Sondheim Review* (Summer 2000, Vol. VII, No. 1), 6.
42 Flahaven, "A glorious *Sweeney*."
43 Stephen Sondheim, program note, New York Philharmonic, May 2000.
44 Barry Singer, "Losing the Present While Waiting for the Future," *New York Times*, July 16, 2000. Singer offers a more in-depth description of the decision-making and implications of the negotiations regarding recording this concert.
45 Sean Patrick Flahaven, "A Halloween treat: *Sweeney Todd* on PBS," *Sondheim Review* (Winter 2002, Vol. VIII, No. 3), 30.

46 Bonnie Weiss, "Getting to the heart of *Sweeney Todd*," *Sondheim Review* (Winter 2002, Vol. VIII, No. 3), 31.
47 Rob Weinert-Kendt, "Alive at last," *Sondheim Review* (Fall 2014, Vol. XX, No. 4), 37–38.
48 Charles Isherwood, "First to Die in *Sweeney Todd*: Decorum at the Philharmonic," *New York Times*, March 6, 2014.
49 Isherwood, "First to Die."
50 Isherwood, "First to Die."
51 Michael Billington, "*Sweeney Todd* review – Bryn Terfel and Emma Thompson in razor-sharp thriller," *The Guardian*, April 1, 2015).
52 Mark Shenton, "Just off Fleet Street, an intimate *Sweeney*," *Sondheim Review* (Fall 2000, Vol. VII, No. 2), 11.
53 Shenton, "Just off fleet Street."
54 Sheridan Morley, "Close-Up with *Sweeney Todd*," *New York Times* (via *International Herald Tribune*), June 14, 2000.
55 Mark Eden Horowitz, "A strong *Sweeney* opens Kennedy festival," *Sondheim Review* (Summer 2002, Vol. IX, No. 1), 6.
56 Nelson Pressley, "*Sweeney Todd*: A Slashing Success," *Washington Post*, May 12, 2002.
57 *The Sondheim Review* (Summer 2002, Vol. IX, No. 1), 7.
58 *The Sondheim Review* (Summer 2002, Vol. IX, No. 1), 8.
59 Horowitz, "A strong *Sweeney*."
60 John Rockwell, "It takes the Sweeney to make the *Sweeney Todd*," *New York Times*, November 6, 2002.
61 Paul Salsini, "Terfel will take *Sweeney* home to Wales," *Sondheim Review* (Winter 2003, Vol. IX, No. 3). 14.
62 Paul Salsini, "She's singing a role she always coveted, " *Sondheim Review* (Winter 2003, Vol. IX, No. 3, 15.
63 John Olson, "Terfel stars in a rich and eerie *Sweeney*," *Sondheim Review* (Winter 2003, Vol. IX, No. 3), 12.
64 Olson, "Terfel stars."
65 Mark Shenton, "Chicago's *Sweeney* moves to London," *Sondheim Review* (Spring 2004, Vol. X, No. 4), 16.
66 Shenton, "Chicago's *Sweeney*."
67 Doyle served as the artistic director for the Swan Theatre in Worcester (1982-1985), the Everyman Theatre in Cheltenham (1986-1989), the Everyman Theatre in Liverpool (1989–1993) and the Theatre Royal, York (1993-1997). He was the associate artistic director of the Watermill Theatre in Newbury (1998-2008), where he first staged *Sweeney Todd*.
68 Charles Isherwood, "Cutting *Sweeney Todd* to the Bone," *New York Times* (October 30, 2005).
69 Rick Pender, "Finding the story: An interview with director John Doyle," *Sondheim Review* (Summer 2006, Vol. XII, No. 4), 34.
70 Mark Shenton, "*Sweeney* spawns a tiny toddler in London," *Sondheim Review* (Fall 2004, Vol. XI, No. 2), 12.

71 Charles Spencer, "Glorious blend of beautiful lyricism, magnificent score – and gallons of blood," *The Daily Telegraph* (February 12, 2004).
72 Doyle's production picked up four additional 2006 Tony nominations: Best Revival of a Musical; Best Actor in a Musical, Best Actress in a Musical, Best Featured Actor in a Musical. The 2006 Tony for Best Revival went to a revival of *The Pajama Game*, a Tony Award winner from 1954. Doyle's *Sweeney Todd* did win the 2006 Drama Desk Award for Outstanding Revival of a Musical.
73 Ken Mandelbaum, "Recent Broadway Nights: 11/23/05," Broadway.com.
74 David Loud, personal correspondence with Rick Pender (May 3, 2024).
75 David Loud, correspondence.
76 David Loud, correspondence.
77 Patricia Cohen, "Sweeney Todd (2005 Revival)" within "Chapter 2: Reunions and Reconsiderations" in a multi-part feature, "What is a Tribe?" *New York Times T Magazine* (April 13, 2020), 86–87.
78 Cohen, "Sweeney Todd."
79 Jesse Green, "Hey, Let's Not Put On a Show!," *New York Times* (August 21, 2005).
80 Christopher Byrne, "Desperate times, desperate measures," *Sondheim Review* (Winter 2005, Vol XII, No. 2), 34.
81 Ben Brantley, "Grand Guignol, Spare and Stark," *New York Times* (November 4, 2005).
82 Peter Marks, "*Sweeney*, Well Done," *Washington Post* (November 17, 2005).
83 Anthony Tommasini, "And by the Way, They Act a Bit, Too," *New York Times* (November 18, 2005).
84 Tommasini, "And by the Way."
85 Rick Pender, "A fearful nightmare: Doyle's inventive revival of *Sweeney* is more distilled, more elemental, " *Sondheim Review* (Spring 2006, Vol. XII, No. 3), 11.
86 J. Wynn Rousuck, "*Sweeney Todd*: Spare staging reveals richness of score," *Baltimore Sun*, December 18, 2005.
87 Micah-Shane Brewer, "Telling the story," *Sondheim Review*, Spring 2006 (Vol. XII, No. 3), 8.
88 Brewer, "Telling the story."
89 Leonard Jacobs, "*Sweeney Todd*'s finely calibrated ensemble," *Sondheim Review*, Summer 2006 (Vol. XII, No. 4), 13.
90 Jacobs, "Finely calibrated ensemble."
91 Jacobs, "Finely calibrated ensemble."
92 Rick Pender, "Finding the story: An interview with director John Doyle," *Sondheim Review*, Summer 2006 (Vol. XII, No. 4), 34.
93 John Fleming, "Less is More in the Broadway Revival of Stephen Sondheim's Musical." *St. Petersburg Times* (June 4, 2006).
94 Robert Hurwitt, "ACT's trimmed *Sweeney Todd* holds its own," *San Francisco Chronicle*, September 5, 2007.
95 Dominic Papatola, "Juniorized: Sondheim provided the impetus for smaller-scale versions of shows," *Sondheim Review*, Winter 2005 (Vol. XII, No. 2), 13–14.
96 Denise Belizar, "A meaty challenge: Florida students bite into *Sweeney Todd*," Sondheim Review, Spring 2008 (Vol. XIV, No. 3), 17–18.

97 Debbie Tedrick, "Attend the tale: *Sweeney Todd* and *Into the Woods* can be performed by youth," *Sondheim Review*, Winter 2011 (Vol. XVIII, No. 2), 38.
98 Belizar, "A meaty challenge."
99 https://www.mtishows.com/sweeney-todd-school-edition.
100 Mark Shenton, "No place like London – or Wales," *Sondheim Review*, Fall 2012 (Vol. XIX, No. 1), 41.
101 Michael Billington, "*Sweeney Todd* – review," *The Guardian*, March 21, 2012.
102 Mark Eden Horowitz, "A dark and a hungry god," *Sondheim Review*, Spring 2015 (Vol. XXI, No. 2), 38–39.
103 Allan Kozinn, "*Sweeney Todd* (Progressive Rock Remix)," *New York Times* (February 12, 2014).
104 Carey Purcell, "*Sweeney Todd* – Prog Metal Version to Play D.C.'s Warehouse Theatre," playbill.com, June 9, 2014.
105 Horowitz, "A dark and a hungry god."
106 Horowitz, "A dark and a hungry god."
107 David Friscic, "An Interview with Andrew and Melissa Baughman on *Sweeney Todd* – Prog Metal Version," dcmetrotheaterarts.com, July 15, 2015.
108 Kozinn, "*Sweeney Todd*."
109 Vanessa Garden, "More hot pies!" *Sondheim Review*, Summer 2015 (Vol. XXI, No. 3), 44.
110 Garden, "More Hot Pies!"
111 Bethany Rickwald, "Why *Sweeney Todd* Is Packing People Into a Strikingly Ordinary British Pie Shop," theatermania.com, February 14, 2017.
112 Rickwald, "Why Sweeney Todd Is Packing People."
113 Hilton Als, "A Wondrous Production of *Sweeney Todd*, T*he New Yorker* (March 13, 2017).
114 Als, "A Wondrous Production."
115 Ben Brantley, A *Sweeney Todd* That Gets Into Your Face," *New York Times* (March 1, 2017).
116 Rob Weinert-Kendt, "*Sweeney Todd* Cuts a Larger Figure," *New York Times*, March 12, 2023.
117 Weinert-Kendt, "*Sweeney Todd* Cuts."
118 Weinert-Kendt, "*Sweeney Todd* Cuts."
119 Weinert-Kendt, "*Sweeney Todd* Cuts."
120 Jeff Lunden, "As *Sweeney Todd* returns to Broadway, 4 Sweeneys dish about a difficult role," "Morning Edition," *National Public Radio*, March 29, 2023.
121 Weinert-Kendt, "*Sweeney Todd* Cuts."
122 Weinert-Kendt, "*Sweeney Todd* Cuts."
123 Peter Marks, "Groban and Ashford ignite the flames of a funny, sexier *Sweeney Todd*," *Washington Post*, March 26, 2023.
124 Alexis Soloski, "In *Sweeney Todd*, a Role That's Filling," *New York Times*, May 14, 2023.
125 Actor Ruthie Ann Miles was a guest for a panel discussion with members of the American Theatre Critics Association in New York City on November 10, 2023.
126 Patrick Ryan, "Josh Groban is out for blood in exhilarating *Sweeney Todd* revival," *USA Today*, April 2, 2023.

127 Leah Putnam, "Gaten Matarazzo and Manoel Felciano Trade Notes on Playing Toby in *Sweeney Todd*," playbill.com, April 20, 2023.
128 Jesse Green, "The Many Thrilling Flavors of a Full-Scale Sweeney Todd," *New York Times*, March 26, 2023.
129 Green, "Many Thrilling Flavors."
130 Green, "Many Thrilling Flavors."
131 Marks, "Groban and Ashford ignite the flames.".
132 Weinert-Kendt, "*Sweeney Todd* Cuts."

Chapter 6

1 Craig Zadan, *Sondheim & Company*, 2nd ed. (New York: Da Capo Press, 1994), 244.
2 Zadan, 246
3 Christopher Bond, *Sweeney Todd: The Demon Barber of Fleet Street – A Melodrama* (London: Samuel French, 1974.
4 Terry Gross, "'Fresh Air' remembers Broadway legend Stephen Sondheim (Part 1)," Fresh Air, National Public Radio, December 1, 2021.
5 Gross, "Fresh Air," Dec. 1, 2021.
6 Ibid.
7 Stephen Sondheim, *Finishing the Hat* (New York: Alfred A. Knopf, 2010), 332.
8 Jeff Lunden, "As *Sweeney Todd* Returns to Broadway, 4 Sweeneys dish about the difficult role," National Public Radio's *Morning Edition*, March 29, 2023.
9 Craig Zadan, *Sondheim & Company* (New York: DaCapo Press, 1992), 249.
10 Sondheim, *Finishing the Hat*, 332.
11 Donal Henahan "Music view: Why can't Verdi voices handle Sondheim?" *New York Times* , October 21, 1984.
12 Martin Gottfried, *Sondheim*, rev. ed. (New York: Harry N. Abrams, 2000), 127.
13 George Martin, "On the Verge of Opera: Stephen Sondheim,", *Musical Quarterly*, Spring 1989, 79.
14 Martin, "On the Verge."
15 "Theater; Musical Or Opera: Which Is It?, *New York Times*, April 30, 2000.
16 "Theater; Musical Or Opera."
17 Martin Gottfried, *Sondheim*, rev. ed. (New York: Harry N. Abrams, 2000), 127.
18 Alan Rich, "Music: Rigging Mortis," *New York Magazine*, March 26, 1979, 94.
19 This point was made and carefully documented by Raymond Knapp and Sam Baltimore in their article "Sondheim's almost-operas" for *The Sondheim Review*, Summer 2015, 10.
20 Stephen Sondheim, interviewed by Jeremy Sams. Lyttelton Theatre, June 1, 1993.
21 Sondheim, Sams interview.
22 Sondheim, *Finishing the Hat*, 332.
23 Graham Skipper, "Stephen Sondheim: Horror's Musical Maestro," posted on fangoria.com, November 30, 2021.
24 Skipper, ibid.
25 Knapp and Baltimore, "Sondheim's almost-operas," 11.

26 Terry Teachout, "Stephen Sondheim's Unsettled Scores," *Commentary*, 2003, 11.
27 Meryle Secrest, *Stephen Sondheim: A Life* (New York: Alfred A. Knopf, 1998), 134
28 Zadan, *Sondheim & Company*, 250.
29 Zadan, *Sondheim & Company*, 248.
30 Secrest, *Stephen Sondheim*, 292.
31 Secrest, ibid.
32 Horowitz, *Sondheim on Music*, 126–127.
33 Terry Gross, "'Fresh Air' remembers Broadway legend Stephen Sondheim (Part 3)," *Fresh Air*, National Public Radio, December 3, 2021.
34 Libretto, *Sweeney Todd*, 23.
35 Ashley Marian Pribyl, Doctoral Dissertation: "Sociocultural and Collaborative Antagonism in the Harold Prince – Stephen Sondheim Musicals (1970-1979)." (St. Louis: Washington University, 2019), 54–57.
36 Joanne Gordon, *Art Isn't Easy: The Theater of Stephen Sondheim* (New York: Da Capo Press, 1992), 211–212.
37 Allen Wallach, "Sweeney Todd," *Newsday*, March 2, 1979.
38 Wallach, ibid.
39 Howard Kissel, "Sweeney Todd," *Women's Wear Daily*, March 2, 1979.
40 Music video by Stephen Sondheim about Jonathan Tunick's orchestrations (2011, Sony Music Entertainment; https://www.youtube.com/watch?v=5uo8bu1RuTM.
41 Darryn King, "The EGOT Winner Behind Sondheim's Signature Sound," *New York Times*, January 10, 2024.
42 Margaret Hall, *Gemignani: Life and Lessons from Broadway and Beyond* (New York: Applause Books, 2022), 73.
43 Mark Stryker, "Composer Stephen Sondheim discusses musical influences, opera and *A Little Night Music*," *Detroit Free Press*, November 8, 2009.
44 Mark Eden Horowitz, *Sondheim on Music* (Lanham, Maryland: Rowman and Littlefield, 2019), 128.
45 Works by renowned composers employing the Gregorian plainchant Dies Irae melodic phrase include Mozart (Requiem, 1791); Berlioz (*Symphonie fantastique*, 1830); Liszt (*Totentanz*: Paraphrase on Dies Irae, 1849); Saint-Saëns (Requiem, 1878); Mahler (Symphony No. 2 in c minor "Resurrection," 1895); and Rachmaninoff (Rhapsody on a Theme of Paganini, 1934).
46 For a more thorough explication of Sondheim's use of the "Dies Irae" theme, see Stephen Banfield, *Sondheim's Broadway Musicals* (Ann Arbor: University of Michigan Press, 1993), 297-300.
47 Zadan, ibid.
48 For a fuller discussion of the actual harmonic structure of the chord: Substack: "*Sweeney Todd*: Prelude," *The Sondheim Hub*, June 2, 2024, https://thesondheimhub.substack.com/p/sweeney-todd-prelude.
49 Zadan, *Sondheim & Company*, 252.
50 Anika Chapin, "Go into the words of 'Epiphany' from *Sweeney Todd*," YouTube video from Signature Theatre (June 13, 2023), https://youtu.be/BEgRBkLCDTc?si=Rbb8W0QjqQ27xCld.
51 Chapin, ibid.

52. Kevin Lynch, "Breaking Down the Score: 'Epiphany,' from *Sweeney Todd*," https://youtu.be/BEgRBkLCDTc?si=IUW6jZAkKgwVmT7N.
53. Chapin, ibid.
54. Porter's songs such as "Let's Do It (Let's Fall in Love)" (1928) "You're the Top" (1934) are good examples of this genre.
55. Mark Eden Horowitz, *Biography of a Song*: "A Little Priest," *The Sondheim Review* (Summer 2006). On p. 24, he provides three columns of the ideas Sondheim generated. Horowitz's in-depth remarks about this song offer profound insights into Sondheim's creative process.
56. *Sweeney Todd*, Libretto, 108.
57. Sweeney Todd, Libretto, 203.
58. *Sweeney Todd*, Libretto, 204.

Chapter 7

1. Thomas Z. Shepard, Monograph, 2022, 1. In advance of Shepard's 2024 publication of his memoir, *Recording Broadway*, he provided access to this singular document and permitted citation of material pertinent to *Sweeney Todd*'s original cast recording. I am grateful to his generosity in making this material available.
2. Shepard, 1. The one exception was the 1971 cast recording of *Follies*, which was made and released by Capitol Records.
3. Robert L. McLaughlin, *Sweeney Todd: The Demon Barber of Fleet Street, added to the National Registry: 2013*, Library of Congress Blogs, August 26, 2023. "Johanna" was moved from its show position (between "The Contest" and "Wait") to precede Anthony and Johanna's "Kiss Me," where it made more narrative sense on the recording.
4. Shepard, 6.
5. Shepard, 7.
6. A 74-minute compact disc of highlights was released in 1984, and a double-compact disk with 106 minutes of material was issued in 1987.
7. John Rockwell, "*Sweeney Todd* on Records – 'Terrific Listening,'" *New York Times*, May 20, 1979.
8. Robert Sandla, *The Theatermania Guide to Musical Theater Recordings*, ed. Michael Portantiere (New York: Back Stage Books, 2004), 354.
9. Alan Rich, "*Sweeney Todd* Triumphs on Disc," *High Fidelity*, August 1979, 80–81.
10. Paul Wittke, "Reviews of Records," *High Fidelity*, April 1980, 314.
11. The addition of the *Sweeney Todd* original cast recording took the total number of sound recordings in the National Recording Registry to 400. Just a dozen original cast recordings are listed on the Registry. In addition to *Sweeney Todd*, the others are *Oklahoma!* (1943), *Four Saints in Three Acts* (1947), *Kiss Me Kate* (1949), *South Pacific* (1949), *Guys and Dolls* (1950), *My Fair Lady* (1956), *West Side Story* (1957), *Gypsy* (1959), *Fiddler on the Roof* (1964), *Hair* (1968), and *The Wiz* (1975). *West Side Story* and *Gypsy* also feature lyrics by Sondheim. *Sweeney Todd*'s 1979 recording is the most recent cast recording to be so honored.

12 Matt Koplik, "*Sweeney Todd*: Original Broadway Cast," castalbumreviews.com/Sweeney-Todd, 2023.
13 For more information about this concert presentation, go to Chapter 5, p. 120.
14 Sean Patrick Flahaven, "And I'm Full of Joy!" www.Theatre.com, November 2000.
15 Following a series of multi-disc, award-winning recording releases of radio-broadcast performances from the Philharmonic's archives, *Sweeney Todd* was the orchestra's first CD-set recorded expressly for commercial release under its own label. As discussed in Chapter 6, Price's staging was repeated in 2001 by the San Francisco Symphony, a performance conducted by Rob Fisher, that was recorded for a PBS audience, airing on Halloween night in October 2001. Featuring many of the same performers from the New York concerts, it won a 2002 Emmy and was subsequently released on DVD. The concert production was reprised once more at Chicago's Ravinia Festival on August 24, 2001, with Price directing and Andrew Litton back on the podium to conduct.
16 Robert Sandla, 354.
17 Steven Suskin, reviewing the recording, noted that the "audience [was] predisposed to whoop and holler for their favorites." Playbill.com, November 12, 2000.
18 As noted elsewhere, the San Francisco Symphony stepped up to make a video recording of Price's *Sweeney Todd* concert presented in three performances at Louise M. Davies Symphony Hall (July 19–21, July 2001). In addition to the video, televised on PBS on October 31, 2001, the DVD includes a bonus: A "making of" featurette about the San Francisco concerts. But no audio cast recording was produced.
19 Steven Suskin, "On the Record," Playbill.com, November 12, 2000.
20 Scott Ross, "The Philharmonic *Sweeney* is resplendent," *Sondheim Review*, Winter 2001, 30.
21 Koplik, *Sweeney Todd*.
22 A "button" is the orchestral punctuation that announces the end of a musical number.
23 Everett Evans, "*Sweeney Todd*, New Broadway Cast Recording," *Houston Chronicle*, March 26, 2006.
24 Ken Mandelbaum, "CDs: Attend the Tale," Broadway.com, March 2, 2006.
25 Donald Rosenberg, "Lean Sondheim cuisine," *Sondheim Review*, Summer 2006, 40.
26 Johnny Depp's longtime friend Bruce Witkin produced the actor's vocals recorded separately at London's Out of Eden studio; recording engineer and mixer was Andy Richards, who also played the Rugby School Chapel Organ for that facet of the film.
27 Recording commentator Matt Koplik described Depp's "crooning, rock-tinged style of singing, less George Hearn and more David Bowie."
28 Mark Eden Horowitz, "The truth of performance," *Sondheim Review*, Winter 2012, 45
29 Michael Billington, "*Sweeney Todd* – review," *The Guardian*, March 21, 2012.
30 David Benedict, "*Sweeney Todd*," *Variety*, March 21, 2012
31 Jonathan Baz, "*Sweeney Todd* – review," jonathanbaz.com/2012/09/sweeney-todd-review.html
32 Jesse Green, "Cast Album Roundup: *Sweeney Todd*, *Parade*, *Camelot* and More, *New York Times*, February 29, 2024.

Chapter 8

1. Meryle Secrest conducted extensive interviews with Sondheim as she assembled her 1998 biography, *Stephen Sondheim: A Life*. From an unpublished transcript of a conversation on November 6, 1995, she reported an interesting remark Sondheim made about working with Wheeler: "It's a little ungallant to say, but it's true: Hugh, being Hugh, deliberately and almost perversely, changed every given sentence of Christopher Bond, just to make it his own, and it was all for the worse. So the only way to retain the territory is to sing it. So everything he wrote, I would turn into words, so that I could get closer to Bond. Hugh did contribute two plot things, or one plot thing anyway, which helped a lot, that had to do with the way the love story is told between the sailor and the young girl, and that was very valuable. Otherwise, I just kept reconstituting the territory, because just perversely – anything that Bond wrote he would just change to make it his own." By and large, however, accounts of the creation of *Sweeney Todd* suggest that Sondheim and Wheeler had a genial working relationship.
2. Craig Zadan, *Sondheim & Company* (New York: Da Capo Press, 1992), 248.
3. Zadan, 244.
4. Zadan, 245.
5. Michael Kantor and Laurence Maslon, *Broadway: The American Musical* (New York: Bulfinch Press, 2004), 364
6. Alison Morooney, "Sweeney Todd" in *Fifty Key Stage Musicals*, Robert W. Schneider and Shannon Agnew, eds. (New York: Routledge, 2022), 166.
7. W. Anthony Sheppard, "Finishing the Line: Wit, Rhythm and Rhyme in Sondheim," in *Sondheim in Our Time and His*, W. Anthony Sheppard, ed. (New York: Oxford University Press, 2022).
8. Sondheim's unusual musical *Pacific Overtures* (1976) predated *Sweeney Todd*. It had an esoteric historical plot about America forcing 19th-century Japan to connect with the larger world. Admired for many of its aspects, especially a score that found ways to evoke Asian music tonalities, it was not a box office hit.
9. The Sondheim parody "A Little Complex" drew elements from his *Into the Woods, Company, A Little Night Music, Sunday in the Park with George*, and — naturally — *Sweeney Todd*. The other four parodies in Bogart and Rockwell's show are "Corn!" in the lyrical style of Richard Rodgers and Oscar Hammerstein; "Dear Abby," in the bouncy style of Jerry Herman; "Aspects of Junita," featuring the bombastic melodies of Andrew Lloyd Webber; "Speakeasy" pokes fun at saucy, tart shows by John Kander and Fred Ebb.
10. The "Schmicago" parodies of *Sweeney Todd* songs can be found on YouTube. An ebullient video of "Good Enough to Eat" (https://youtu.be/4buUVhA3FdQ?si=E5KhY8EtZ6T9Vomn) is delightfully dark. Also available as audio tracks are "Worst Brats in Town" (https://youtu.be/gFfA4fwdeFo?si=b_vRgeDzBQLiJpWo) and "There Was a Butcher" (https://www.youtube.com/watch?v=cxacrA61YIg).
11. The YouTube video of the cast of *Hamilton*'s 2017 Easter Bonnet parody of *Sweeney Todd* is available online (https://www.youtube.com/watch?v=bruTOQoNtO4). On May 5, 2023, the cast of *Hamilton* celebrated the Broadway revival of *Sweeney Todd*

receiving eight Tony Award nominations with a "Ham4Ham" pre-performance reprise rendition of the *Sweeney* parody. They were joined before an adoring throng at the Richard Rodgers Theatre by members of the *Sweeney Todd* revival cast, including Josh Groban, Annaleigh Ashford and Gaten Matarazzo. National Public Radio produced a news feature about the event: (https://www.npr.org/2023/05/05/1174264880/lin-manuel-miranda-and-josh-groban-hamilton-sweeney-todd).

12 Zachary Scott, "The 10 Indispensable American Musicals," Theatermania.com, August 5, 2024.
13 Joanne Gordon, *Art Isn't Easy, The Theater of Stephen Sondheim* (New York: Da Capo Press, 1992), 254.

Appendix 1

1 Suzanne Yanko, "Victorian Opera: *Sweeney Todd*," ClassicMelbourne.com, July 17, 2015.
2 Cameron Woodhead, "*Sweeney Todd* review: Teddy Tahu Rhodes' gravelly bass breaks new ground as demon barber," *The Age*, July 19, 2015.
3 Freeman Cebu, "A Dream Come True for Theater Stalwarts," *PhilStar Global*, October 26, 2009.
4 Vincen Gregory Yu, "*Sweeney Todd*: Bobby Garcia's reinvention of the musical a triumph of Vision and staging," *Philippine Daily Inquirer*, October 19, 2019.
5 Mark Fisher, "*Sweeney Todd*," *The Guardian*, 2010.
6 A YouTube video of the first act of the 2007 Seoul production of *Sweeney Todd*, performed in a Korean translation, can be found at: https://youtu.be/lYxy7CXLFvI?si=GF-gQ8C1wTfwP45n
7 Yoo Hu-hyun, "*Sweeney Todd* is back for revenge," *Korea JoonAng Daily*, November 12, 2019
8 Yoo Hu-hyun, "Musical *Sweeney Todd* is back and better than ever," *Korea JoongAng Daily*, December 6, 2022.
9 'Musical *Sweeney Todd* is back," *Korea JoongAng Daily*.
10 Park Ga-young "Musicals that are treats for the ears, feasts for the eyes," *The Korea Herald*, January 28, 2023.
11 Mariana Mijares, "*Sweeney Todd*: A minimalist, but effective, approach to Sondheim," *Cartelera de Teatro*, October 2023.
12 Gunilla Brodrej, "The corpse slides toward opera's meat grinder," *Expressen*, January 29, 2023.
13 Dan Backman, "Skillful play in bloody horror musical," *Svenska Dagbladet*, January 29, 2023).

Appendix 2

1 Joanne Gordon, *Art Isn't Easy: The Theater of Stephen Sondheim* (New York: Da Capo Press, 1992), 214

2. Sondheim said, "The opening organ chords are based on 'Kyrie eleison,' and I drew on the medieval 'Dies Irae' from the requiem mass, because Sweeney is in love with death ... The opening creates a rumble, something is about to happen. The dissonance is not resolved, which is creepy, the feeling is one of lifting and dropping the audience." Foster Hirsch, *Harold Prince and the American Musical Theatre* (expanded edition) (New York: Applause Theatre & Cinema Books, 1989), 123

3. Mark Eden Horowitz, *Sondheim on Music: Minor Details and Major Decisions* (Lanham, Maryland: Rowman and Littlefield, 2019), 219

4. Stephen Citron, *Sondheim and Lloyd-Webber: The New Musical* (London: Chatto & Windus, 2001), 248.

5. Paul Wittke, "Review of Records: Sweeney Todd. Original cast recording," *Musical Quarterly*, April 1980, 310–311.

6. Larry Avis Brown, "Sondheim Notes," https://larryavisbrown.com/sondheim-sweeney-todd/ (2018).

7. The chorus first declares of Sweeney's bloody mission with "Lift your razor high, Sweeney" (Libretto, 43). After the barbering contest we are told "Sweeney pondered, and Sweeney Planned" (Libretto, 67.) Three tenors harmonize and describe how "His hands were quick, his fingers strong" (Libretto, 81). In the second act, a quintet is assembled following the Wigmaker sequence to remind us that "Sweeney'd waited too long before" (Libretto, 169) and goes on to voice the letter that Sweeney composes to lure Judge Turpin back to his barbershop. As Anthony approaches Fogg's Asylum, the chorus sets the foreboding tone with "The engine roared, the motor hissed" (Libretto, 183-184). And when the Judge is finally in Sweeney's clutches once more, they repeat his charge, "Lift your razor high, Sweeney" (Libretto,196). According to Music Director Paul Gemignani, "My biggest job was to try to get variety in who was singing ... in harmonization." He memorized the individual singers' voices so he could mix and match their vocal performances . "We never used the same person twice for solo lines. So over the course of the evening, the same tune sounded just a little different each time you heard it." – Craig Zadan, *Sondheim & Company* [New York: Da Capo Press, 1992], 252.

8. In a note in *Finishing the Hat*, Sondheim explained that the Beggar Woman's song is "an amalgam of pure invention, authentic Cockney, American slang and universal poetry," 334.

9. According to Sondheim, "Those of us who write songs should stage each number within an inch of its life in our own heads when we write. . . . They may not use anything in your blueprint at all, but they have something to work on, something to build from." Stephen Sondheim, "The Musical Theater: A Talk by Stephen Sondheim," *The Dramatist's Guild Quarterly*, Volume 15 (1978. 17. Writer Carey Blyton described how the song's rapid changes of meter emphasize Mrs. Lovett's "attempts to swat the flies that plague her as she kneads the dough: 4/4, 2/4, 3/4, 4/4, 5/4, 3/4, 4/4, etc." Blyton, "Sondheim's *Sweeney Todd*," *Tempo* 149 (1984).

10. It's "first a giddy beerhall waltz, then a 6/8 quasi-tarantella," according to Kim Kowalke, "Sweeney's Identity Crisis and the Dynamic Potential of Generic Hybridity" in *Sondheim in Our Time and His*, W. Anthony Sheppard, ed. (New York: Oxford University Press, 2022), 260.

11 Jeff Lunden, "As *Sweeney Todd* returns to Broadway, 4 Sweeneys dish about the difficult role," Morning Edition, National Public Radio, March 29, 2023.
12 Brown, 6.
13 Youtube.com/watch?v=DBCVaFqGJwg. Sondheim, in a master class with students at London's Guildhall School of Music and Drama in 1984.
14 Brown, 6.
15 Terry Gross, "'Fresh Air' remembers Broadway legend Stephen Sondheim (Part 3)," National Public Radio (December 3, 2021).
16 In the libretto Sweeney declares, "My right arm is complete again!" In the original Broadway production it had to be revised because Len Cariou, playing Sweeney was left-handed. When George Hearn replaced Cariou, he too was left-handed. Citron, 250 (footnote).
17 Steven Suskin, *The Sound of Broadway Music* (New York: Oxford University Press, 2009), 286. He makes this observation in \his fascinating account of sitting in the Kennedy Center's Eisenhower Theater's orchestra pit during a performance of *Sweeney Todd* during the 2002 Sondheim Celebration.
18 When playwright Christopher Bond adapted the Dibdin Pitt script in 1973, he intended the role of Tobias for himself.
19 Diegetic numbers are performances that characters onstage can hear, such as these songs by Toby and Pirelli. It's sometimes called "actual sound." The term derives from the Greek word *diegesis*, which means "to narrate."
20 Citron, *Sondheim and Lloyd-Webber*, 254.
21 Paul Wittke, "Reviews of Records," *High Fidelity* (April 1980) 313.
22 Stephen Sondheim, *Finishing the Hat* (New York: Alfred A. Knopf, 2010), 349.
23 Martin Gottfried, *Sondheim* (New York: Harry N. Abrams, Inc., 1993), 135.
24 Stephen Sondheim, quoted by David Savran, *In Their Own Words: Contemporary American Playwrights* (New York: Theatre Communications Group, 1988), 230.
25 Brown, 7.
26 Citron, *Sondheim and Lloyd-Webber*, 251.
27 Foster Hirsch, *Harold Prince and the American Musical Theatre* (New York: Applause Books, 2005; expanded edition of Cambridge University Press, 1989).
28 Ethan Mordden, *One More Kiss* (New York: Palgrave Macmillan, 2003), 229.
29 "The orchestra [is] blasting a five-note *fortissimo* dissonant chord that dissolves eerily into a four-note *piano* crazed shadow chord (F#-B-D-F), vividly signifying Todd's schizophrenic breakdown. Although this is the ending that appeared in the first edition of the published piano-vocal score, it is seldom heard in major productions or on recordings."– Kowalke, "Sweeney's Identity Crisis," 252.
30 Terry Gross, "Fresh Air remembers Broadway legend Stephen Sondheim (Part 1)," National Public Radio, December 1, 2021.
31 Gottfried, *Sondheim*, 137. That description is often applied to "Rose's Turn," the culminating number sung by the furious stage mother in *Gypsy*, for which Sondheim wrote the lyrics.
32 Brown, 7.
33 Christopher Bond, *Sweeney Todd, The Demon Barber of Fleet Street: A Melodrama* (London: Samuel French, 1974), 22.

34 Kowalke, "Sweeney's Identity Crisis," 265.
35 Josh Groban in Lunden interview on NPR (March 29, 2023).
36 Wittke, 313.
37 Mark Eden Horowitz, "Biography of a Song: 'A Little Priest,'" (Summer 2006), 24.
38 Horowitz, 26.
39 Ashley Marian Pribyl, "Sociocultural and Collaborative Antagonism in the Harold Prince-Stephen Sondheim Musicals (1970–1979)" (PhD dissertation, Washington University, 2019.
40 Citron, *Sondheim and Lloyd-Webber*, 251.
41 Sondheim told Lansbury, "I wrote a song for you so crowded there is no place to breathe." Gottfried, *Sondheim*, 141.
42 Sondheim looked through a book of English folk songs for possible numbers to use in this scene. He thought he would "do one about a maiden; and then do one about something that has many choruses . . . the fun of it is it's got go be a song where he gets her to agree to sing with him, and then there turn out to be endless verses, and she doesn't know how to get rid of him." Sondheim, interviewed by Mark Eden Horowitz, *Sondheim on Music*, 143. This material is, by the way, another example of diegetic music, actual tunes that are played for entertainment between characters.
43 Libretto, 204.

Index

Abell, David Charles   122, 200
Adelphi Theatre (London)   138, 181
Ahmanson Theatre (Los Angeles)   119
Allen, Thomas   126
American Conservatory Theatre (San Francisco)   130
Annual Register   17, 30
Arbo, John   130–1
Armfield, Neil   124–6
Armstrong, Alun   115
Arnold, Malcolm   29
Ashford, Annaleigh   144–5, 147–8, 170, 182
Ashley, Christopher   123
Atwood, Colleen   85–6
Avalon Club (London)   141
Avery Fisher Hall (Lincoln Center, New York City)   120–1, 175, 177

Ball, Michael   138, 181
Baranski, Christine   119, 123–4
Baron Cohen, Sacha   86, 98–9, 180
Barr, Richard   35, 37–9
Barre, Gabriel   116
Barrow Street Theatre (New York City)   141–3
Batalla, Roser   198
Baughan, G. A.   27
Baughman, Andrew L.   139
Baughman, Melissa   139
Bean, Sawney   16–17

Bernstein, Leonard   2, 35, 187
Billington, Ken   50
Blackwell, Harolyn   175
Blakeley, Lee   200
Blank, Larry   123
Bluma Appel Theatre (Toronto)   201
Bogart, Joanne   190
Bond, Christopher   5–6, 31–7, 39, 59, 108, 112, 149–50, 185, 218
Bonham Carter, Helena   83, 85, 92, 95–8, 101, 104, 170, 180
Bower, Jamie Campbell   100–1, 180
Bridewell Theatre (London)   123
Buckhurst, Bill   141
Burton, Tim   81–92, 94, 96, 99, 102–6, 161, 170, 179

Cariou, Len   37, 40, 47–8, 52–6, 59, 61–3, 70, 72, 77, 80, 91, 117, 144, 151, 158, 166, 169, 173–4, 217
Carmello, Carolee   142
Castle, Joyce   110
Catnach, James   18
Cerveris, Michael   121, 129, 134, 144, 170, 188, 210
Charlotte Theater (Seoul, South Korea)   202
Chicago Symphony Orchestra   121
Chichester Festival Theatre (U.K.)   138
Christin, Judith   125
Cia de Teatro Musical Salle (Mexico City)   203

Circle in the Square (New York City) 113
Coleman, Jim 75
Cottesloe Theatre (Royal National Theatre; now the Dorfman Theatre) 109, 115, 129
Cranko, John 29
Cruikshank, George 48–9, 206

Dang, Tim 116
Davies Symphony Hall (San Francisco) 120–1
Delavan, Mark 111
DeMain, John 110
Depp, Johnny 83, 86, 87, 89, 92–6, 101–2, 106, 170, 180, 190
Dewhurst, George 27
Dexter, John 34
"Dies Irae" theme 54, 162–4, 168, 171, 205, 210, 212, 215–17, 219, 224
Donnellan, Declan 108–9, 115–16
Doyle, John 126–32, 169–70, 177, 179
Dundee Rep (Scotland) 201

East West Players (Los Angeles) 116, 143
Edelen, Sherri L. 114
Edwards, Rachel 140–1
Eisenhower Theater (Washington, D.C.) 123
Elias, Rosalind 111
English National Opera (London Coliseum) 122
Eugene O'Neill Theatre (New York City) 129

Factory whistle 11, 42, 48–9, 51–2, 156, 158–61, 172, 182, 206, 224
Ferretti, Dante 84–5
Finnish National Opera (Helsinki) 198
Fisher, Rob 121
Fleet Street Collective 139
Forrest, Michael 114
Fowler, Beth 112–13
Fryer, Robert 38
Fuller, Larry 49–50

Gaines, Davis 117, 119, 120, 175
Garber, Victor 61–4, 174
Gas, Mario 198
Gelbart, Larry 2
Gemignani, Alexander 129–30, 135
Gemignani, Paul 48, 51–3, 60, 67, 75, 90–1, 101, 111, 124, 126, 151, 159, 161, 164, 171–2, 175, 179, 210–11
Gemora, Audi 199
Gero, Edward 114
Gerould, Daniel 5
Gilbert, Alan 121
Gilfry, Rod 200
Goldman, James 3, 4
Goodspeed Opera House (East Haddam, Connecticut) 116
Grammer, Kelsey 119
Grammy Awards 174, 179
Grand Guignol 5–6, 92, 103–5, 108, 115, 156
"Great Performances" (PBS) 77, 120, 176
Greene, Leon 112
Groban, Josh 140, 144, 170, 182
Groenendaal, Cris 68, 75
Gunton, Bob 112

Haining, Peter 29–31
Half Moon Theatre 108
Hammerstein, Jimmy 10
Hammerstein, Oscar II 10, 157
Hancock, Sheila 110
Hangover Square 10–11, 151, 155–6
Hanna, Gillian 112
Harrington's Pie & Mash Shop (London) 140–1
Harris, Neil Patrick 119, 120, 175
Hazleton, Frederick 26
Hearn, George 62, 75–7, 120–1
Hegarty, Paul 128
Herman, Jerry 56, 157, 190
Herrmann, Bernard 3, 11, 151–2, 155, 163, 185
Hess, David 130
Higham, Mike 89–90, 101, 179

Hollywood Bowl (Los Angeles)   118
Holmes, James   118
Horowitz, Mark Eden   219
Houston Grand Opera   110, 116, 152, 169

Icelandic Opera   198
Imperial Theater (Tokyo)   197
Israeli National Opera   198

James, Richard   123
Jennings, Ken   55, 61–3
Johnson, Mary Lea   38, 171
Joslyn, Betsy   68, 75

Kail, Thomas   143–4, 147, 170
Kalbfleisch, Jon   115
Kaufman, Welz   121
Kaye, Judy   117, 130
Kelly, Laura Michelle   100, 180
Kennedy Center for the Performing Arts (Washington, D.C.)   75, 123–4
Kennedy Center Sondheim Celebration   123–4
Kent, Jonathan   138, 180–1
Kerryson, Paul   117
King, George   27–8
Klein, Beverly   118
Koshiro, Matsumoto   197
Krasker, Tommy   176
Krass, Ellen M.   77, 121

Lacamoire, Alex   143, 147, 170, 183
Landless Theatre Company   138–40
Lansbury, Angela   2, 5, 40–1, 47, 49, 55–61, 63, 69–70, 72, 74–7, 115, 157–8, 173, 186–7
Lapine, Sarna   114
Lauchengo-Yulo, Menchu   199
Laurents, Arthur   2, 7, 35, 149, 157
Lee, Eugene   45–9, 71
Lee, Franne   49, 69, 71
Leicester Haymarket Theatre (U.K.)   117
Leitmotifs   40, 157, 162, 164
Lewis, Norm   114, 142

Lincoln Center (New York City)   111, 175
Litton, Andrew   120–1, 176–7
Liverpool Playhouse   108
Lloyd, Edward   19–20
Logan, John   80–2, 85, 87–9, 92, 93, 99, 105
Loud, David   130–1
Loudon, Dorothy   62
Louise, Merle   65–6
Lucas, Craig   68
Lunt-Fontanne Theatre (New York City)   143–8
LuPone, Patti   98, 115, 120–1, 129, 170, 175, 177
Lyndeck, Edmund   66, 75, 174, 214
Lyric Opera of Chicago   124–5, 189
Lyttelton Theatre (London)   115

McCarthy, Siobhán   141–2
McDonald, Audra   120, 122
McKenzie, Julia   109, 115
Mackintosh, Sir Cameron   141
McLean, Michael   123
McVicar, David   118
Mackintosh, Sir Camero141
Manahan, George   111
Mann, Karen   128
Manos, Dean & Judy   37
Marineau, Barbara   116
Marmousets, Rue de   13–15
Marriott, Moore   27
Martin, Jessica   123
Masella, Arthur   111
Mauceri, John   118
Melbourne Theatre Company (Australia)   196
Mendes, Sam   80–1
Mendoza, Orville   116
Merman, Ethel   2, 57, 79, 157
Migliaccio, Donna   114
Milan Theatre (Mexico City)   203
Miles, Ruthie Ann   145–6, 182
Mitchell, Brian Stokes   123–4
Miyamoto, Amon   197

Index

Montecasino Theatre (Johannesburg, South Africa)   202
Music Theatre International (MTI)   136-7

National Theatre, Drury Lane (London)   100, 112
New Ambassadors Theatre (London)   127
Newgate Prison, Calendar   16, 30-1
New York Choral Artists   120
New York City Opera   111, 116, 152, 169
New York Philharmonic   120-2, 169
Nolen, Timothy   110-11, 116, 121, 125, 198

O'Connor, Caroline   200
Old Bower Saloon (London)   26
Opéra de Toulon (France)   200
Opera North (Leeds, UK)   118, 189
Opernhaus Zurich (Switzerland)   204

Page, Steven   118
Paige, Elaine   111
Palmer, Felicity   126
Parham, Bryonha Maria   115
Peña, Roger   198
Peña, Vicky   198
Penny Dreadfuls   6, 18-20, 26, 29, 92, 107, 140
Perkins, Anthony   3, 104
Pitt, George Dibdin   23-6, 32
Prest, Thomas Peckett   21
Price, Lonny   120-2, 175-7
Prince, Harold (Hal)   1, 4, 6-7, 11, 37-40, 63, 69, 72, 74, 107-11, 116, 132, 135-6, 152, 157, 160, 169, 175, 185-7, 207
    original creative team   41-53
    "Prog-Metal" *Sweeney Todd*   138-40

Quaine, J. P.   27
Quast, Philip   122
Quilley, Denis   110, 115

Ran, Otori   197
Ranger, Jeanette   117
Ravinia Festival (Chicago)   121
Redgrave, Lynn   118
Remsberg, Calvin   119
Repertory Philippines   199
Reprise! Broadway's Best in Concert (Los Angeles)   119
Rice, Sarah   64-5
Richards, Martin   38, 171
Rickman, Alan   98
Robbins, Jerome   35
Roberts, Flora   35-6
Rockwell, John   190
Romaguera, Joaquin   66-7
Romero, Constantino   198
Royal Brittania Saloon & Tavern   24
Royal Danish Opera   204
Royal Festival Hall (London)   117
Royal National Theatre (London)   109, 115
Royal Opera House, Covent Garden (London)   29, 125, 189
Royal Swedish Opera (Stockholm)   204
Rue de la Harpe   15, 22
Rymer, James Malcolm   21-3

Saks, Jay David   172-3
Salisbury Square   19-23
Sanders, Edward   101, 180
Sandler, Zak   114
San Francisco Symphony Orchestra   120-1
Schaeffer, Eric   113-14, 123
Schulman, Susan H.   112
Secomb, Jeremy   141-2
Septién, Miguel   203
Sesma, Thom   142
Shaw, Maxwell   32
Shen, Freda Foh   116
Shepard, Thomas Z.   171-4
Shevelove, Burt   2, 7, 79, 149
Signature Theatre (Arlington, Virginia)   113-15

Sills, Beverly   111
Slaughter, Tod   27–8
Sondheim, Stephen; *see also* "Dies Irae" theme
   and book writing   7–8, 149
   choral writing   164
   convincing Hal Prince to direct *Sweeney Todd*   6–7, 11, 38–9
   defining a genre for *Sweeney Todd*   152, 156–7
   imagining a horror movie   9–12
   influence of Bernard Herrmann   150–2, 155, 163
   love of movies   80, 154
   melodrama and farce   6–9
   musical theater or opera   69, 71–2, 74, 151–4, 156, 162
   necessary changes to make a movie of *Sweeney Todd*   88–9; *see also* "Dies Irae" theme
Spall, Timothy   99–100, 180
Stampley, Nathaniel   115
Starstruck Performing Arts Center (Stuart, Florida)   137
State Opera of South Australia (Adelaide)   196
Staunton, Imelda   138, 180
Stewart, Patrick   118–19
Stratford East Theatre (London)   5, 6, 33, 35
String of Pearls, "Penny Dreadful"   21–3
   stage melodrama   23–6
Styne, Jule   2, 57, 74
Sweeney Todd School Edition   136–7

Tadashi, Suzuki   197
Taylor, Elizabeth   37, 80
Teatre Rozrywki (Chorzow, Poland)   200
"Teeny Todd"   112–13, 189
Terfel, Bryn   120–2, 125, 175, 189
Terkel, Studs   58
Théâtre Capitol de Québec   201

Théâtre du Châtelet (Paris)   200
Theatre Royal, Drury Lane   110
Thompson, Emma   121–2
Todd, Sweeney: a real person?   18, 27, 29–31
Tokuda, Marilyn   116
Tony Awards   73–4, 129, 148
Tooting Arts Club (London)   140
Travis, Sarah   126, 177, 179
Triplett, Sally Ann   142
Tunick, Jonathan   50–1, 90–1, 101, 126, 133, 151, 153, 161, 175–81
Tveit, Aaron   148

Uris Theatre (New York City)   38, 46–7, 51, 61, 72, 169, 172

Verlizzo, Frank (FRAVER)   68–9
Victoria Theatre (Stoke-on-Trent, U.K.)   31

Wales National Opera   201
Watermill Theatre (Newbury, U.K.)   126–7
Webber, Andrew Lloyd   157, 190
Wermland Opera (Sweden)   204
West, Walter   27
Wheeler, Hugh   4, 7–8, 39, 41–2, 150, 171, 185
Whitehall Theatre (London)   127
Willetts, Dave   117
Williams, Jack Erick   67
Williams, Joss   87
Wisener, Jayne   100, 180
Witkin, Bruce   94
Wolski, Darius   86
Woodward, Charles   35, 38, 40

York Theatre Company (New York City), "Teeny Todd"   112

Zanuck, Richard D.   85, 87, 94, 96, 99

About the Author

Rick Pender, author of *The Stephen Sondheim Encyclopedia* (2021), is a respected authority about Sondheim and the composer/lyricist's eighteen Broadway musicals. In 1999, he began contributing features and reviews to *The Sondheim Review*. He became its managing editor in 2004 and served in that role until it ceased publication in 2016. In 2017, he launched the website EverythingSondheim.org, now operated by Signature Theatre in Arlington, Virginia. For more than three decades, he has been a theater critic in Cincinnati, Ohio, reviewing local, regional, and national productions for *CityBeat*, Cincinnati's alternative newsweekly, where he also served as arts and entertainment editor (1998–2006). From 2005 to 2022, he recorded theater interviews for Cincinnati's NPR affiliate WVXU-FM, including several in-studio conversations with Stephen Sondheim. A longtime member of the American Theatre Critics Association, he was its chair in 2005–2006.